Cobol 85
for Programmers

Cobol 85
for Programmers

Jim Inglis

Department of Computer Science
Birkbeck College
University of London
UK

JOHN WILEY & SONS
Chichester · New York · Brisbane · Toronto · Singapore

Library of Congress Cataloging-in-Publication Data:

Inglis, J.
   Cobol 85 for programmers / J. Inglis.
      p.   cm.
   Includes index.
   ISBN 0 471 92156 4
      1. COBOL (Computer program language)   I. Title.   II. Title: Cobol
eighty-five for programmers.
QA76.73.C25154   1989
005.13'3—dc 19   88-13874
                                                                              CIP

British Library Cataloguing in Publication Data:

Inglis, J.
   Cobol 85 for programmers.
   1. Computer systems.   Programming languages:
   Cobol language
   I. Title
   005.13'3

ISBN 0 471 92156 4

Typeset by Photo · Graphics, Honiton
Printed and bound in Great Britain by
Courier International Ltd, Tiptree, Essex

To

Bryan and Kate Dean

Contents

Preface

There are better ways of spending one's time than writing a book. My own reluctance was overcome initially by the needs of the students to whom I teach Cobol every year. Most of these students are mature part-time postgraduates, nearly all of them have programming experience, and many are professional programmers. I have never found a Cobol textbook which I could with any enthusiasm recommend to such people.

It occurred to me that a book which would suit these students would also meet the needs of other readers who are ill-served by the texts currently available. I have in mind professional programmers generally; those academic colleagues who ask me how they can learn Cobol quickly; undergraduates who already have a grounding in one or more other programming languages; and those many people who, having gained some programming proficiency, for one reason or another want to learn about Cobol.

People like these are quickly alienated by the typical Cobol textbook. They become impatient with tedious explanations (so necessary for absolute beginners) of what computers are, how arithmetic expressions are evaluated, what an **if** statement does, and the seemingly obligatory chapters on structured programming. They already know about these things; what they want is a book which will give them a concise but reasonably comprehensive introduction to the language, and which will enable them to compare the strengths and weaknesses of Cobol with those of the languages they already know. This is the book I have tried to write.

An added incentive to write this book was the approval in September 1985 of a new ANSI and ISO standard definition of the language. The book should enable programmers who are already familiar with the 1974 Standard to update their Cobol knowledge. Those who are new to Cobol should if possible avoid learning the 1974 version, the version taught by a vast majority of the textbooks currently available. The differences between the 1974 and 1985 versions are not merely matters of detail — the programming styles encouraged by the two are fundamentally different. There is little point in learning to overcome the control structure limitations of 1974 Cobol when a more natural approach is possible with the 1985 version. Nevertheless, some readers may for a time find themselves having to use a 1974 compiler or having to maintain old programs written by other people. I have therefore included a chapter dealing with the more significant differences between the two versions.

As far as I know, this is the first Cobol textbook to present Cobol programs in lower-case letters with reserved words in bold type. This method of presentation has always been used to good effect in the Algol-based languages and may have contributed more than we think to the alleged comprehensibility of programs presented in these languages. Certainly I have found it very successful over the years in teaching Cobol and its use is especially suitable now, when the standard allows programs to be written in lower-case.

Cobol is a big language, and this is a relatively small book. Inevitably some language features are given only outline treatment and others are omitted altogether. The omissions will not please everyone. Few people, I think, will regret the absence of the communication module or, at the other extreme, of alphabetic pictures. On the other hand there will be those who feel that indexing or the report writer should have had more than the scant mention I have given them. The report writer facilities in particular are likely to be superseded by fourth-generation tools more quickly than other features of the language. The omitted features will be easily mastered by anyone who understands the fundamentals. A textbook's function is to give general understanding; when serious programming begins, the textbook is replaced by the implementor's manual.

My experiments in teaching Cobol have shown that, when I do not mention certain specific points of detail, I am invariably asked about them, but also that there are other areas where students appear to be perfectly happy with the principles and become bored with the details. The varying depths of treatment accorded to different topics in the book reflect this experience.

The book contains no exercises. Most exercises in programming textbooks fall into one or other of two main categories — the 'repeat what I've just told you' type of question, which I have never liked, and the specification of a simple, or not so simple, program which the reader is expected to prepare and run. Programs which are easy for me to specify and for the reader to understand, such as those to calculate means and standard deviations, give the misleading impression that Cobol is just a verbose alternative to Fortran. Good exercises in more appropriate areas like data validation, file manipulation, and string handling suffer from complex definitions and the need for sizeable data files to be available on the system which the student is using. Where this book is used in conjunction with a taught course, the instructor will no doubt follow the traditional Cobol teaching method of providing files appropriate to the exercises which he or she considers worth setting. Where the book is used for private study, readers will have in mind the application areas which led them to investigate Cobol, and they can create files, and write programs, related to these areas.

In a few places I have adopted the traditional English usage of a masculine pronoun as encompassing both male and female. I have done so only where there seemed to be no other way to achieve equivalent clarity of expression, and I hope that female readers will forgive these lapses. I have reluctantly (I am British) adopted American usages which are enshrined in the Cobol language — 'organization' instead of 'organisation', when the word is used in its technical sense, and 'alternate' instead of 'alternative'. I also accept the use of 'data' as a singular noun, a use common to both sides of the Atlantic. Unattributed quotations are from the current ANSI Standard.

I am grateful to Roger Mitton, Carol Small, and Bill Willcox, who read earlier versions of this work in manuscript form and made very helpful suggestions for improvement; I have not always followed their suggestions, and any errors are mine alone. I would also like to thank Kevin Brunt for technical help, and a whole generation of Birkbeck students for their unwitting role as guinea-pigs.

I include the following acknowledgement at the request of the American National Standards Institute:

COBOL is an industry language and is not the property of any company or group of companies, or of any organization or group of organizations.

No warranty, expressed or implied, is made by any contributor or by the CODASYL COBOL Committee as to the accuracy and functioning of the programming system and language. Moreover, no responsibility is assumed by any contributor, or by the committee, in connection therewith.

The authors and copyright holders of the copyrighted materials used herein

FLOW-MATIC (trademark of Sperry Rand Corporation), Programming for the UNIVAC (R) I and II, Data Automation Systems copyrighted 1958, 1959, by Sperry Rand Corporation; IBM Commercial Translater Form No. F 28–8013, copyrighted 1959 by IBM; FACT, DSI 27A5260–2760, copyrighted 1960 by Minneapolis-Honeywell

have specifically authorized the use of this material in whole or in part, in the COBOL specifications. Such authorization extends to the reproduction and use of COBOL specifications in programming manuals or similar publications.

1. Background and approach

1.1 BACKGROUND

In 1985, the American National Standards Institute (ANSI) published a new specification of the Cobol language. That specification, referred to here as the 1985 Standard, is a milestone in the history of a language which originated from a meeting held in Washington, D.C., in May 1959.

In 1959 most programmers were writing in machine-code. If they were programming commercial or administrative applications, they were further impeded by the unsuitability of the machine languages, which at that time were designed for the manipulation of binary representations of numbers. Fortran and various 'autocodes' were emerging as a means of simplifying the production of programs for numerical applications, and the Algol 60 report was on its way; but these developments did not touch commercial programmers. What was the value to them of a programming language whose data universe consisted of integers and real numbers? Could they, if they heard of Algol at all, do anything but laugh at a language which lacked the concepts of file, record, and character and had no provision at all for input and output? Their contempt for these unusable tools, together with the failure of most academics to take commercial programming seriously, resulted in a regrettable dichotomy of programming expertise. It was to be many years before these academics discovered that files were interesting, and just as many before the commercial programming world came to appreciate Algol 60 for the remarkable achievement it was.

What was needed in 1959 was a 'commercial autocode' — a language which would do for commercial applications what Fortran was beginning to do for numerical work — and a number of hardware manufacturers were engaged in designing and implementing such languages. This development was viewed with alarm by organizations with potentially large computing requirements who might buy machines from more than one supplier. They feared that one of the virtues of a high-level language — the ability to transfer programs and programmers from one machine to another — would be lost. The US Department of Defense (itself of course a huge user of computers) therefore called the Washington meeting for the purpose of considering the desirability and feasibility of establishing a common high-level language.

A body known as CODASYL (Conference on Data Systems Languages) developed out of that meeting. CODASYL's Programming Languages Committee — now known as the Cobol Committee — is still responsible for the development of Cobol and for the submission of Cobol language specifications to be considered

1

for standardization by ANSI. The Cobol standards published by ANSI have been adopted internationally by the International Standards Organization.

In April 1960 a committee of CODASYL produced the initial specification of Cobol, and a revised version appeared in 1961. From then on, the days of the other commercial programming languages were numbered, for the US federal government stipulated, in effect, that it would not buy or rent for data processing purposes any computer which did not have a Cobol compiler. Further official specifications of Cobol were published in the 1960s and an American standard appeared in 1968. Later standards were the ANSI 1974 Standard and the ANSI 1985 Standard referred to above.

Software vendors — *implementors* — provide *implementations* of a standard language by writing compilers which produce, from programs written in accordance with the standard, interpretable or executable code for use on particular computers. Some implementors provide only a subset of the standard language facilities, and some include *extensions* for areas in which the standard language facilities are deficient.

Cobol has continued to be the major language used in commercial applications programming — even PL/1, backed by the might of IBM, failed to supplant it. With the adoption of program generators, application generators, and fourth-generation languages generally, the use of Cobol will increasingly be as a target language, rather than as a language for application programming. But as long as application programs are written in the conventional way, Cobol's predominance will continue.

Cobol is a language which in many respects shows its age, a language encrusted with accretions, a language of redundancies, incongruities, and long-windedness. It could not be otherwise. Over the last quarter-century, applications and techniques have changed, and Cobol has changed with them (or somewhat after them). Because of the problem of forward compatibility, changes to the language have almost inevitably made some features redundant and have increased its size. The need for forward compatibility arises from the very heavy investment represented by probably millions of programs throughout the world written in Cobol. It is — indeed it has to be — an aim of CODASYL and ANSI that programs which conform to earlier specifications of the language will continue to be valid syntactically, and to have the same interpretation, when processed by a compiler which conforms to a later standard. As far as possible, the only kinds of language features actually removed are those which are generally recognized as being little-used or downright dangerous, or whose removal will cause only minor changes to existing programs.

This situation is not always appreciated by critics of Cobol, who tend to come from backgrounds where throw-away programs are the norm, and who have little idea of what it means to have many production programs evolving over the years. The critics are also inclined to underestimate the managerial problems and financial cost of moving to a new language. Programs have to be converted; programmers have to be persuaded of the advantages of the change and have to be trained; experience of using the language has to be gained, and that experience has to be embodied in installation programming standards which the programmers have to be persuaded to observe. All this activity distracts staff from their major task and seriously affects development schedules. To justify such cost and disruption, a language to replace Cobol must have a clearly demonstrable superiority, which in practice means that the language of programming must move closer to the application area and further from the machine. Such 'fourth-generation' tools are already in use, and they will eventually replace Cobol for most routine commercial applications. However, many of these tools generate Cobol code, and a number of them allow the programmer to escape into Cobol when appropriate. There are application areas which cannot conveniently be handled by many fourth-generation languages, there are sometimes efficiency constraints which the languages cannot meet, and the world is full of operational Cobol programs which have to be maintained. The situation will slowly improve, but knowledge of Cobol will still be an asset to commercial programming professionals for some years to come.

Compared with other conventional programming languages, Cobol has much to offer in those application areas where it is commonly used. There are few other languages, and certainly none so generally available as Cobol, which offer all the following advantages *entirely within the standard language*:

(1) Uniform treatment of all data as records in the form of character strings.
(2) Extensive capabilities for defining and handling files. (Try taking your file-handling programs in 'extended' Pascal or Basic to another machine, and you will appreciate the point being made here.)
(3) Incorporation of many functions which in other contexts would be regarded as the province of system utilities. Compared with their colleagues who use other languages in comparable applications, Cobol programmers have little need to concern themselves with the system command language of the particular machine they are using, and their programs are more readily portable to other machines.
(4) The ability to construct large programs from independently compiled modules which communicate with each other by passing parameters or by using common files. Those who speak of Cobol programs as being monolithic do so from a position of ignorance.
(5) The ability to 'tune' programs to improve their performance on particular hardware. Performance is still an important issue in relation to critical response time requirements and in programs which are in use continuously or repeatedly over a period of years. Such tuning can have an adverse effect on program portability, but its use is of course optional.
(6) Facilities for compile time incorporation into a program of text from a library — particularly useful for descriptions of files used by several programs — and facilities for aiding program debugging.

These and many other advantages are taken for granted by Cobol programmers. Beside them, criticisms of such aspects of Cobol as its lower-level control structures are relatively trivial and in any case usually turn out to be criticisms of earlier versions of the language.

1.2 APPROACH

In the remaining chapters, the various Cobol features are not given uniform attention. Emphasis is on those aspects of the language which are essential to basic understanding and those which are likely to be unfamiliar to most readers. Files receive quite detailed attention, since many of the concepts involved in file organization and access are likely to be new to most readers other than those with a background in PL/1 or Fortran 77. The last few chapters deal with features which have practical importance, but treat them only in summary form; the purpose is to make you aware of their existence. In practical situations which call for the use of these features, you will have no problem in understanding the details given in your implementor's manual if you have first mastered the essentials of the language.

Little attention is given to familiar features like boolean and arithmetic expressions, where Cobol is broadly similar to other programming languages. But the most familiar concept of all — assignment — is treated in considerable detail, because failure to grasp the basic rules of Cobol assignment is a major source of trouble for newcomers to the language. In particular, they often fail to appreciate that the Cobol standard does not require run-time type-checking to be done. For example, it is perfectly valid to assign, to an unsigned integer variable, the value of a character-string variable; if at run time the program fails to check that the character-string consists only of numeric digits (the check can be achieved by a single statement), then a value such as "*A-" may be assigned to the integer variable. The Cobol standard does not require the implementor to give a run-time warning or to abort execution. If the implementor chooses not to check for the error, what will happen when the integer variable is subsequently involved in an arithmetic operation? Again, the standard leaves this to the implementor; some implementors may give a run-time message and abort execution, while others may regard the characters as being numeric (e.g. by using only the four low-order bits of their internal representation) and produce nonsensical results.

With most programming languages, programmers can regard the variables they use as abstract entities — an integer is an integer, irrespective of any representation in a computer store. Programmers may, however, become painfully aware of storage considerations when arithmetic accuracy is suspect, or when a program which runs satisfactorily on one machine gives curious results on another; they may also find that the consistency of approach for which a language is praised stops short at the input and output interfaces, where relationships have to be defined between the abstraction of internal data and the character-string representation used externally. Many languages appear to have been designed 'from the inside out', with input and output being added almost as an afterthought.

Cobol, in contrast, appears to have been designed 'from the outside in', with the notion that character strings are received from input and file storage devices, and that character strings are transmitted to output and file storage devices. Programs are therefore seen as algorithms which operate on character strings, and numbers are seen as strings of decimal digits. This emphasis on representation is carried further — a variable declaration is seen as naming *a storage area in a computer*. You cannot describe Cobol without talking about storage.

Finally, a few words about Cobol syntax. (Experience has shown that, even during an introductory lecture when general concepts are being illustrated, students ask questions about the detailed syntax of the language). The major 'symbols' in the language are **words** and **literals**. Cobol 'words' are similar to words in the English language, but there are differences — arithmetic operators, for example, are words in Cobol. A literal is either a character string enclosed in quotation marks or a number in conventional notation. Nearly always, there is at least one space character between one symbol and the next in a program. Two or more contiguous spaces are equivalent to one space, and in most contexts a 'new line' is equivalent to a space. Cobol thus follows normal English usage but is in marked contrast to the Algol-based languages. The role of the space character as a separator extends to its compulsory use between operators and operands in expressions. *Comma, semi-colon,* and *period* follow the conventions of printed English in being followed by one or more spaces. Comma and semi-colon are optionally used for readability only *and have no other significance.* Use of the period (full stop) is compulsory to terminate certain syntactic units of the language. Executable statements require no general terminator or separator because every executable statement begins with a reserved word. More details on these matters will be found in Appendix 1, which need not be read at this stage.

Appendix 1 presents a summary of detailed syntax rules which, in Cobol manuals, tend to be scattered around in diverse places. The Appendix is intended for quick reference during preparation of the reader's first few Cobol programs, and to satisfy any syntactic curiosity which may arise from the examples.

In program examples throughout this book, words appearing in **bold** type are Cobol **reserved words**. Appendix 2 gives the alarmingly long list of reserved words for the 1985 Standard, but you should always consult your implementor's list which may include additional words. Reserved words are words, like 'if' and 'read', which have special significance to a compiler and cannot be used for any other purpose, for example as the name of a file or a variable or a procedure. In actual program text prepared for compilation, reserved words are not distinguished typographically from the rest of the text and, except within non-numeric literals, upper-case and lower-case letters are equivalent.

Appendix 3 is a syntax definition of the language, copied from the 1985 Standard. The reserved words are shown in upper-case rather than in bold type. The metalanguage used is straightforward. Reserved words which are not underlined may be omitted. Brackets, [ ], enclose options which may be omitted; braces, { }, enclose alternatives, one of which must be chosen, or they enclose a piece of syntax to be regarded as a single unit for the purpose of a following ellipsis. The ellipsis (. . .) indicates that the immediately preceding syntactic unit may be repeated one or more times. The symbols | | enclose options from which one or more may be chosen, but from which any given option may be chosen only once.

2. Files, records, and data items

2.1 THE COBOL VIEW OF DATA

Cobol was intended primarily as a programming language for use in commercial and administrative applications. These applications are concerned with the storage, retrieval, and manipulation of large numbers of records. An organization usually keeps many collections of records. One such collection may be a customer file, in which each record relates to one customer and contains such information as the customer's name, address, credit rating, and trade classification. In Cobol, a **record** is a string of characters, and a **file** is a collection of records. Typically, many files are kept in a computer system and each file may be accessed by a number of different programs. The characters which make up a record can include upper- and lower-case letters, numeric digits, and the other characters from the character set of the computer on which the Cobol program is to be run.

In most other programming languages we define the variables and data structures on which a program is to operate; similarly in Cobol we define the files and record types which will be used. Here is a very simple Cobol definition of a file (*note the use of spaces, which are important in Cobol programs*):

> **fd** *mailing-list.*
> 01 *addressee* **pic** x(95).

(The word **pic** is a standard abbreviation of **picture**; **fd** means 'file description'.) This says that the program may make use of a file which it will call *mailing-list*, and that that file is a collection of records of the 'type' *addressee*, i.e. each record is a string of 95 characters. The special **level-number** 01 indicates that what follows is the description of a type of record.

While this description may be adequate for use in some programs, most programs will require the specification of more information about the format of an *addressee* record. On the assumption that our mailing list contains only private individuals, the same file might be defined as in Figure 2.1. The definition now says that the character string forming an *addressee* record consists of four contiguous substrings, the name of each substring being preceded in the definition by level-number 02. The first of these substrings, called *name*, is further divided into two substrings called *initials* and *surname*. (The subdivision is indicated by the use of level-number 03.) If we regard a record of type *addressee* as a string of characters numbered 1, 2, 3,. . . then the string of characters 1 to 6 is called *initials*, characters 7 to 26 are called *surname*, characters 1 to 26 are called *name*, characters 27 to 56 *address-line-1*, characters 57 to 86 *address-line-2*, characters 87 to 95 *post-code*, and characters 1 to 95 *addressee*.

```
fd   mailing-list.
01   addressee.
     02   name.
          03   initials   pic x(6).
          03   surname    pic x(20).
     02   address-line-1  pic x(30).
     02   address-line-2  pic x(30).
     02   post-code       pic x(9).
```

Figure 2.1: A simple description of a file

As seen through Cobol, the main store of a computer is divided into a large
number of 'character positions' each of which can contain one character of data.
Each record description in a program defines and names a **record area** in main
store. The record description in Figure 2.2 defines a record area eleven characters
in length, and specifies the names by which the program may refer to that area
and to sequences of character positions within it. Figure 2.3 shows how the names
a, b, c, d, e and *f* are mapped on to that area. Every reference to *a* in the
program will be a reference to the same fixed eleven-character-position area,
every reference to *b* will be a reference to the first two character positions of
that area, and so on. Thus, if, at some time during program execution, record
area *a* has the value "71JIM∗&A,B.", then the value of *d* is "JIM", the value of
c is "JIM∗", etc.

In the example, *a, b, c, d, e* and *f* are **data-names** (akin to variable names in
other languages); they are the names of **data items** (akin to variables). The name

---

```
*  In pictures, x is equivalent to x(1), xx to x(2), etc.
01  a.
    02  b        pic xx.
    02  c.
        03  d    pic xxx.
        03  e    pic x.
    02  f        pic x(5).
```

*Figure 2.2: A simple record description. A comment line, which has no
effect on the compiled program, is indicated by '∗' in a fixed position at
the start of the line*

---

*Figure 2.3: Storage mapping defined by the record description in Figure
2.2*

a, since it is defined at level 01, is also a **record-name**; a record-name is a name of a **record area**. Since data items are primarily considered as areas of storage, Cobol programmers often speak of the 'content' rather than the 'value' of a data item.

The description of *addressee* in Figure 2.1, therefore, was not really defining a record 'type', but rather defining a record area in store. Throughout the program, every reference to *addressee* is a reference to that same record area which is 95 characters in length, every reference to *post-code* is a reference to character positions 87 to 95 of that area, and so on. Now, the file *mailing-list* contains many records which have the same format, but there is only a single record area *addressee*. So, if a program wants to make use of a particular record from the file, it first of all obtains a copy of that record in the record area *addressee*.

Record areas are discrete areas of store; there is no necessary relationship between the storage position of any record area and the position of any other.

The two commonest operations involving data items are assignment and comparison. When data items are of the kinds introduced so far — i.e. defined by x-type pictures or by concatenation of lower-level data items — the rules governing these two operations are straightforward.

2.2 ASSIGNMENT

In other languages, an assignment operation is denoted by such statements as

$p:=q$

or

$P=Q$

or

$LET\ P=Q.$

In Cobol the equivalent statement is

move *q* **to** *p*

the effect usually being that the current value of *p* is replaced by the current value of *q*, the latter remaining unchanged. Execution of a **move** statement is not affected by the level-numbers of the operands — *p* and *q* may have the same or different level-numbers.

When *p* and *q* are the names of data items of the same length, the effect of the statement

move *q* **to** *p*

is obvious, and is not affected by level-numbers:

			before	*after*
05	*q*	**pic** x(3).	JIM	JIM
05	*p*	**pic** x(3).	TOM	JIM

or:

				before	*after*
03	*q*	**pic** x(3).			
03	*p*.			JIM	JIM
		04	*m* **pic** x.	T	J
		04	*n* **pic** xx.	OM	IM

When *q* is longer than *p*, and the statement

> **move** *q* **to** *p*

is executed, truncation occurs on the right:

			before	*after*
03	*q*	**pic** x(5).	ROYAL	ROYAL
02	*p*	**pic** x(3).	TOM	ROY

When *q* is shorter than *p* the extra character positions in *p* are filled with space characters:

			before	*after*
02	*q*	**pic** x(3).	JIM	JIM
02	*p*	**pic** x(5).	KEVIN	JIM⎵⎵

The same rules apply when the first operand of a **move** statement is a literal (i.e. an actual value, rather than a data-name). So, if *p*'s picture were x(5), the result of executing the statement

> **move** "FRED" **to** *p*

would be that *p*'s value would become FRED⎵.

2.3 COMPARISON

Unless special steps are taken, comparison of two characters is according to the 'collating sequence' of the machine on which a program is executed. A machine usually has a unique internal binary representation (encoding) for each character in its character set, and the collating sequence of a machine is normally nothing more than a simple listing of the characters in order of their binary encodings, listed from low to high value. Thus if, in a particular machine, the character "A" were encoded as 11010001 (binary 209) and "*" as 10001011 (binary 139), then the value "A" would be greater than the value "*". In another machine, however, the internal representations might be such that "A" was *less* than "*". This is clearly an undesirable situation, since a program can give different results when run on different machines, and we will see in a later chapter how Cobol provides a means of overcoming the difficulty. For the present, it is enough to note that all collating sequences are such that "A" is less than "B", "B" is less than "C", etc., that "a" is less than "b", "b" is less than "c", etc., and that "0" is less than "1", "1" is less than "2", etc.

The relational operators in Cobol are $<$ (less than), $=$ (equal to), $>$ (greater than), $<=$ (less than or equal to), and $>=$ (greater than or equal to). The first three of these may be preceded by the word **not**. *Every relational operator must be preceded and followed by at least one space.*

When two character strings of equal length are compared, comparison may be regarded as proceeding from left to right, each corresponding pair of characters being compared until either an unequal pair is found or the rightmost pair is reached and found to be equal. So, given

> *p* **pic** x(3).   JIM
> *q* **pic** x(3).   TOM

comparison of the first characters (J and T) is enough to establish $p < q$. Given

> *p* **pic** x(6).   JOHN⎿⎾⏌
> *q* **pic** x(6).   JOANNA

comparison of the third pair of characters (H and A) establishes $p > q$. Given

> 01 *p* **pic** x(4).   JOHN
> 01 *q*.
>   02 *r* **pic** x(3).   JOH
>   02 *s* **pic** x.   N

all four character pairs have to be compared to establish $p = q$. The same method is used when one of the operands is a literal, as in

> $p >$ "JOHN"

When the operands are of different lengths, the shorter (whether it be a data item or a literal) is considered as being extended to the length of the longer by the addition of space characters on the right. Thus, given

> *p* **pic** x(3).   JIM
> *q* **pic** x(6).   JIM⎿⎾⏌

the condition

> $p = q$

is true, and the condition

> $q =$ "JIM"

is also true. But, given

> *p* **pic** x(3).   TOM
> *q* **pic** x(6).   TOMATO

the conditions

> $p = q$

and

$$q = \text{"TOM"}$$

are both false, and whether such conditions as

$$p < q$$

and

$$q > \text{"TOM"}$$

are true or false depends on the relative positions of the space character and the character "A" in the collating sequence. Conditions of the kind shown may be terms in a more complex expression which includes the familiar boolean operators **and**, **or**, and **not**, e.g.

$$a > b \text{ and } a < c$$

Such expressions are considered further in a later chapter.

2.4 INTERACTION WITH TERMINALS

Values may also be assigned to data items by input from a terminal. Cobol does not provide a satisfactory standard method of screen management, and extended facilities in this area are often provided by implementors of the language. This book is intended to cover only standard Cobol, so only the crudest form of screen management is used in the examples. Sequentially organized files (to be described in Chapter 8) can be assigned to terminals, but initially we will restrict our consideration of terminal input and output to the **accept** and **display** statements. (These statements may also be used for devices other than terminals.)

The Cobol standard leaves the details of these statements to be defined by the implementor, but the simple uses described below are typical. The **accept** statement receives one line of input and assigns it to the data item named in the statement, truncating or space-filling on the right as necessary. For example the statement

> **accept** y

takes a line of input from the user and assigns it as a character string to data item y.

The **display** statement sends a line of output to the screen and may specify several values which are to be placed in the line. For example, if the value of the data item *depot-location* is "Leeds", then execution of the statement

> **display** "Depot is ", *depot-location*

will result in output, left-aligned, of the line

> Depot is Leeds

Because only minimal specifications of **accept** and **display** are given in the Cobol standard, you should consult your implementor's manual before using these statements.

3. Files and file access

3.1 THE COBOL VIEW OF STORAGE

Figure 3.1 shows a conceptual model of computer storage during execution of a program which accesses three files called a, b, and c. The **data division** consists of the record areas defined in the program. The record areas in the **file section** have a special property — each is exclusively associated with a file used by the program, and there is one record area in the file section corresponding to each file. The record area ar, for example, is the record area associated with file a. Every record read from file a is read into area ar and every record written to file a is written from area ar. *No data can be written to a file or read from a file except through the record area associated with that file.*

In storage terms, then, we can visualize the **file section** of the data division as containing one record area for each file used by the program. The **working-storage section** consists of as many record areas as the program requires for records which are not associated with files. Data cannot be read directly from files into working-storage record areas, nor can data in these areas be written directly to files. If a working-storage record is to be written to a file, it must first be moved to the record area associated with that file. (Notice that there is no similar restriction on input and output using the **accept** and **display** statements; but these statements are intended for 'low-volume data' only and they cannot be used to access files.)

Figure 3.2 shows in outline the form of a Cobol program corresponding to the model of Figure 3.1. The **identification division** gives the name *example1* to the program; if the program were called as a sub-process of another program, *example1* is the name by which the calling program would identify it.

The **environment division** contains a **select** sentence for each file. The files are known as a, b, and c in this program, but the operating system under which the program is run may know them by different names or may have to know to which input or output channel or device a file is to be assigned. The names $x1$, $x2$, and $x3$ in Figure 3.2 are arbitrary, as are all names following the words **assign to** in examples throughout this book; the implementor's manual for a particular compiler should be consulted to determine what should be specified here.

In the **file section** of a program's data division, each file is named and a record description is given of the associated record area. The **working-storage section** in the program describes all record areas not associated with files. The **procedure division** contains only the executable program code. No special statement is needed to terminate the text of a program.

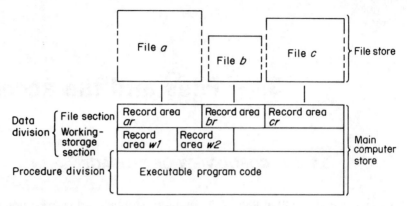

Figure 3.1:   The Cobol programmer's model of computer storage

---

3.2 FILE-ACCESSING STATEMENTS

Consider again the file *mailing-list* and its associated record area *addressee* (Figure 3.3). Like any file, *mailing-list* is accessed one record at a time. The following operations can be performed by statements in the procedure division:

   (**1**) We can assign to *addressee*, or to its constituent data items individually, the name and address of a person who is to be added to the mailing list. Then we can insert this new record into the file by using the statement

   write *addressee*

The effect of executing this statement is to copy the content of *addressee* into the file *mailing-list* (since that is the file associated in the data division with the area *addressee*) as a new record. As a result, the file contains one record more than it did before. The content of *addressee* is undefined after successful execution of the **write** statement.

   (**2**) Execution of the statement

   read *mailing-list*

obtains, in the record area *addressee*, a copy of some record from the file. (We will see later how the program can identify which one of the records in the file is to be read.) The file is unchanged.

   (**3**) Execution of the statement

   delete *mailing-list*

does not delete the complete file, as the syntax may suggest. In fact it removes *one record* from the file. (Again, we will see later how the program identifies which one of the records is to be removed.) As a result, the file contains one record fewer than it did before. The content of *addressee* is unchanged.

   (**4**) Execution of the statement

   rewrite *addressee*

```
identification division.
  program-id. example1.

environment division.
  input-output section.
  file-control.
     select a    assign to x1 ... .
     select b    assign to x2 ... .
     select c    assign to x3 ... .

data division.
  file section.
  fd   a ... .
  01   ar.
       02 ...
       -
       -
       -
  fd   b ... .
  01   br.
       02 ...
       -
       -
       -
  fd   c ... .
  01   cr.
       02 ...
       -
       -
       -
  working-storage section.
  01   w1.
       02 ...
       -
       -
       -
  01   w2.
       02 ...
       -
       -
       -

  procedure division.
       -
       -
       -
```

Figure 3.2: Outline Cobol program corresponding to the model of Figure 3.1

---

causes the content of *addressee* to be placed in the file *mailing-list* in such a way that it replaces (or 'overwrites') an existing record in the file; the number of records in the file is thus unchanged. The content of *addressee* is undefined after successful execution of the **rewrite** statement. The method of determining which one of the records in the file is to be replaced by a **rewrite** statement will be explained later. The **rewrite** statement is commonly used in the 'updating' of a record, which a program carries out by:

```
(a) Description of mailing-list file:

    fd  mailing-list.
    01  addressee.
        02  name.
            03  initials    pic x(6).
            03  surname     pic x(20).
        02  address-line-1  pic x(30).
        02  address-line-2  pic x(30).
        02  post-code       pic x(9).
```

```
(b) Partial diagram of storage:
```

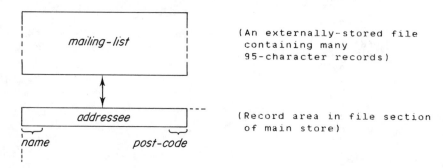

Figure 3.3:   The file mailing-list *and its record area* addressee

---

(a) using a **read** statement to obtain a copy of a specified record; then
(b) assigning new values to one or more data items in the record area; then
(c) using a **rewrite** statement to replace (in the file) the record originally read
 by its updated version.

   (**5**) A statement in the form

   start *mailing-list*

enables a program to set a file cursor (pointer) to a particular logical position in
the file. Neither the file nor the record area is affected by execution of a **start**
statement.

   These five statements, together with

(a) the **open** statement, which makes a specified file or files available to the
 program, and
(b) the **close** statement, which makes a specified file or files no longer available
 to the program,

constitute the complete repertoire of executable file-handling statements.

   It may seem strange that **read**, **delete**, and **start** name the file, while **write** and
rewrite name the record area. This seeming inconsistency will be explained later.

3.3 SUCCESSFUL AND UNSUCCESSFUL EXECUTION

Execution of a file-accessing statement may be successful, in that the primary function of the statement is successfully carried out (e.g. a **read** statement retrieves a record) or it may be unsuccessful (e.g. the record to be read cannot be found in the file). It is important to note the effects of successful and unsuccessful execution in relation to the content of the record area associated with the file. These effects are summarized in Figure 3.4. In the circumstances shown there as resulting in the record area content being undefined, some Cobol implementations in fact act consistently — for example, after successful execution of a **write** statement, a copy of the record written may still be available in the record area — but a program which relies on such implementation-dependent features may not be portable to another implementation.

3.4 FILE ORGANIZATION AND ACCESS

Precisely how the five basic file-accessing statements described above are used depends on:

(a) the **organization** of the file being accessed;
(b) the **access method** employed by the program; and
(c) the current **open mode** for that file.

The logical structure of a file is referred to as its **organization**. (British readers should note the 'z' in this spelling. Use of the spelling 'organisation' is one of the commonest errors which people make in their first Cobol programs, and the compiler's error message is unlikely to indicate clearly what is wrong). Cobol provides three methods of organization (**sequential**, **relative**, and **indexed**), one of which is chosen by the programmer for any file which a program creates. When a file has been created, it retains its organization throughout its life; its organization is therefore a fixed property of a file.

Statement	Content of record area after: successful execution	unsuccessful execution
write	undefined	unchanged
read	copy of retrieved record	undefined
delete	unchanged	unchanged
rewrite	undefined	unchanged
start	unchanged	unchanged

Figure 3.4: How record area content is affected by execution of file accessing statements

Access method, by contrast, is a property of a program in relation to a particular file. Cobol provides three methods of accessing a file (**sequential**, **random**, and **dynamic**) and, subject to certain restrictions, a program may choose to access a file using any one of these methods.

When a program opens a file, it may do so in one of four modes:

input: the file already exists; it may be used as a source of data but cannot be changed;

output: the file is a new one, to be created by the program; records once written cannot be changed or deleted;

i-o: usually, the file already exists; it may be used as a source of data and, subject to certain limitations, may also be changed by the addition of new records or deletion or amendment of existing records;

extend: usually, the file already exists; all that the program can do is add new records to the end.

Chapters 4, 5, 6, 8, 11, and 12 describe the Cobol file organization methods and the application of the access methods to each of them.

4. Indexed files – random access

4.1 INTRODUCTION

In a file whose organization is *indexed*, each record can be uniquely identified by a **record key** value. The record key is a specially designated data item in the record description which has a different value in every record in the file. In other words, there is some data item in the record format whose set of assigned values has a one-to-one correspondence with the set of records forming the file. The record key position within a record is established at the time when the file is created, and cannot later be changed.

Let us suppose that our *mailing-list* file has indexed organization and that the record key is the data item *surname*, i.e. character positions 7 to 26 of a record. There are two consequences.

(a) By specifying a value of *surname*, say 'Strachan', we immediately identify the record in the file in which *surname* = "Strachan", if such a record exists.

(b) Since the function of the record key is to identify a unique record, there cannot be two or more records in the file with *surname* = "Strachan". So our file cannot be used if two people on our mailing list have the same surname! We will see later that this is a limitation of our file design rather than a limitation of Cobol, and that the limitation can easily be overcome, but for the moment let us accept it.

Figure 4.1 shows how the file is described. The **select** sentence in the environment division now specifies that the file organization is indexed, and that the record key is *surname*.

The words **access random** indicate that, when this program wants to access a record in the file, it will identify the particular record by specifying its record key value. In other words, the statements **read**, **delete**, and **rewrite** will each make use of the current value of *surname* in the record area *addressee* in order to identify that record in the file to which the operation is to be applied.

4.2 SOME TYPICAL REQUIREMENTS

(**1**) *Mrs Leighton wishes to have her record removed from the mailing list.*
This change can be effected by the two statements

```
         -
         -
         -
      environment division.
        input-output section.
        file-control.
          select mailing-list, assign to xyz
                 organization indexed
                 access random
                 record key  surname.
         -
         -
         -
      data division.
        file section.
        fd  mailing-list.
        01  addressee.
            02  name.
                03  initials    pic x(6).
                03  surname     pic x(20).
            02  address-line-1  pic x(30).
            02  address-line-2  pic x(30).
            02  post-code       pic x(9).
```

Figure 4.1: Details of the indexed file mailing-list, *which is to be accessed randomly*

> **move** "Leighton" **to** *surname*
> **delete** *mailing-list*

Three practical observations should be made at this stage. Firstly, if this were part of a real program, the name "Leighton" would not appear as a literal in the **move** statement. (If it did appear as a literal, special statements would have been written to delete the "Leighton" record; most programs are intended to be more general in their application.) Rather, the name "Leighton" would have been obtained from a terminal or from another file and might have been assigned to a working-storage data item. Thus a statement such as

> **move** *requested-name* **to** *surname*

would probably be used instead of

> **move** "Leighton" **to** *surname*

This observation applies also to the examples which follow, but will not be repeated; the use of literals makes the examples easier to read.

Secondly, it is not usual practice to delete a record without first archiving it in some other file; such archiving enables the record to be reconstituted easily if it has been deleted in error, and may in general be useful for statistical analysis at a later date. Valuable information might otherwise be lost. Thus, a more likely sequence of statements is

> **move** "Leighton" **to** *surname*
> **read** *mailing-list*
> **move** *addressee* **to** *archive-record*
> **write** *archive-record*
> **delete** *mailing-list*

where *archive-record* is the record area associated with some other file which is used for storing archive records. Notice that there is no need to assign "Leighton" to *surname* again before the **delete** statement — the record read from *mailing-list* has "Leighton" as the value of *surname*, and the intervening statements have not changed the content of the record area *addressee*.

Thirdly, and most importantly for this chapter, it is possible that there is no "Leighton" record in the file. Perhaps there never was, or perhaps it has already been deleted, or perhaps the name has been wrongly spelt. In any of these cases, the program should inform the person responsible for the deletion request that there is no "Leighton" record. In this chapter we will assume that requests come from a terminal or from the keyboard of a micro, when the statement

> **display** "not in mailing-list"

may be adequate.

In random access, as here, an **invalid key** condition arises when execution of one of the statements **read**, **write**, **delete**, and **rewrite** is attempted but is unsuccessful because the state of the file is inconsistent with the operation to be performed. Unless a suitable declarative procedure (explained later) is provided, Cobol requires that each of these four statements be extended by an **invalid key** phrase, in which the words **invalid key** are followed by statements which are to be executed only in the event of an invalid key condition arising. We may choose also to include a **not invalid key** phrase containing statements to be executed only in cases where the invalid key condition does *not* arise. So we can change the above program to that shown in Figure 4.2(a), the logic of which is shown in flow-chart form in Figure 4.2(b). Notice, in Figure 4.2(a), the use of the word **end-read** to delimit the **read** statement — **end-read** separates the statements embedded in the **read** statement from those which follow the **read** statement. (Indentation of statements which are subordinate to another statement, as in the case of the **display** statement here, is not required but it is generally regarded as making programs more readable. Bear in mind too that commas and semi-colons have no syntactic or semantic significance.)

But this is not the end of the story. The **delete** statement too must have an **invalid key** phrase, as shown in Figure 4.3. The invalid key condition can arise during execution of this **delete** statement only if there is no record in the file whose record key matches that in the record area. Yet our program logic ensures that the **delete** statement is executed only if we have successfully read a "Leighton" record. Should the invalid key condition arise during execution of the **delete** statement, there must be an error in the program logic. In such a case there may

```
move "Leighton" to surname
read mailing-list;
invalid key
    display "not in mailing list"
not invalid key
    move addressee to archive-record
    write archive-record
    delete mailing-list
end-read
```

*Figure 4.2(a):   The use of **invalid key** and **not invalid key** phrases*

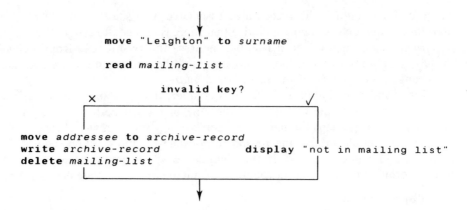

Figure 4.2(b): A flow chart showing the logic of the program in Figure 4.2(a)

```
move "Leighton" to surname
read mailing-list;
invalid key
     display "not in mailing list"
not invalid key
     move addressee to archive-record
     write archive-record
     delete mailing-list;
     invalid key
          display "logic error 8 - program stopped"
          stop run
     end-delete
end-read
```

Figure 4.3: Deleting the "Leighton" record

be little point in proceeding with the program, so we can notify the user, then use the **stop run** statement which terminates execution of the program. Note that we resort to this expedient only very exceptionally, in cases where the error must arise from causes like a program logic error or a hardware failure, and not from bad data. It seems entirely appropriate to handle such a 'panic abort' situation in this way; indeed, if the language did not force us to include an **invalid key** phrase, we would not even test for the possibility of an error. In this case (and in similar cases) we have chosen to include an identifying number (here 8) in the error message. The terminal user is expected to pass this number on to programming staff who will investigate the cause of the error. (For the sake of simplicity, we are assuming here, as we shall in similar situations throughout the book, that the file is not being accessed simultaneously by another program, or by another activation of this program.)

Figure 4.3 shows the final version of our program fragment. Notice first that, just as the **read** statement is delimited by the word **end-read**, so the **delete** statement is delimited by the word **end-delete**. Notice also that we have not made use of a **not invalid key** phrase in the **delete** statement, since there is no special action to be taken in the case where the record is successfully deleted. (The absence of an **invalid key** phrase in the **write** statement which archives the deleted record is due to an assumption that the archive file is sequentially organized; sequential organization will be introduced in a later chapter. Thus no other statements are embedded within this **write** statement; the statement is therefore *not* delimited by the word **end-write**).

(**2**) *J. Kennedy of 6 The Mansions, Potters Bar, EN6 3XY is to be added to the mailing list.*

The program code to meet this requirement is given in Figure 4.4. In a real program, the first operands of the **move** statements would not, of course, be literals.

When a **write** statement is executed, the system checks that the value of the record key in the record area is not already present as the value of the record key in any record in the file. If it is, the record cannot be written (since that record key value would no longer identify a unique record), the invalid key condition exists, and the content of the record area is unchanged. Otherwise, the content of the record area is copied to the file as a new record and the content of the record area becomes undefined. So, in this example, the invalid key condition probably indicates that there is already a record with *surname* = "Kennedy" in the file; but the invalid key condition can also indicate that the space assigned to the file is full — hence the message output by the **display** statement. (If a program is to establish which of these two situations exists, it can do so by defining a **file status** data item whose value can be tested when the invalid key condition has been detected. File status will be introduced in a later chapter.) Notice that in this program we have chosen to place the words **invalid key** on the first line of the **write** statement, rather than on the line following; this makes no difference at all to the program logic.

(**3**) *Mr Rougvie's post-code is to be corrected to "AB1 5AB"*

The program code to meet this requirement is given in Figure 4.5, and is straightforward. The invalid key condition arises during execution of the **rewrite** statement if there is no record in the file whose record key value matches that in the record area. In this program the condition should not arise — the record for "Rougvie" *must* be present in the file since the program has just read it. The 'panic abort' action is justified for the same reasons as it was in example (1) above.

4.3 A PROGRAM TO MAINTAIN THE MAILING LIST FILE

In the rest of this chapter we develop a program by means of which a user at a terminal can keep the mailing list up to date. The file design, as we have noted,

```
move "    J." to initials
move "Kennedy" to surname
move "6 The Mansions" to address-line-1
move "Potters Bar" to address-line-2
move "EN6 3XY" to post-code
write addressee; invalid key
    display surname, "already in file, or space full"
end-write
```

Figure 4.4: Adding the "Kennedy" record

```
move "Rougvie" to surname
read mailing-list;
invalid key
    display "not in mailing list"
not invalid key
    move "AB1 5AB" to post-code
    rewrite addressee; invalid key
        display "logic error 9 - program stopped"
        stop run
    end-rewrite
end-read
```

Figure 4.5: Changing Rougvie's post-code

---

is unrealistic — it cannot accommodate two persons with the same surname. The user dialogue which the program implements is also far from ideal: the program itself is unsophisticated in form, and neglects proper validity checking; it also fails to archive deleted records. But at this stage practicality and elegance are secondary objectives — the maintenance of a mailing list is an application which every reader will understand; the dialogue is simple and the program is short, yet it introduces just enough of the Cobol language to enable you to prepare and run your own programs.

4.3.1 THE DIALOGUE TO BE REALIZED BY THE PROGRAM

When the program is activated, it displays

ready

to which the user responds by entering the name of a function:

show	to display a record on the screen
remove	to delete a record
add	to insert a new record in the file
change	to update an existing record
finish	to sign off.

(a) If the user enters anything other than these five words, a suitable message is displayed, followed by

ready

again.

(b) If the user enters *finish*, the program responds

goodbye

and the session ends.

(c) Otherwise the program displays

surname?

to which the user responds by entering the surname of the person whose record is to be operated on or added. The form of dialogue (if any) from this point on depends on which function the user has chosen. When the operation is complete, or when an error has been detected and notified to the user, the word

ready

is again displayed.

4.3.2 THE PROGRAM IN GENERAL

The program presented in Figure 4.6 is nearly complete; the only omission is the procedure *update-procedure*, which will be considered later. Line numbers are provided purely as an aid to discussion; they are not part of the program.

Any line with "*" at the beginning is a comment line. Any line with "/" at the beginning is also a comment line, but, if the program is listed on a printer, a "/" comment line will be printed as the first line of a new page. So, if this program is listed by the compiler, each division will start at the top of a new page.

Since the only file used by the program is *mailing-list*, the environment division and the file section of the data division are those we have already used in this chapter. In the working-storage section of the data division, the record areas *in-line* and *orig-surname* will be used in later development of the program and can be ignored for the present.

The procedure division of this program consists of five paragraphs, named *main* (lines 33 to 50), *show-procedure* (lines 53 to 63), *delete-procedure* (lines 66 to 70), *insert-procedure* (lines 73 to 94) and *get-surname* (lines 97 to 99). Each paragraph is headed by its name, followed by a period (.), and a period also follows the last statement in a paragraph. The first statement in a paragraph may begin on the same line as the paragraph name (as at line 33), but need not do so (see line 53).

Execution of a program begins at the start of the first paragraph (in this program, the paragraph *main*), and ends when a **stop run** statement is executed.

4.3.3 THE PARAGRAPH MAIN

(1) The statement

open i–o *mailing-list*

makes the file and its record area available to the program. The word **i–o** is a standard abbreviation of **input–output**. In random access mode, as here, **open i–o** enables a program to use the statements **read**, **write**, **delete**, and **rewrite**.

Often a program uses an existing file only as a source of data and does not amend it in any way. In such a case the mailing list file would be opened by the statement

open input *mailing-list*

```
1      identification division.
2         program-id.  change-mailing.
3      /
4       environment division.
5       input-output section.
6          file-control.
7             select mailing-list  assign to xyz
8                   organization indexed
9                   access random
10                  record key surname.
11     /
12      data division.
13      file section.
14      fd  mailing-list.
15      01  addressee.
16          02  name.
17              03  initials   pic x(6).
18              03  surname    pic x(20).
19          02  address-line-1 pic x(30).
20          02  address-line-2 pic x(30).
21          02  post-code      pic x(9).
22
23      working-storage section.
24      01  command          pic x(6).
25      01  in-line.
26          02  op           pic x(5).
27          02  val          pic x(30).
28      01  orig-surname     pic x(20).
29      01  inserted-surname pic x(20).
30
31     /
32      procedure division.
33      main.  open i-o mailing-list
34             display "ready"
35             accept command
36             perform until  command = "finish"
37                 evaluate command
38                     when "show"    perform show-procedure
39                     when "remove"  perform delete-procedure
40                     when "add"     perform insert-procedure
41                     when "change"  perform update-procedure
42                   . when other     display "valid commands are add,
43      -                             " change, remove, show, finish"
44                 end-evaluate
45                 display "ready"
46                 accept command
47             end-perform
48             close mailing-list
49             display "goodbye"
50             stop run.
51
52
53      show-procedure.
54          perform get-surname
55          read mailing-list;
56          invalid key
57              display "not in mailing list"
58          not invalid key
59              display name
60              display address-line-1
61              display address-line-2
62              display post-code
63          end-read.
```

```
64
65
66    delete-procedure.
67         perform get-surname
68         delete mailing-list;   invalid key
69              display "not in mailing list"
70         end-delete.
71
72
73    insert-procedure.
74         perform get-surname
75         move surname to inserted-surname
76         read mailing-list;
77         invalid key
78              move inserted-surname to surname
79              display "initials?"
80              accept initials
81              display "first line of address?"
82              accept address-line-1
83              display "second line?"
84              accept address-line-2
85              display "post-code?"
86              accept post-code
87              write addressee;   invalid key
88                   display "logic error 1 or file space full - progr
89    -                    "am stopped"
90                   stop run
91              end-write
92         not invalid key
93              display "already in file"
94         end-read.
95
96
97    get-surname.
98         display "surname?"
99         accept surname.
100
```

Figure 4.6:   The program change-mailing, *with* update-procedure *as yet undefined*

---

and, in random access, the only operation permitted on *mailing-list* would be **read**.

To create a new file called *x* to which only the **write** statement will be applied, the statement

open output *x*

is used. File *x* must, of course, have been defined in the environment and data divisions.

(2) The statements appearing between

perform until *command* = "finish"

(line 36) and

end-perform

(line 47) are executed repeatedly until the condition

    command = "finish"

is true. This is demonstrated by Figure 4.7, which shows the logic of the paragraph *main* in flow-chart form.

Programmers who have used an Algol-based language such as Pascal should be careful — Cobol's **perform until** normally tests the terminating condition *before*, rather than after, each iteration, so that, if the condition is initially true, the 'repeated' code is not executed at all. (But it is possible in Cobol to specify that the test be made *after* each iteration.)

(3) Within the **evaluate** statement (lines 37 to 44), **perform** happens to be used in a different way. Here, because the word **perform** is followed by the name of a paragraph, it is the equivalent of a procedure or subroutine call. For example, when the value of *command* is "remove" (line 39), the paragraph *delete-procedure* will be executed as a sub-process. (The **perform** statement has no provision for parameter-passing, but we will see later that another Cobol statement, **call**, does provide for parameters.)

(4) The semantics of the **evaluate** statement, as used in lines 37 to 44, should be obvious. (In general, it is a very powerful "case" statement.) The value of *command* is examined and, depending on its value, an appropriate procedure (paragraph) is called. If the value is one which is not provided for by the program (**when other**), a suitable message is displayed. After execution of the appropriate statements, control returns to the statement following the **evaluate** statement (**display** "ready", at line 45). Then a further command is accepted and evaluated, unless the user enters "finish", in which case control passes to the statement following **end-perform**.

(5) The statement

    close *mailing-list*

'detaches' the file *mailing-list* from this program; the file could later be made available again in the same program by another **open** statement. The **close** statement is included in this program only to illustrate its syntax. Its use here is unnecessary since the **stop run** statement closes all files which are still open.

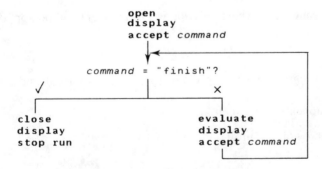

Figure 4.7: The logic of the paragraph main

4.3.4 *THE PARAGRAPHS* SHOW-PROCEDURE *AND* DELETE-PROCEDURE

These paragraphs introduce no new concepts. Both of them cali *get-surname* as a procedure; *get-surname* obtains the surname from the user and places it in the record key position in the record area *addressee*. In order to keep the program simple, no archive file has been defined, and *delete-procedure* does not archive the deleted record.

4.3.5 *THE PARAGRAPH* INSERT-PROCEDURE

Here a further dialogue is conducted with the user to obtain the details of the record to be inserted. The procedure could have been specified as:

> **perform** *get-surname*
> **display** "initials?"
> [Lines 80 to 86 unchanged]
> **write** *addressee*; **invalid key**
>   **display** *surname*, "already in file or file space full"
> **end-write**

But, if the surname were already in the file, the user would not be told that the new record was unacceptable until he or she had entered a great deal of unnecessary data. Therefore *insert-procedure* in Figure 4.6 (lines 73 to 94) includes a **read** statement (line 76) which establishes initially whether or not a record for the given surname already exists in the file. Since unsuccessful execution of a **read** statement leaves the content of the record area undefined, it is necessary to preserve the value of *surname* in working-storage — hence the move to *inserted-surname* (defined at line 29) — and to reinstate it after the **read**. The **write** statement (line 87) can be executed only when the **read** statement gave rise to the invalid key condition, i.e. when there is no record in the file for the given *surname* value. Therefore, if the invalid key condition arises during execution of the **write** statement, it is either because there is no space left in the file store allocated to *mailing-list* (as noted in example 2, earlier) or because of an error in the program logic.

4.3.6 *UPDATING A RECORD*

In our dialogue, when the user enters the word "change", he or she is indicating a wish to change the values of one or more data items in a record. So we have a further dialogue in which we first prompt the user by showing the options available. We display the two lines:

> *enter one of the following:*
> *surn= init= add1= add2= post= done*

Then if, for example, the user wants to change the second line of the address to "Edinburgh", he (let us assume that the user is male) responds

    add2 = Edinburgh

after which the word

    another?

is displayed, and he can enter a change to another data item. When he has made all the changes he wants to, he responds

    done

which indicates that he has finished with this record and results in return to the

    ready

state.

    This dialogue is implemented in *update-procedure*, given in Figure 4.8. It:

(a) reads the required record from the file; then
(b) places each new value obtained from the user in the appropriate part of the record area *addressee*, thus replacing the value already there; then
(c) rewrites the changed record into the file.

But notice that the procedure leaves changes of surname to be handled by another procedure, *change-key*, which is as yet unspecified. At first sight, it might appear that line 113 in Figure 4.8 could be simply:

    when "surn=" **move** *val* **to** *surname*

but, because *surname* is the record key, this will not do. Suppose that the record read from the file had "Miller" as the value of *surname*, and that the user entered

    surn = Hiller

then the value of *surname* would become "Hiller". So, when the **rewrite** statement was reached, the system would try to place the amended record in the file in such a way that it replaced an existing "Hiller" (instead of "Miller") record. If there were no such record, the invalid key condition would cause the program to stop; if there were such a record, that record would be wrongly replaced by the amended record and lost. In either event, the original "Miller" record would remain in the file unchanged.

    What the procedure *change-key* must do, therefore, is delete the old "Miller" record and **write** a new "Hiller" record, while ensuring that any changes which the user makes to other data items of the record, both before and after the change of surname, are correctly effected. One possible solution is that shown in Figure 4.9. The explanation below assumes that the surname "Miller" is to be changed to "Hiller".

    Lines 131 and 132 store "Miller" as the value of *orig-surname* and set *surname* = "Hiller".

    Lines 133 to 148 write the current form of the record (with *surname* = "Hiller") to the file as a new record, and test whether the operation was successfully completed.

```
101
102    update-procedure.
103        perform get-surname
104        read mailing-list;
105        invalid key
106            display "not in mailing list"
107        not invalid key
108            display "enter one of the following:"
109            display "surn=  init=  add1=  add2=  post=  done"
110            accept in-line
111            perform until  op = "done"
112                evaluate op
113                    when "surn="  perform change-key
114                    when "init="  move val to initials
115                    when "add1="  move val to address-line-1
116                    when "add2="  move val to address-line-2
117                    when "post="  move val to post-code
118                    when other    display "?"
119                end-evaluate
120                display "another?"
121                accept in-line
122            end-perform
123            rewrite addressee;  invalid key
124                display "logic error 2 - program stopped"
125                stop run
126            end-rewrite
127        end-read.
128
```

Figure 4.8: Update-procedure. *The storage area* in-line, *which includes* op *and* val, *is defined at lines 25–27 (see Figure 4.6)*

```
129
130    change-key.
131        move surname to orig-surname
132        move val to surname
133        write addressee
134        invalid key
135            display "already in file, or file space full"
136            move orig-surname to surname
137        not invalid key
138            move orig-surname to surname
139            delete mailing-list;  invalid key
140                display "logic error 3 - program stopped"
141                stop run
142            end-delete
143            move val to surname
144            read mailing-list;  invalid key
145                display "logic error 4 - program stopped"
146                stop run
147            end-read
148        end-write.
```

Figure 4.9: Change-key

   Lines 135 and 136 deal with the case where the **write** was unsuccessful, by displaying a message, then restoring "Miller" as the value of *surname*. The record area *addressee* still reflects all other changes made since the original record was read. (The record area content is not affected by unsuccessful execution of a **write** statement.)

Lines 138 to 147 deal with the case where the **write** was successful. The value "Miller" is assigned to *surname*, so that the **delete** statement deletes the "Miller" record originally read. Since the successful execution of the **write** statement left the record area content undefined, the "Hiller" record which was written at line 133 has to be read back again. This record, now in the record area (*addressee*), therefore reflects all changes made so far by the user. Any subsequent user changes will of course be made in the record area and, when the user enters *done*, the **rewrite** statement in *update-procedure* (line 123) will replace the "Hiller" record which was written at line 133 by the version in the record area.

4.3.7 THE COMPLETE PROGRAM

The complete program for our little application is simply that shown in Figure 4.6, with the procedures of Figures 4.8 and 4.9 added to the end. It must be stressed again that the object of this program is to introduce the reader to essential features of the language; the object is assuredly not the presentation of a good production program.

You should now be able to write a small indexed file of your own and to write and run a program to access it. Your very first program can simply open your file as an output file and then close it again, thus creating an empty file. You could also display a message on the terminal, just to convince yourself that the program actually runs. Your second program can then open the file you have created as an i–o file, which enables the program to write records to it and to carry out some of the other functions mentioned in this chapter. You will probably find Appendices 1 to 3 useful during the preparation of your programs.

5. Indexed files — sequential access

5.1 INTRODUCTION

Random access, despite its convenience and simplicity, is not suitable for some of the things we want to do with a file. For example, we may want to:

(a) look through the file for records having certain characteristics, and perhaps change or delete these records; or
(b) count the number of records in the file; or
(c) make a copy of the file.

For these and many other uses, what we need is a method of access which does not require a knowledge of the record key values and which guarantees that we can access the file in such a way that every record is accessed precisely once.

When we use **sequential** access, an *ordering* is applied to the set of records which constitute a file. We see a file as a *sequence*, rather than just a collection, of records, and we access the records according to that sequence. In random access we specify the key of the record we want to access; in sequential access we specify that we want to access the *next* record in the sequence. In sequential access, therefore, we can ensure that we access every record in the file by starting at the first record in the ordering and continuing to access each "next" record until we reach the last record in the ordering.

5.2 INPUT FILES AND OUTPUT FILES

Suppose that we want to make a copy of our mailing list for security purposes. In the event of the file *mailing-list* being corrupted or lost, the copy can be used in its place.

It should perhaps be emphasized at this stage that a name following **fd** in the data division is a name which is local to the program in which it appears. (We will meet an exception to this rule later.) The file *mailing-list* which we are using in a number of our programs can actually be any file which

(a) has indexed organization; and
(b) contains fixed-length records each 95 characters in length; and
(c) has its record key located in character positions 7 to 26 of the record format.

33

The operating system will usually check that the actual file used on any occasion matches the program's definition in these respects, but it is the programmer's responsibility to ensure that the record description used in the program, and the operations performed, make sense in terms of the application. The program developed in Chapter 4 could be used with several different files at different times as long as these files were consistent with the definition in the program. The **assign** phrase in the environment division and the operating system's job control language together link the file name used in the program with an actual file.

But let us return to the business of copying the mailing list. A Cobol program to do so will illustrate in simple form the use of sequential access to indexed files. The original file *mailing-list* is an **input** file, read sequentially record by record, and the copied version, *mailing-list-backup* is an **output** file, written sequentially record by record. The strategy used is illustrated in Figure 5.1 and the program, called *copy-mailing-list*, is given in Figure 5.2.

Looking first at the environment and data divisions, we see that, naturally enough, both files have indexed organization and are accessed sequentially. But we notice that the record description for *mailing-list* is different from that used in earlier examples. This program is merely making a record-by-record copy of the file and has no interest in the detailed record format. Since the file has indexed organization, the position of the record key in the record area has to be established but no names need be given to other parts of the record area. The three **pic**s together establish the record length and the position of the record key.

In the working-storage section there is a single data item *eof* (a common abbreviation in programming for 'end of file'), which will, regrettably, have to be used as a 'flag'. Cobol has no boolean variables, so we choose here to define *eof* as a single-character data item, to which we will assign one of the values "t" (by which we mean 'true') and "f" (for 'false').

At lines 36 to 47 of Figure 4.6, we saw the use of a **perform until** statement to cause repeated execution of a number of statements. The terminating condition

    command = "finish"

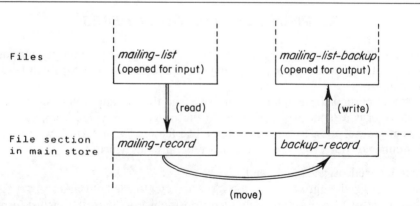

Figure 5.1:   Program strategy for copying a file

```
      identification division.
        program-id.   copy-mailing-list.

      environment division.
        input-output section.
        file-control.
          select mailing-list  assign to xyz
              organization indexed
              access sequential
              record key surname.
          select mailing-list-backup   assign to wxy
              organization indexed
              access sequential
              record key b-surname.

      data division.
        file section.
        fd mailing-list.
        01 mailing-record.
          02          pic x(6).
          02   surname pic x(20).
          02          pic x(69).

        fd mailing-list-backup.
        01 backup-record.
          02          pic x(6).
          02   b-surname pic x(20).
          02          pic x(69).

        working-storage section.
        01 eof   pic x.

      procedure division.
      main. open input mailing-list
              output mailing-list-backup
        perform, with test after, until eof = "t"
            read mailing-list next;
            at end
                move "t" to eof
            not at end
                move "f" to eof
                move mailing-record to backup-record
                write backup-record;   invalid key
                    display "sequence error or no room - stopped"
                    stop run
                end-write
            end-read
        end-perform
    * the stop run statement closes the files
        stop run.
```

*Figure 5.2:   Sequential access to two indexed files, one in input mode and
one in output mode*

---

was tested *before* each execution of the statements enclosed between the words
perform and **end-perform**. In the procedure division of Figure 5.2, we see the
same kind of statement, but this time with the words **with test after** appearing
before **until**. This too causes repeated execution of the statements between
perform and **end-perform** until the terminating condition (*eof* = "t") is true, but

the difference is that the terminating condition is tested *after* each execution of these statements. The **read** statement in Figure 5.2 is therefore always executed at least once.

In the procedure division of Figure 5.2 there is only a single paragraph. On entry, both files are opened, one as an input file (precluding the use of **write**, **delete**, and **rewrite**) and the other as an output file (allowing the use of **write** only). The **open** statement also places a conceptual pointer at the beginning of *mailing-list* to indicate that the "next" record in that file is its first record. Thus, when the **read** statement in the fourth line is executed for the first time, the record retrieved will be that first record. Thereafter successive executions of the **read** will progress through the file until there is no "next" record, i.e. until the end of the file has been reached. When this happens, and only then, the statement in the **at end** phrase (**move** "t" **to** *eof*) is executed. On all earlier reads, the statements in the **not at end** phrase (two **move** statements and a **write**) are executed.

In sequential access, as here, the **read** statement

(a) includes the word **next** (in fact, this word is optional in sequential access, though it is obligatory in dynamic access),
(b) includes an **at end** phrase instead of the **invalid key** phrase used in random access, and
(c) may include a **not at end** phrase and does not include a **not invalid key** phrase.

Cobol, like a number of other languages, provides no method of testing whether the end of a file has been reached other than by attempting to read a record. The effect of a sequential **read** statement is that

either a copy of the next record from the file is presented in the record area
or the **at end** condition arises (no next record existed) and the content of the record area is undefined.

This accounts for the use of the flag *eof* in the program. Its function is to transmit the end-of-file status from the **read** statement which establishes it to the **perform** statement which controls exit from the loop. The use of flags, arguably more even than the use of **go to** statements, is best avoided where possible, but there is no escape from using one or other of these techniques when an end-of-file terminating condition is to be detected within a loop. (Pascal manages things better in this respect by allowing the end-of-file condition to be tested independently of the **read** operation, thus removing the need for a flag.)

Notice that, though we are using sequential access, the **write** statement in Figure 5.2 retains its **invalid key** phrase. The need for this arises from the ordering of the records in sequential access. In the absence of any other stipulation in the program, *the ordering applied to an indexed file when it is accessed sequentially is ascending order of record key value.* Since we have defined *surname* as its record key, our *mailing-list* file will be read in surname order, starting perhaps "Abbey", "Abbot", . . ., and ending "Zves", "Zwingli". This ordering does not apply only to input files, so each record sent to the copy file *mailing-list-backup* is checked by the system to ensure that it has a higher key value than the preceding record; if this is not so, the **write** is unsuccessful and the invalid key condition arises. Clearly the situation should never exist in our program; if it does, it is another case for a 'panic abort'.

After these explanations, you should have no difficulty in following the logic of the program in Figure 5.2.

5.3 THE START STATEMENT AND OPEN EXTEND

Suppose that, on some earlier occasion, instead of copying the whole mailing list, a program had copied all records up to and including that with *surname* = "Macmaster", and that we now wish to write a program to copy the remaining records to the same backup file.

In order to meet the requirement, we need make only two changes to the program of Figure 5.2. We change the mode in which the file *mailing-list-backup* is opened, and we introduce a **start** statement. The new version of the procedure division is shown in Figure 5.3.

The file *mailing-list-backup* is now opened in **extend**, rather than **output**, mode. This means that the file already exists and that records are to be added to the end; so, in the case of an indexed file, as here, the first record written to the file must have a higher record key value than any record already in the file. If it does not, an invalid key condition will occur.

Recall that an **open input** statement establishes the first record in ascending key order as the "next" record, i.e. as the record to be retrieved by the first

```
procedure division.
main.
    open input mailing-list
         extend mailing-list-backup
    move "Macmaster" to surname
    start mailing-list,  key > surname;
    invalid key
         continue
    not invalid key
         perform, with test after, until eof = "t"
              read mailing-list next;
              at end
                   move "t" to eof
              not at end
                   move "f" to eof
                   move mailing-record to backup-record
                   write backup-record;  invalid key
                        display "sequence error or no room - pr
                                      "ogram stopped"
                        stop run
                   end-write
              end-read
         end-perform
    end-start
    stop run.
```

*Figure 5.3: Procedure division illustrating a use of the **start** statement in sequential access*

execution of a **read next** statement following the **open**. A **start** statement enables us at any time to change our current position within the file, so that the "next" record is the *first* in record key order *which satisfies the* **key** *condition in the* **start** *statement*. In the program of Figure 5.3, since the value of *surname* is "Macmaster", the "next" record is established as the first record in the *surname* ordering which has a value greater than "Macmaster", i.e. the record following the "Macmaster" record. Thus that record will be retrieved by the first execution of the **read next** statement, and subsequent executions will progress through the file from there to the end. If no record in the file satisfies the condition specified in the **start** statement, then the invalid key condition arises. During execution of the program of Figure 5.3, the invalid key condition arises if there is no record in the file with a *surname* value greater than "Macmaster". In such a case there are no records to be copied to the back-up file, and no special action is needed. But (in the absence of a declarative procedure) the **start** statement must have an **invalid key** phrase, so the single-word statement **continue** is used; **continue** is a null statement, meaning 'do nothing'.

The content of the record area is unaffected by execution of a **start** statement. The condition specified in the **start** statement must always begin with the word **key**, followed by one of the operators $>$, $=$, $>=$, and **not** $<$. (It should be obvious why the choice of operators is restricted in this way.) The operator cannot be followed by a literal. The data item whose name follows the operator must be *either* the key item itself *or* an item which is shorter than the key item and whose leftmost character position in store is the same as that of the key item.

To illustrate this last rule, we now look at a program (Figure 5.4) which, instead of copying the whole file, copies only the records for those people whose surnames begin with letter S or T. Notice that the program takes care of the case where there are no surnames beginning with these letters (in which case an empty output file will be produced) and the case where the last record in the file has a *surname* value beginning with one of these letters. Notice also that, because we use only the leftmost character position, the only assumption we make about the collating sequence is that letter T immediately follows letter S.

In this program, exit from the **perform** loop takes place either when the end of the file is detected or when a record whose *surname* starts with a character greater than 'T' has been read. Thus the appropriate point in the loop to test for these conditions is immediately after the reading of each record. With the test at the head of the loop, we must ensure, by a 'priming' **read** statement, that the first record is in the record area before the loop is entered.

(Where a loop is terminated by an end-of-file condition, many programmers and programming methodologies insist that it is good practice *always* to test for the exit condition at the head of the loop. The examples in this and succeeding chapters are not stylistically consistent — they are intended to illustrate a variety of approaches. Also, many programmers would exclude the **not at end** phrase from the second **read** statement of Figure 5.4 since it is logically redundant. This is a matter of programming style which need not be pursued here.)

The identity of the "next" record may be changed by a **start** statement at any time during sequential processing of an input or input–output file.

```
identification division.
  program-id.  copy-st.

environment division.
  input-output section.
  file-control.
    select mailing-list  assign to xyz
        organization indexed
        access sequential
        record key  surname.
    select st-file  assign to vwx
        organization indexed
        access sequential
        record key  s.

data division.
  file section.
  fd  mailing-list.
  01  mailing-record.
        02            pic x(6).
        02  surname.
            03  start-of-surname  pic x.
            03            pic x(19).
        02            pic x(69).
  fd  st-file.
  01  st-record.
        02    pic x(6).
        02  s  pic x(20).
        02    pic x(69).

  working-storage section.
  01  eof  pic x.

procedure division.
main.
    open input  mailing-list
         output  st-file
    move "S" to surname
    start mailing-list,  key >= start-of-surname;
    invalid key
        continue
    not invalid key
        read mailing-list next; at end
*               [This situation should not arise - the start
*               statement has identified a record]
            stop run
        end-read
        move "f" to eof
        perform until  eof = "t"  or  start-of-surname > "T"
            move mailing-record to st-record
            write st-record;  invalid key
*               [This situation should not arise]
                stop run
            end-write
            read mailing-list next;
            at end      move "t" to eof
            not at end  move "f" to eof
            end-read
        end-perform
    end-start
    stop run.
```

Figure 5.4: A program to copy all records with surnames beginning "S" or "T"

You may have noticed that random retrieval of a record can be simulated in sequential access mode, as shown in Figure 5.5. Such redundancy of language facilities is not uncommon in Cobol.

5.4 DEFAULT CONDITION IN THE START STATEMENT

Omission of the condition phrase in the **start** statement implies that the condition is equality with the record key. Thus in Figure 5.5(b) the statement

> **start** *mailing-list*, **key** = *surname*; **invalid key** . . .

could be replaced by the shorter equivalent

> **start** *mailing-list*; **invalid key** . . .

5.5 INPUT–OUTPUT FILES

When file *x* is accessed sequentially, the statement

> **open i–o** *x*

means that the statements **read**, **start**, **delete**, and **rewrite** may be applied to file *x*. In sequential access, new records cannot be written to a file opened in the **i–o** mode.

The facilities available for accessing an i–o file are all of those just described for accessing an input file, but with the added provision that *at any time between the execution of a* **read next** *statement and the execution of the next* **read next** *or* **start** *statement, a single* **delete** *or* **rewrite** *statement may be executed*. The **delete** or **rewrite** operates on the record most recently read; the invalid key condition arises if the record key value in the record area at the time of execution of a **rewrite** is not the same as that in the record last read. The **rewrite** operation

---

```
move query-name to surname
read mailing-list;
invalid key   perform p
end-read
```

Figure 5.5(a): Retrieval of the record whose key is stored as the value of query-name *using* **random** *access. Assume that the undefined procedure* p *deals with the case where no such record exists*

```
move query-name to surname
start mailing-list,   key = surname;
invalid key
    perform p
not invalid key
    read mailing-list next;
    at end
        stop run
    end-read
end-start
```

Figure 5.5(b): An equivalent program, using **sequential** *access statements to simulate random access. (The* **at end** *condition should not arise)*

therefore cannot be used to change the record key value. In sequential access, the **delete** statement has no **invalid key** (or **not invalid key**) phrase, and therefore has no **end-delete** to terminate it.

The use of these facilities is illustrated in Figure 5.6, which shows a program whose function is to remove from the mailing list all records in which the post-code begins with the character-string "AB1⎵". Notice that, because a four-character data item is compared with a three-character literal, the literal is regarded as being extended on the right by one space character. Records whose post-codes begin with, for example, "AB12" will not be deleted by this program.

This example also introduces the Cobol **if** statement, the semantics of which should be obvious. As in many other languages, an **else** phrase may follow the **then** phrase. An **if** statement is terminated by the word **end-if**.

```
        identification division.
          program-id. delAB1.

        environment division.
          input-output section.
          file-control.
            select mailing-list   assign to xyz
                organization indexed
                access sequential
                record key surname.

        data division.
          file section.
          fd    mailing-list.
          01    addressee.
                02              pic x(6).
                02    surname   pic x(20).
                02              pic x(60).
                02    post-code.
                      03    post-code-area   pic x(4).
                      03                     pic x(5).

          working-storage section.
          01    eof   pic x.

        procedure division.
        main. open i-o mailing-list
            perform, with test after, until  eof = "t"
                read mailing-list next;
                at end
                    move "t" to eof
                not at end
                    move "f" to eof
                    if  post-code-area - "AB1"
                    then   delete mailing-list
                    end-if
                end-read
            end-perform
            stop run.
```

Figure 5.6: A program to remove all records with post-codes starting "AB1⎵"

6. Indexed files — dynamic access

6.1 INTRODUCTION

An indexed file may be accessed randomly, as described in Chapter 4, or it may be accessed sequentially, as described in Chapter 5, or access may be **dynamic**, as described in this chapter. Of the three methods of file access, **dynamic** is by far the most useful when applied to a file opened in **i–o** mode. For files opened in other modes, dynamic access adds little that is useful. A file which is accessed dynamically cannot be opened in **extend** mode. Applied to a file opened in **output** mode, dynamic access is equivalent to random access, since only the random **write** statement is available.

6.2 INPUT FILES

Dynamic access to a file opened in **input** mode makes three statements available:

(a) the **start** statement;
(b) the sequential **read** statement

      (**read** *x* **next**; **at end** . . .);

(c) the random **read** statement

      (**read** *x* **invalid key** . . .).

Applied to an input file, therefore, dynamic access combines full sequential access facilities with full random access facilities. We have already noticed that a random **read** can be simulated by the **start** and **read next** statements; so, in relation to an input file, there is nothing we can do using dynamic access that we could not do using sequential access. However, the sequential access statements

      move "Bell" **to** *surname*
      start *mailing-list*; **invalid key** . . .
      read *mailing-list* **next**; **at end** . . .

are more cumbersome than the dynamic access statements

      move "Bell" **to** *surname*
      read *mailing-list*; **invalid key** . . .

especially when we bear in mind that program code has to be written to provide for the (impossible) **at end** condition. The random **read** statement, like the **read next** statement, adjusts our position in the file so that, if in either of the above cases the next access to *mailing-list* is through a **read next** statement, the record retrieved will be the record following "Bell".

(In the above examples, successful execution of the file accessing statements is assumed; in other words, we assume that the **invalid key** and **at end** conditions do not occur. This assumption will be made in all the examples in this chapter. The object is to enable you to concentrate on the sequence in which records are accessed, undistracted by aspects of the program which are not relevant to our purpose; so only the 'bare bones' of the program extracts are shown. In a real program, of course, the ellipses (. . .) would have to be replaced by appropriate statements.)

The effects of successful execution of the various statements available for accessing an input file are summarized in Figure 6.1. It will be seen that, though every one of the four statements establishes a 'position' in the file, only the sequential **read** statement makes use of that position.

6.3 INPUT–OUTPUT FILES

When a file with dynamic access is opened in **i–o** mode, the facilities available are:

(a) all the facilities available for a **dynamic** access file in **input** mode (see above); and

(b) all the facilities available for a **random** access file in **i–o** mode (see Chapter 4).

It is possible therefore to use the full range of random access facilities and to change at will between random access to individual records and sequential reading of all or part of the file. The statements available are listed in Figure 6.2.

Statement	Accessed record is	"Next" record becomes
open	(None)	First record in file
start	(None)	Record identified by **start**
(random) **read**	Record with record key value matching that in record area	Record following accessed record
(sequential) **read next**	"Next" record	Record following accessed record

Figure 6.1: Statements in dynamic access to an input file—effects of successful execution. (The file is assumed to have no alternate record keys)

Statement	Accessed record is	"Next" record will be the first record in the file whose record key value satisfies the condition:
open	(None)	≥ lowest possible value
start	(None)	≥ record key value in record identified by **start**
(random) **read**	Record with record key value matching that in record area	> record key value in accessed record
(sequential) **read next**	"Next" record	> record key value in accessed record
delete	Record with record key value matching that in record area	(Not affected)
rewrite	Record with record key value matching that in record area	(Not affected)
write	(New record written to file)	(Not affected)

Figure 6.2: Statements in dynamic access to an i–o file—effects of successful execution. (The file is assumed to have no alternate record keys)

The full potential of these facilities will become evident when we reach Chapter 11. For the present, it is important to be aware of one consequence of mixing random and sequential access — we must be very clear about which record is the "next" record at any point during program execution, for:

(a) the record which was "next" a moment ago may now have been deleted; or
(b) after a record has been read, another record may be written whose key value lies between that of the record which was read and that of the record which became "next" as a result of the **read** statement.

Such possibilities call for a more rigorous examination of the concept of "next" record". Instead of thinking of a particular record as the "next" record, we now think of a *condition* which is *established when any* **read**, **read next**, **open** *or* **start** *is executed* and *which is evaluated when the next* **read next** *is executed. The condition, once established, is unaffected by intervening* **write**, **rewrite** *or* **delete** *statements*. The record retrieved by the **read next** statement is the *first* record (in record key order) which satisfies the condition at the time of execution of the **read next**. The final column of Figure 6.2 shows the conditions established by the various statements.

You will find the preceding paragraph more intelligible after you have studied Figure 6.2 in conjunction with the examples which follow. Each example assumes that initially the file contains records with the following *surname* values:

> *Bell*
> *Black*
> *Gibson*
> *Kennedy*
> *Leighton*
> *Macleish*
> *Macmaster*
> *Miller*
> *Rougvie*
> *Strachan*
> *Weir*

(1) After execution of

> **move** "Strachan" **to** *surname*
> **read** *mailing-list*; **invalid key** . . .
>
> —
>
> —
>
> —
>
> **move** "Black" **to** *surname*
> **rewrite** *mailing-record*; **invalid key** . . .
>
> —
>
> —
>
> —
>
> **move** "Macadam" **to** *surname*
> **write** *mailing-record*; **invalid key** . . .
> **read** *mailing-list* **next**; **at end** . . .

the *Weir* record would be in the record area. The sequential position in the file is not affected by **rewrite** or **write**.

(2) After execution of

> **open i–o** *mailing-list*
> **read** *mailing-list* **next**; **at end** . . .
>
> —
>
> —
>
> —
>
> **move** "Macleish" **to** *surname*
> **delete** *mailing-list*; **invalid key** . . .
> **read** *mailing-list* **next**; **at end** . . .

the *Black* record would be in the record area. The sequential position in the file is not affected by **delete**.

(3) After execution of

> **open i–o** *mailing-list*
>
> —
>
> —
>
> —
>
> **move** "Adamson" **to** *surname*
> **write** *mailing-record*; **invalid key** . . .
> **read** *mailing-list* **next**; **at end** . . .

the *Adamson* record just written would have been read back into the record area.

(4) But after execution of

> **move** "Brazil" **to** *surname*
> **start** *mailing-list*, **key** $>=$ *surname*; **invalid key** . . .
>
> —
>
> —
>
> —
>
> **move** "Ferguson" **to** *surname*
> **write** *mailing-record*; **invalid key** . . .
>
> —
>
> —
>
> —
>
> **read** *mailing-list* **next**; **at end** . . .

the *Gibson* record (not the *Ferguson* record) would be in the record area, because:

(a) the record identified by the **start** statement was the *Gibson* record;
(b) the **read next** statement therefore retrieved the first record in the file which satisfied the condition $>=$ "Gibson".

(5) After execution of

> **move** "Strachan" **to** *surname*
> **read** *mailing-list*; **invalid key** . . .
>
> —
>
> —
>
> —
>
> **move** "Weir" **to** *surname*
> **delete** *mailing-list*; **invalid key** . . .
> **read** *mailing-list* **next**; **at end** . . .

the **at end** condition would exist.

(6) After execution of

>   **move** "Leighton" **to** *surname*
>   **start** *mailing-list*; **invalid key** . . .
>   —
>
>   —
>
>   —
>
>   **move** "Leighton" **to** *surname*
>   **delete** *mailing-list*; **invalid key** . . .
>   —
>
>   —
>
>   —
>
>   **move** "Lochhead" **to** *surname*
>   **write** *mailing-record*; **invalid key** . . .
>   —
>
>   —
>
>   —
>
>   **read** *mailing-list* **next**; **at end** . . .

the *Lochhead* record would be in the record area.

6.4 SUMMARY OF CHAPTERS 4, 5, AND 6

In determining how the records of a file may be accessed, there are three important parameters.

(1) The file's organization method, which may be **sequential**, **relative**, or **indexed**. These three chapters have been devoted to **indexed** organization, in which a record can be identified by an embedded **record key** value. Indexed files will be considered further in Chapter 11.

(2) The access method used by the program in relation to the file. In relation to an indexed file, access may be:
   (a) **random**: the record key value in the record area determines which record is to be accessed;
   (b) **sequential**: the file is regarded as being ordered on ascending record key values; the record accessed is the next in that ordering;
   (c) **dynamic**: random access is combined with sequential retrieval.

(3) The mode in which a file is open at a particular stage of execution. Open modes are **input**, **output**, **i–o**, and **extend**.

Figure 6.3 relates to indexed organization (and also, incidentally, to relative organization) and is a modified version of a table which appears in the Cobol standard. It indicates, for each combination of access method and open mode, the statements which may be used.

Access	Statement	Open mode			
		input	output	i-o	extend
sequential	**read** (*random*)				
	read next	X		X	
	write		X		X
	rewrite			X	
	delete			X	
	start	X		X	
random	**read** (*random*)	X		X	
	read next				
	write		X	X	
	rewrite			X	
	delete			X	
	start				
dynamic	**read** (*random*)	X		X	
	read next	X		X	
	write		X	X	
	rewrite			X	
	delete			X	
	start	X		X	

Figure 6.3: Permissible statements for an indexed file (and for a relative file). For any combination of access and open mode, only those statements indicated by 'x' may be used

7. Numbers, arithmetic, and initialization

7.1 NUMBERS AND ARITHMETIC

Up to now, the only data items we have considered have been those which are regarded simply as strings of characters. These data items are of two kinds:

(1) **elementary alphanumeric** items, described in the program by pictures like xx, x(6), and x(130);
(2) **group** items, defined as the concatenation of other (**subordinate**) data items. The program description of a group item does not include a picture.

Depending on the requirement of the program, a record (level 01) may be defined as an elementary item, as in

01 *addressee* **pic** x(95).

or as a group item.

A **group** item is invariably alphanumeric; any value which it assumes is treated purely as a string of characters. But, instead of being alphanumeric, an **elementary** item may be **numeric**. Usually numeric items too are character strings, but they have special properties.

The definition of a numeric item differs from that of an alphanumeric item in that the character '9' rather than 'x' is used in its picture. The definition

03 *a* **pic** 9(3).

indicates that *a* occupies three character positions, and that the three characters stored as the value of *a* should be numeric digits. It also indicates that the characters represent an integer value (i.e. a whole number) in the range 0 to 999. (Notice that the picture could have been specified as "999" rather than as "9(3)".) Similarly, the definition

04 *b* **pic** 99.

indicates that *b* occupies two character positions and that the two numeric digits stored as the value of *b* represent an integer value in the range 0 to 99. The names *a* and *b* can therefore be included in arithmetic expressions in the program. So, if *a* and *b* contained the character strings "024" and "12" respectively, the result of evaluating the expression

$a - b + 5$

would be 17.

In the above expression, 5 is a **numeric literal**, i.e. a number written in everyday notation, but not ending with a decimal point. Other examples are −20, 18.6, .23, and −0.23. The sentence you have just read demonstrates why a numeric literal must not end with a decimal point — the final "." is the period that terminates the sentence. Cobol too uses "." both as a decimal point and as a period.

Notice that, instead of having the concepts of 'real' and 'integer' common in other languages, Cobol regards each numeric data item as a sequence of decimal digit positions. The number of positions specified determines the range and accuracy of numbers which the data item can accommodate.

Arithmetic expressions in Cobol are like those in many other languages; priority of operators during evaluation is the familiar one; unary operators (+ and −) first, exponentiation (∗∗) second, multiplication (∗) and division (/) third, and addition (+) and subtraction (−) last. Parentheses (round brackets) may be used to override the normal priorities, and evaluation at any priority level is left to right. Every operand must be a numeric data item or a numeric literal or a sub-expression enclosed in parentheses. Programmers coming to Cobol from other languages must be careful not to write expressions like

$$a-b+5$$

since in Cobol each operator, even a unary operator, must be preceded and followed by at least one space. This requirement arises from the view of operators as 'words' and from the fact that the minus sign and the hyphen are the same character (see Appendix 1).

Returning to numeric data items, we now look at the methods of defining **signed** numeric items. The **unsigned** data item c, defined

c **pic** 9(5) (or **pic** 99999)

occupies five character positions of storage and may take any value in the range 0 to 99999. A **signed** data item d, defined

d **pic** s9(5), **sign leading**, **separate**

occupies six character positions of storage and may take any value in the range −99999 to +99999. The character 's' in the picture means 'signed', and '**leading, separate**' means that the sign is represented by a separate character in the leftmost character position. Thus the value 118 would be represented in d as the character string

+00118

If e is defined

e **pic** s9(4), **sign trailing**, **separate**

then e occupies five character positions and may take any value in the range −9999 to +9999. The representation of −62 as the value of e would be

0062−

If the **sign** clause is omitted from the definition of a signed item, the sign does not occupy a separate character position in the representation. Thus the data item f, defined

   f **pic** s9(4)

is only four character positions in length, since the sign representation is combined with the representation of either the leftmost or the rightmost digit. If you are accustomed to machine level programming you will have some idea of how this is achieved; if not, you need not be too concerned about it.

Signed data items which, like f, do not include a separate character position for the sign offer these advantages over items like e which do include a separate character position:

(a) they *may* give faster arithmetic;
(b) they occupy less storage;
(c) they involve the programmer in less writing or typing,
but have these disadvantages:
(a) since each implementor of Cobol is free to choose his own method of representing a non-separate sign, data files including these items are not easily portable between machines;
(b) if an item with a non-separate sign is displayed on a screen or sent to a file for printing the output will look odd to a human reader. For example, in a particular machine the representation of 1234 may be "123D" and that of −1234 may be "123M". (However, such problems are unlikely to arise except in programmer-oriented outputs such as store dumps; as we shall see, a program normally 'edits' numeric data before sending it to an output device.)

The examples given later in this chapter will make heavy use of **separate** signs, but this fact is not to be construed as implying that **separate** signs are preferable — in fact, many programmers never use them at all. They are over-used here because they are independent of individual machine representations and because they make the examples easier to read.

A **non-integer** data item is one whose value need not be a whole number. The decimal scaling of the item is indicated by a "v" in its picture. Thus an item g may be defined

   g **pic** 9(3)v9(2)

equivalents of which are

   g **pic** 999v99
   g **pic** 999v9(2)

and

   g **pic** 9(3)v99

The item g is five character positions in length and may take any value in the range 0 to 999.99, with two places after the decimal point. The character "v" indicates the position of the *implied* decimal point; the decimal point is not explicitly stored. So if *g* contained the character-string

   12345

the value represented would be 123.45. If the definition of *h* were

   h **pic** v9(4)

then the value .0125 would be stored as

   0125

   Non-integer items can of course be signed. If the definition of *i* were

   i **pic** s9v99 **sign leading, separate**

then the value −.5 would be stored as

   −050

and, in general, *i* could accommodate values in the range −9.99 to +9.99, with two places after the decimal point. Below are listed several data item definitions together with, in each case, the appropriate representation of the integer 22.

j	**pic** 99		22
k	**pic** 9(4)		0022
l	**pic** s9(5)	**sign leading, separate**	+00022
m	**pic** s999v9	**sign leading, separate**	+0220
n	**pic** 9(3)v9(4)		0220000
o	**pic** s99v99	**sign trailing, separate**	2200+

   Evaluation of an arithmetic expression takes account of the sign and scaling of each data item named in the expression. Values of unsigned items are regarded as positive. Thus, given the following data item definitions and values (or, more accurately, contents)

p	**pic** 99v9		051
q	**pic** sv99	**sign leading, separate**	−42
r	**pic** 9(4)		0038

the result of evaluating the expression

$$2 * (r - p + q)$$

is 64.96.

   Recall from Chapter 2 that, when the values of alphanumeric items are compared, comparison proceeds from left to right on a character-by-character basis. Thus, given

s	**pic** x(3)	051
t	**pic** x(4)	0038

the condition

   $s > t$

would be true. But, if the two items being compared are numeric data items, then, instead of the character strings being compared, *the numeric values which they represent are compared*. Thus, given

```
p  pic 99v9    051
r  pic 9(4)    0038
```

the condition

$p > r$

would be false, since the values compared would be 5.1 and 38. The conditions

$p = 5.1$
$p > 3$

and

r **not** < 24.99

would all be true.

Recall from Chapter 2 that, given the definition

u **pic** x(5)

execution of

move "123" **to** *u*

will result in *u* containing

123␣␣

However, if a *numeric* literal and a *numeric* data item are involved, as with the definition

v **pic** 9(5)

and the statement

move 123 **to** *v*

then execution of the **move** will result in the numeric value specified by the literal being correctly represented in *v* as

00123

(Notice that the redundant digit positions are filled with zeros, not with spaces.) Similarly, given the definition

w **pic** s99v9 **sign leading**, **separate**

execution of

move 8 **to** *w*

will result in *w* containing

+080

and execution of

> **move** −5.2 **to** *w*

will result in *w* containing

> −052

When both operands of a **move** are numeric data items, execution results (where possible) in both items containing a representation of the same value. Thus, given the definitions and contents

> *x*   **pic** 9   3
> *y*   **pic** s99v99   **sign leading, separate**   −1234

execution of

> **move** *x* **to** *y*

will result in *y* containing

> +0300

Since *x* is unsigned, a positive sign is generated in *y*. A **move** from a signed item to an unsigned item results in the absolute value being moved. Thus, given the definitions and contents

> *a*   **pic** s99   **sign leading, separate**   −12
> *b*   **pic** 9(4)   5678

execution of

> **move** *a* **to** *b*

will result in *b* containing

> 0012

If a data item is too small to accommodate a value which is moved to it, then excess digits are truncated. Note that no execution-time warning is given. In an extreme case, truncation may occur at both ends of the item. Given the definitions and contents

> *c*   **pic** 99v999   96128
> *d*   **pic** 9v9   12

execution of

> **move** *c* **to** *d*

will result in *d* containing

> 61

representing the value 6.1. Such an assignment could be used purposely to obtain part of a number, or in situations where it is known that no non-zero digits will be lost at the more significant end, e.g.

if $c < 10$
then move c **to** d
else . . .

Zero-filling and truncation may occur together, as they will if the value .12 is moved to d.

Another means of assigning a value to a numeric data item (or to a numeric edited data item, as explained later) is by the use of one of the arithmetic statements **compute**, **add**, **subtract**, **multiply**, and **divide**. One of these statements *must* be used when the assigned value is to be calculated. It is illegal to say

move $d + 1$ **to** c

The statement

compute $y = x$

is almost equivalent to

move x **to** y

where x and y are numeric data items. The only difference in execution is that, in the event of y being too small to accommodate one or more non-zero digits at the more significant (left-hand) end (e.g. if x's value were 123.4 and y's picture 99v9):

(a) the **move** statement results in loss of these digits and a truncated value being stored in y (e.g. y's value in the above case would be 23.4);
(b) the **compute** statement leaves the value of y undefined.

In a **compute** statement any arithmetic expression may appear on the right of the assignment operator '='. For example, given the definitions

credit   **pic** s9(4)v99   **sign leading**, **separate**
capital **pic** 9(5)

the statement

compute *credit* = *credit* + *capital* * .083

may be executed. Consider now three possible combinations of the initial values of *credit* and *capital*, and the result of evaluating the arithmetic expression:

(a) *credit* = 1022.5,   *capital* = 20,000,   result = 2682.5;
(b) *credit* = 1022.5,   *capital* = 20,012,   result = 2683.496;
(c) *credit* = 9000,   *capital* = 20,000,   result = 10,660.

During execution, when the result of evaluating the expression is assigned to *credit*, case (a) above presents no problems. The content of *credit* becomes

+268250

In case (b), truncation occurs on the right, and the content of *credit* becomes

+268349

In practice, two digits of fraction may indeed be the degree of accuracy required by the application, but usually *rounding* is required, i.e. if (and *only* if) the leftmost truncated digit is 5 or greater, 1 is added in the rightmost retained digit position. This effect can be obtained by adding the word **rounded** to our original **compute** statement:

> **compute** *credit* **rounded** = *credit* + *capital* ∗ .083

so that execution in this case results in the content of *credit* becoming

> +268350

In case (c) above, the integer part of the result has five significant digits, but the picture of *credit* allows for only four. In this case a **size error** exists, and the content of *credit* is undefined. (Incidentally, a size error condition always arises when division by zero is attempted or when certain rules regarding exponentiation are broken.) The size error condition can be detected by appending to the **compute** statement a **size error** phrase which specifies the actions to be taken in the event of a size error condition arising. If a size error condition arises and there is no **size error** phrase in the statement, the value of *credit* becomes undefined; but if there *is* a **size error** phrase, the value of *credit* is unchanged.

As in the cases of the **at end** and **invalid key** phrases, there is a corresponding **not** phrase. Figures 7.1 and 7.2 show examples of the use of the **compute** statement with a **size error** phrase.

The existence of the **compute** statement in the language means that the remaining arithmetic statements are redundant. Very little attention can be given to them here, though they are on occasion more natural, more convenient, or more efficiently executed, than the **compute** statement.

Several different forms of the **multiply** and **divide** statements are available in the standard language. Some of them have dreadful syntax — the statement

> **multiply** *a* **by** *b*

actually changes the value of *b* rather than that of *a*. Statements like

> **divide** *c* **into** *d*

(which divides *d* by *c*) give little indication of their semantics — certainly, as someone once observed, they are not akin to the normal English usage 'divide cake into three'. There is a useful variant of the **divide** statement which gives results in quotient and remainder form.

```
compute credit rounded = credit + capital * .083;
size error
        display "credit amount exceeds storage capacity"
not size error
        -
        -
        [normal program code]
        -
        -
end-compute
```

*Figure 7.1: Use of **size error** phrase when execution continues*

```
compute credit rounded = credit + capital * .083;
size error
    display "credit amount exceeds storage capacity"
    stop run
end-compute
    -
    -
[normal program code]
    -
    -
```

*Figure 7.2:   Use of **size error** phrase when execution is terminated*

Statements such as

> **add** 1 **to** *count-a*

and

> **subtract** *payment* **from** *debt*

are, at least in this author's opinion, more natural than the statements

> **compute** *count-a* = *count-a* + 1

and

> **compute** *debt* = *debt* − *payment*

Like **compute**, the **add**, **subtract**, **multiply**, and **divide** statements all provide optional **rounded** and **size error** phrases.

All the arithmetic statements allow multiple assignment. Be careful if you are accustomed to using multiple assignment in another language. In Cobol, execution of the statement

> **compute** *a*, *b*, *c* = *d* / (*e* + 1); **size error** . . .

involves a single evaluation of the expression $d / (e + 1)$ and (conceptually at least) the temporary storage of the result as the value of some 'very large' data item. The value of that data item is assigned to *a*, then it is assigned to *b*, then it is assigned to *c*. A size error arising during assignment to *a* does not prevent the assignments to *b* and *c* being made. When execution ends, all valid assignments have been made after which the size error statements have been executed once if one or more of the assignments gave rise to a size error condition. Rounding may be specified for each destination item individually — if only *b* is to have a rounded result, the statement begins

> **compute** *a*, *b* **rounded**, *c* = ...

In commercial computing applications there are often situations in which multiple assignments in the **add** and **subtract** statements may be used to good effect. For example,

> **add** 1 **to** *area-count*, *district-count*, *security-count*

is clearly preferable to

    compute *area-count = area-count* + 1
    compute *district-count = district-count* + 1
    compute *security-count = security-count* + 1

and

    subtract *payment* **from** *debt, account-balance,*
        total-balance

is clearly preferable to

    compute *debt = debt − payment*
    compute *account-balance = account-balance − payment*
    compute *total-balance = total-balance − payment*

especially when, as a safety measure, a **size error** phrase would have to be appended to each of three **compute**s rather than to a single **add** or **subtract** statement.

A final warning before we leave the subject of numbers and arithmetic: if a program includes the definition

    02 *x.*
        03 *y* **pic** 99.
        03 *z* **pic** 999.

the data item *x* is *not* a numeric item. It is alphanumeric, and is regarded as a string of characters. For most purposes it is treated as though it had the picture x(5).

7.2 INITIALIZATION

The data item description

    01 *top-line* **pic** x(60), **value** "List of products".

besides defining the item *top-line* in the usual way, also ensures that, at the start of program execution, the value of *top-line* is as specified (space-filled on the right, as after execution of a **move** statement). Similarly

    05 *count-1* **pic** s9(6), **value** 1.

ensures that the initial value of *count-1* is 1. Notice that in this case the type of the literal (1) is numeric because *count-1* is defined as an elementary numeric data item; the initial value of any other type of data item is specified as a non-numeric literal (i.e. a character-string bounded by quotation marks).

A **value** clause may be used in the description of a group item in order to avoid specifying individually the initial values of subordinate items; an example is shown in Figure 7.3. A **value** clause cannot be used in the **file section** of the data division, because the record area associated with a file does not become available to the program until the file is opened at run time.

```
02   a,   value "abc0025".
     03   b    pic x(3).
     03   c    pic 9(4).
```

*Figure 7.3:   Use of the **value** clause at group level. The initial value assigned to b is "abc", and that assigned to c is 25*

Initialization (or indeed assignment at any stage of program execution) may also be effected in the procedure division by the **initialize** statement. If a, b, and c are group data items, execution of the statement

initialize a, b, c

causes the values of all elementary numeric and numeric edited data items subordinate to a, b, and c to be set as though zero had been **moved** to them, and the values of all other elementary items subordinate to a, b, and c to be set as though **spaces** had been **moved** to them. It is also possible to use the **initialize** statement in such a way that it sets all subordinate elementary items of a particular category to a specified value, as in

initialize a **replacing numeric data by** -1

which results in every elementary numeric item subordinate to a being treated as though the value -1 were moved to it.

Many programmers believe that programs are less confusing to read when routine initialization is effected by **move** or **initialize** statements in the procedure division, rather than by **value** clauses in the data division. Very often these programmers use the **value** clause almost exclusively for defining what we may call 'pseudo-constants'.

If you have evolved a good programming style in another language, you may be surprised by the absence thus far of any mention of constants in Cobol. In fact, Cobol provides no means of defining constants. The nearest we can come to defining and using a constant is to initialize the value of a data item and thereafter, where permissible, to use the name of the data item in place of a literal. We must then, of course, take care not to change the value of that data item during execution of the program, for data items, unlike constants, can be freely assigned new values.

8. Sequential files

8.1 INTRODUCTION

Sequential files differ from indexed files in a number of significant ways:

(a) In a sequential file, records have no keys by which file-accessing statements can identify them; *the only structural property of the file is that the records have a fixed ordering*, determined by the order in which the records were placed in the file. Of course, this does not mean that records cannot have unique identifiers or that the ordering of the records cannot reflect an ordering of values of some subordinate data item. What it *does* mean is that when these properties are present in a sequential file they are entirely the concern of the application program — they are not properties of sequential file organization and therefore cannot be made use of in file-accessing statements.

(b) As a consequence of (a), random and dynamic access cannot be used with a sequential file. The only access mode available is **sequential**.

(c) As another consequence of (a), the **start** statement is not available for accessing a sequential file.

(d) The **delete** statement cannot be used to remove a record from a sequential file.

(e) Indexed files must be stored on what the Cobol standard calls 'a mass storage medium' (nearly always disk storage), but sequential files can be stored on either mass storage media or serial access media such as magnetic tapes or paper tapes.

(f) Both indexed and sequential files may be read and written by computer programs; in addition, a sequential input file may be prepared outside the computer and read by a program, and a sequential output file may be written by the program for use outside the computer. For example, a sequential output file may be sent to a line printer.

Like an indexed file, a sequential file may be opened in one of the four modes **input**, **output**, **i–o**, and **extend**. The operations which can be performed in each mode are very limited.

8.2 CREATING A SEQUENTIAL FILE

A sequential file is created by opening it as an **output** file and placing records in it by a sequence of **write** executions. The sequence in which records are written

determines their ordering in the file, an ordering which is permanent throughout
the life of the file. As an example, the program in Figure 8.1 creates a sequential
file containing records from the indexed file *mailing-list* which was used in
Chapters 4 and 5. The program produces a file called *mail-tape*, which contains
all records from *mailing-list* for persons having surnames beginning with the letters
A to L.

Notice that in Figure 8.1 the organization of *mail-tape* is **sequential** and its
access mode is **sequential**. Neither of these facts need have been stated by the

```
        identification division.
          program-id.   copy-start.

        environment division.
          input-output section.
          file-control.
            select mailing-list   assign to xyz
                organization indexed
                access sequential
                record key surname.
            select mail-tape   assign to stu
                organization sequential
                access sequential.

        data division.
          file section.
          fd  mailing-list.
          01  addressee.
              02              pic x(6).
              02   surname.
                   03 start-s  pic x.
                   03          pic x(19).
              02          pic x(69).

          fd  mail-tape.
          01  tape-record   pic x(96).
      *         the last character of tape-record is a space

          working-storage section.
          01  eof    pic x.

        procedure division.
        main.
            open input mailing-list
                output mail-tape
            perform get-addressee
            perform until  eof = "t"   or   start-s > "L"
                move addressee to tape-record
                write tape-record
                perform get-addressee
            end-perform
            stop run.
        get-addressee.
            read mailing-list next;
            at end       move "t" to eof
            not at end move "f" to eof
            end-read.
```

*Figure 8.1: Copying mailing list records, for persons whose surnames
begin with letters in the range A to L, to a sequential file*

program since the default organization and access for any file are both **sequential**. Two points are worthy of note regarding the record description associated with *mail-tape*:

> 01 *tape-record* **pic** x(96).

Firstly, the file is sequential, so there is no record key position to be defined; and since the program is doing little more than copying records there is no need for the detailed record format to be described — it is enough to give the name and length of the record area. Secondly, every record written to *mail-tape* consists of the corresponding record from *mailing-list* with one character added at the right-hand end; the added character is always a space. The space character is appended by the statement

> **move** *addressee* **to** *tape-record*

which, since *tape-record* is longer than *addressee* by one character position (their lengths are 96 and 95 positions respectively), generates a space character in the last position in *tape-record* (see Chapter 2). We will make use of this extra character position in later examples.

The procedure division in Figure 8.1 has features which require some explanation. Firstly, a **write** statement, when applied to a sequential file, has no **invalid key** phrase. Indeed, the **invalid key** phrase is never present in any statement used in the processing of a sequential file because the records of sequential files have no keys.

Secondly, there is a procedure *get-addressee* whose 'output parameters' are *eof* and *addressee*. After execution of *get-addressee*:

either the value of *eof* is "f", and the next record from *mailing-list* is in the record
      area *addressee*;
or the value of *eof* is "t" and the content of *addressee* is undefined.

(You must not be given the impression that procedures in Cobol are always so unsatisfactory. We shall see later that procedures can be specified in a better way, with disjoint name scopes and explicitly declared parameters.)

Thirdly, the existence of *get-addressee* draws our attention again to an unsatisfactory feature of the language which we have already met briefly in Chapter 4. If you have used an Algol-based language, you may believe that you have found an error in Figure 8.1 — surely, despite the indentation, the **end-perform** terminates the preceding statement

> **perform** *get-addressee*

rather than the **perform until** statement? Surprisingly, it does not, and the program is correct. Let us see why.

An **explicit scope terminator** (i.e. a reserved word which begins with **end-**) is normally used *when other statements are nested within the statement which it terminates*. Notice for example that the statement

> **write** *tape-record*

in Figure 8.1 is not terminated by an **end-write** — the **write** has no **invalid key** or other phrase appended, and therefore does not contain other statements. It is implicitly terminated by the **perform** statement that follows it. The function of a **perform** statement is the 'performance' (i.e. execution) of other statements either once or repeatedly. These other statements may:

either (a) be nested within the **perform** statement itself (e.g. the three statements nested within the **perform until** in Figure 8.1), in which case **end-perform** serves to mark the end of these nested statements;

or (b) constitute a procedure, in which case the **perform** statement names the procedure (e.g. *get-addressee* in Figure 8.1). In this case no **end-perform** is allowed. Thus a Cobol compiler translating the program in Figure 8.1 would not expect an **end-perform** to terminate the statement

>**perform** *get-addressee*

and would correctly interpret the **end-perform** as terminating the **perform until**.

In certain syntactic contexts, explicit scope terminators which would otherwise be required can be omitted, but the examples in this book do not demonstrate such omissions, nor are they recommended.

In order to demonstrate the repeated execution of a procedure, Figure 8.2 shows an alternative, over-refined, version of the procedure division of Figure 8.1.

8.3 EXTENDING A SEQUENTIAL FILE

Records can be added to the end of a sequential file by opening the file in **extend** mode and placing the records into it by a sequence of **write** executions. As an example, the program in Figure 8.3 adds to the end of the file *mail-tape* (written by the program in Figure 8.1) all records from *mailing-list* for persons having surnames beginning with the letters M to Z. Only the procedure division is shown — the environment and data divisions are identical to those in Figure 8.1.

```
procedure division.
main.
    open input mailing-list
         output mail-tape
    perform get-addressee
    perform copying until  eof = "t"  or  start-s > "L"
    stop run.

copying.  move addressee to tape-record
          write tape-record
          perform get-addressee.

get-addressee.  ...
```

Figure 8.2: An over-refined version of the procedure division in Figure 8.1 (get-addressee is unaltered)

```
procedure division.
main.
     open input mailing-list
          extend mail-tape
     move "L" to surname
     start mailing-list, key > start-s; invalid key
          stop run
     end-start
     perform get-addressee
     perform until  eof = "t"
          move addressee to tape-record
          write tape-record
          perform get-addressee
     end-perform
     stop run.
get-addressee.  ...
```

*Figure 8.3:   Adding the remaining records from the mailing list file to the file created by the program in Figure 8.1 (*get-addressee *is as shown in Figure 8.1)*

8.4 READING A SEQUENTIAL FILE

When a sequential file is opened in **input** mode, only the sequential **read** statement (**read next**, though the word **next** may be omitted) is available. Records are retrieved according to their ordering in the file. The program in Figure 8.4 counts how many records in the file *mail-tape* (written by the programs of Figures 8.1 and 8.3) have a post-code beginning "MA".

8.5 UPDATING A SEQUENTIAL FILE

If a sequential file is stored on a mass-storage medium and is opened in **i–o** mode, records can be changed as the file is read sequentially. An **i–o** file is accessed in the same way as an input file but additionally, at any time between one execution of a **read** statement and the next, a single **rewrite** may be executed. The **rewrite** replaces the last record read by the content of the record area. The program in Figure 8.5 finds any records which have "Kirkcaldy" followed only by spaces as the second address line and amends them so that that line becomes "Kirkcaldy, Fife" followed by spaces. When used to access a sequential file, the **rewrite** statement has no **invalid key** phrase.

8.6 'DELETING' RECORDS FROM A SEQUENTIAL FILE

No **delete** statement is available for files with sequential organization, but we may occasionally want to remove records from such files. One method of achieving the effect of deletion is to make a file which is a copy of the original file, but without copying the records which are to be removed. Another, which does not involve copying, is to ensure that 'deleted' records are 'rewritten' so as to contain some special value which cannot occur naturally in real data. A third method is

```
identification division.
  program-id.  count-ma.

environment division.
  input-output section.
  file-control.
     select mail-tape  assign to stu
        organization sequential
        access sequential.

data division.
  file section.
  fd  mail-tape.
  01  tape-record.
       02  name              pic x(26).
       02  address-line-1    pic x(30).
       02  address-line-2    pic x(30).
       02  post-code.
           03  pc12          pic xx.
           03                pic x(7).
       02  d-mark            pic x.

  working-storage section.
  01  eof        pic x.
  01  ma-count pic 9(5).

procedure division.
 main.
     open input mail-tape
     move 0 to ma-count
     perform, with test after, until  eof = "t"
        perform get-record
        if  eof = "f"  and  pc12 = "MA"
        then  add 1 to ma-count
        end-if
     end-perform
     display ma-count, " records with post-code MA"
     stop run.
 get-record.
     read mail-tape next;
     at end       move "t" to eof
     not at end move "f" to eof
     end-read.
```

Figure 8.4: Counting the number of records in the sequential file which have post-code *beginning "MA"*

---

to design the record format so that every record contains a data item whose function is to indicate either that the record is a 'live' record or that it has been 'deleted'.

This third method can be used in our *mail-tape* example since (for this very reason) the programs in Figures 8.1 and 8.3 ensured that each record had an extra character added, the value of which was a space character. In Figure 8.4 this extra character position is the data item *d-mark*, and we can adopt a convention that when the value of *d-mark* is a space the record is 'live', but when the value is "D" the record has been deleted.

```
procedure division.
main.
      open i-o mail-tape
      perform get-record
      perform until  eof = "t"
          if   address-line-2 = "Kirkcaldy"
          then move "Kirkcaldy, Fife" to address-line-2
               rewrite tape-record
          end-if
          perform get-record
      end-perform
      stop run.
get-record.  ...
```

*Figure 8.5: Amending the second address line of selected records.
Environment division, data division, and* get-record *are as in Figure 8.4*

Suppose now that, instead of changing them, we want to 'delete' all records whose second address line is "Kirkcaldy" followed only by spaces. The program of Figure 8.5 can serve our purpose if we change the **if** statement to:

> **if** *address-line-2* = "Kirkcaldy"
> **then move** "D" to *d-mark*
>   **rewrite** *tape-record*
> · **end-if**

Naturally, our convention requires that any program which reads the file should ignore the 'deleted' records. Since our accessing programs so far make use of the procedure *get-record*, all we have to do is substitute another *get-record* procedure which does not pass 'deleted' records to the calling program; a possible version is shown in Figure 8.6.

8.7 SEQUENTIAL FILES AND THE EXTERNAL ENVIRONMENT

The only kind of file we have so far considered is the kind created, maintained, and read only by computer programs – the programmer need not know anything about how records are represented on the file storage medium. However, streams of characters received from the outside world through an input device, or sent to the outside world through an output device, are also normally regarded as sequential files in Cobol. In these cases, the implementor's manual should be

---

```
get-record.
      perform, with test after,
          .until  eof = "t"  or  d-mark not = "D"
          read mail-tape next
          at end       move "t" to eof
          not at end   move "f" to eof
          end-read
      end-perform.
```

Figure 8.6:   A version of get-record *which 'skips' the 'deleted' records*

consulted for the meaning of 'record' in relation to a given external data medium.
A 'logical' record in the Cobol sense is usually, for such files, equivalent to one
'physical' record. Two traditional examples are a file consisting of punched cards,
where each record normally starts at the first column of a card, and an output
file assigned to a printer, where each record normally starts at the beginning of
a line. There is usually no need for the logical record length to match the standard
number of character positions in a card or in a line of print; for example, if a
record sent to a printer is 20 characters long and a print line is 120 characters
long, most compilers will ensure that the rightmost 100 character positions of the
line are blank.

8.8 PRINTED OUTPUT FILES

Special facilities exist for output files which are to be assigned to printers, or to
other devices for which the concept of a 'page' is useful. If *r* is a record-name
associated with such a file, then the statement

> **write** *r*

results in the printer advancing one line before the record is printed. In other
words, each record written by this form of **write** statement normally appears on
the line following that on which the preceding record was printed. An equivalent
statement is

> **write** *r* **after advancing** 1 **line**

but fortunately the words **advancing** and **line** (or **lines**) are optional, so most
programmers quickly adopt the form

> **write** *r* **after** 1

The statement

> **write** *r* **after** 2

results in the printed record being preceded by one blank line, the statement

> **write** *r* **after** 3

results in its being preceded by two blank lines, and so on. An integer data item
may be used to specify how many lines are advanced, as in

> **write** *r* **after** *n*

where the number of lines advanced is the value of *n*. The value of *n* may be
zero, or the statement

> **write** *r* **after** 0

may be used, in which cases no paper advance occurs and overprinting of
characters may result. (It may not, for the program may have ensured that, in
every character position, at most *one* of the two records — the record written
by this statement and the record preceding it — contains a non-space character.)

The statement

write *r* **after page**

results in the record being printed at the top of the next page.

It is also possible to specify that the record is to be printed on the current line, *followed* by several blank lines or by a page throw, as in

write *r* **before** 2

or

write *r* **before** *n*

or

write *r* **before page**

The words **after** and **before** cannot both be used in the same statement. For most purposes it is advisable to use *either* **after** (expressed or implied) *or* **before'** throughout a program; using both in the same program is not normally necessary and easily leads to mistakes in printed output.

In the application areas where Cobol is used, precise positioning of output on a printed page is very important. Output frequently has to be written on preprinted continuous stationery, such as invoice forms, delivery note forms, etc., each form being separated from the next by perforations in the paper. It is, of course, a trivial matter in Cobol to position characters correctly within one line of output, since the string of characters forming an internal record (in the record area associated with the print file) appears in exactly the same form on the printed line. Vertical positioning, however, is not quite so easy — it requires that a program maintain information about its current position within a page so that output records appear in the correct positions on printed forms, preprinted matter is not overwritten by computer output, and the ends of pages are not overrun.

As an aid to vertical positioning, a **linage** clause may be used in the **fd** sentence which describes a file. The simplest form of linage clause is exemplified in:

```
fd pfile, linage 40.
01 prec.
    02 . . .
```

The **linage** clause specifies the total number of lines over which printing and line advancing can occur in each logical page, i.e. it specifies the page size. Any **linage** clause results automatically in the existence of a special integer data item called **linage-counter** which may be referenced, but not modified, by procedure division statements. (If more than one file used by a program has a **linage** clause specified, then **linage-counter** must be *qualified* by the appropriate file name when it is referenced in the program, e.g. "**linage-counter of** *pfile*".) The value of **linage-counter** at any time is the current line number within a page. The programmer is thus relieved of the task of maintaining a count of lines.

Let us return for a moment to the file *mailing-list*. Suppose that we have blank peel-off adhesive labels attached to continuous stationery according to the dimensions given in Figure 8.7 and that we want to print address labels for all

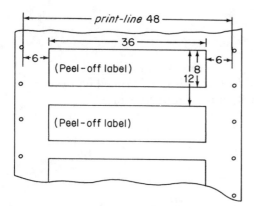

Figure 8.7: Stationery dimensions for mailing labels. Horizontal measures are expressed as character positions, vertical dimensions as lines

people on the mailing list. If the stationery is initially set up at, say, the second line of a label, then the program can treat the second line of every label as being the first line of a twelve-line 'page'; only the first four lines of a page will be used for printed characters.

A program to print the address labels is shown in Figure 8.8. Notice how it ensures that each line of output begins with nine spaces, so that printed characters start in the fourth position after the left-hand edge of a label. Since in standard Cobol the successful execution of a **write** statement leaves the record area content undefined, it is necessary to reset the space characters for each line printed. Spaces at the end of each line are generated by the statements which **move** data to *label-line*. The reserved word **spaces** used in the procedure division is an example of a **figurative constant**. Figurative constants are words which can be employed in place of certain frequently used literals. In this very simple program we are printing a fixed number of lines on each 'page', so there is no need to concern ourselves with the value of **linage-counter**.

8.9 PAGE CHANGES

(*This section may safely be omitted on your first reading.*)

Repeated execution of **write** statements may give rise to a situation in which a **write** statement cannot be completely executed within the current page, i.e. where execution would result in the value of **linage-counter** exceeding the file's **linage** value. In this situation, called 'page overflow', a **write** statement containing (or implying the use of) the word **after** is treated as though it had specified **after page**, and a **write** statement containing the word **before** is treated as though it had specified **before page**. In either case, therefore, the value of **linage-counter** is reset to 1. It is possible, though of limited usefulness, for the program to detect that page overflow has occurred and that these actions have been taken.

In practice, it is usually important to detect that output is *nearing* the end of a page in order to take some action *within the current page*. Consider a situation

```
      identification division.
        program-id.  print-labels.

      environment division.
        input-output section.
        file-control.
          select mailing-list  assign to xyz
              organization indexed
              access sequential
              record key surname.
          select label-file  assign to px1
              organization sequential
              access sequential.

      data division.
        file section.
        fd  mailing-list.
        01  addressee.
            02  name.
                03  inits        pic x(6).
                03  surname      pic x(20).
            02  address-line-1   pic x(30).
            02  address-line-2   pic x(30).
            02  post-code        pic x(9).

        fd  label-file,  linage 12.
        01  print-line.
            02  left-margin      pic x(9).
            02  label-line       pic x(39).

        working-storage section.
        01  eof    pic x.

      procedure division.
      main.
          open input mailing-list
              output label-file
          read mailing-list next;
          at end     move "t" to eof
          not at end move "f" to eof
          end-read
          perform until  eof = "t"
              move spaces to left-margin
              move name to label-line
              write print-line after page
              move spaces to left-margin
              move address-line-1 to label-line
              write print-line
              move spaces to left-margin
              move address-line-2 to label-line
              write print-line
              move spaces to left-margin
              move post-code to label-line
              write print-line
              read mailing-list next;
              at end      move "t" to eof
              not at end move "f" to eof
              end-read
          end-perform
          stop run.
```

Figure 8.8: Printing the mailing labels

in which the output records are lines of an invoice, each page being a preprinted invoice form. When the number of output records exceeds the number of lines provided for on the invoice form, it is necessary to continue to a second form. But it is normal practice to place at the foot of the first form one or more lines, indicating that the invoice continues on a second sheet and showing the total cash amount carried forward. Likewise, at the top of the second form, certain information (such as the customer's name and address) is repeated, there is an indication that the form is a continuation sheet — probably with a sheet number — and there is a note of the cash amount brought forward from the preceding sheet.

To provide for such cases, it is possible to specify a **footing** value, as in:

> **fd** *pfile*, **linage** 40, **footing** 36.
> 01 *invoice-line* . . .

The effect is that an **end-of-page** condition exists whenever the value of **linage-counter** equals or exceeds 36. If a **write** statement is in the form

> **write** *invoice-line* **after** 2; **end-of-page**
>   **perform** *page-change*
> **end-write**

then the procedure *page-change* is executed only when an end-of-page condition exists after execution of the **write** statement. (Mercifully, **eop** is a standard abbreviation for **end-of-page**.) In terms of the preceding paragraph, *page-change* will be a procedure which writes any lines required at the foot of the current page, advances to the next page, and writes any heading lines on that page.

A preprinted form is often designed so that all printing by the computer takes place within a limited area of the form, called the 'page body'. For example, the form may be headed with information like the organization's name and address, and at the foot there may be explanatory notes or advertising material, all of which is preprinted. If a file is described with

> **linage** 40, **footing** 36, **top** 12, **bottom** 4

then each page consists of 56 lines:

(a) a *top area*, consisting of 12 lines;
(b) a *page body*, consisting of 40 lines; and
(c) a *bottom area*, consisting of 4 lines.

with no intermediate lines between pages. When execution of a **write** causes a page advance, the advance is to the first line of the *page body*. The value of **linage-counter** is the number of the current line *within the page body*, and page overflow occurs when the **linage-counter** value would exceed 40. Thus a **write** statement cannot result in a record being printed in the top area or the bottom area. These areas are passed over by each page advance.

The **footing**, **top**, and **bottom** 'phrases' are all optional parts of the Cobol **linage** 'clause' and so cannot appear unless a **linage** value is specified. Absence of a **footing** phrase means that the end-of-page condition will occur simultaneously with the page overflow condition; absence of the **top** or **bottom** phrase indicates that there is no top or bottom area respectively.

Any of the characteristics of a page may be specified dynamically at run time if the appropriate phrase of the **linage** clause specifies a data-name instead of an integer. For example,

>   **linage** m, **footing** n

has the effect that the number of lines in the page body and the footing value are determined:

(a) for the first page, by the values of m and n when the file is opened;
(b) for subsequent pages, by the values of m and n at the time of page advance.

9. Editing data

(Towards the end of this chapter there are detailed examples which have been included in order to illustrate the potential of Cobol's editing facilities. On a first read-through, there is no need for you to try to memorize the detailed rules; knowledge of these is not required in later chapters.)

9.1 INTRODUCTION

Figure 9.1 shows two record descriptions and a fragment of procedure division code from a grossly oversimplified stock valuation program. The idea is that successive inventory records are read from a file, and the procedure division code shown converts each into a line of print and prints it.

A Cobol data-name, unlike variable names in most languages, can begin with a numeric digit, and Figure 9.1 illustrates a useful programming technique for making procedure division statements more intelligible — all data-names associated with a particular file begin with a digit identifying that file. (The same intelligibility could be achieved by *qualifying* the data-names, e.g.

    stock-no **in** *print-line*

but experience has shown that the simple technique illustrated makes for programs which are more readable as well as being easier to write or type; it also avoids the inadvertent use as data-names of reserved words such as *value* and *report*.)

In Figure 9.1, the object of the statement

    move spaces to *2print-line*

is to ensure that the unnamed data items, which 'space out' the output line, contain spaces. An alternative approach would be to define the subordinate items of *2print-line* as

02	*2stock-no*	**pic** x(7).
02	*2item-name*	**pic** x(23).
02	*2quantity*	**pic** 9(5).
02	*2filler*	**pic** x.
02	*2value*	**pic** 9(9)v99.

and to replace the above statement by

    move space to *2filler*

```
01      1inventory-record.
        02    1item-name     pic x(20).
        02    1stock-no      pic x(5).
        02    1quantity      pic 9(5).
        02    1unit-price    pic 9(4)v99.
        -
        -
        -
01      2print-line.
        02    2stock-no      pic x(5).
        02                   pic xx.
        02    2item-name     pic x(20).
        02                   pic xxx.
        02    2quantity      pic 9(5).
        02                   pic x.
        02    2value         pic 9(9)v99.
        -
        -
        -
        move spaces to 2print-line
        move 1stock-no to 2stock-no
        move 1item-name to 2item-name
        move 1quantity to 2quantity
        compute 2value = 1quantity * 1unit-price
        write 2print-line
```

Figure 9.1:   Two record descriptions (assumed to be associated with files) and a procedure division fragment

---

thus relying on the **move** statements to supply the spaces following the stock number and the item name. Notice that we cannot extend this technique to the space following *2quantity* by changing *2quantity*'s picture to 9(6) since

> **move** *1quantity* **to** *2quantity*

is a *numeric* **move**. Overall, the approach used in Figure 9.1 results in a program which is more intelligible and more maintainable.

Nevertheless, the output presented to the user is far from satisfactory. The statements in Figure 9.1 would give output lines like

> 1678Y Widget − half-inch   00024 00000001248

which no user should be expected to accept.

An **edited data item** can be informally considered as a data item in which the value is represented in a user-oriented form. It is distinguished from other kinds of data item by the presence in its picture of at least one of the symbols "z", "*", ".", ",", "$", "+", "−". "CR", "DB", "/", "b". and "0". The pictures of edited data items are often called 'editing pictures'. The syntactic and semantic rules which govern the definition and use of edited data items are complex, but the practical use of these items is very simple. The following description therefore consists largely of examples accompanied by explanatory notes.

9.2 NUMERIC EDITING

Perhaps the most alarming aspect of the sample output line from Figure 9.1 was that the value 12.48 looked, when printed, like an integer 1248 (with leading zeros printed). This, of course, was a consequence of the fact that the "v" in the picture of *2value* indicates the position of an *implied* decimal point and that the data does not include an *explicit* representation of the decimal point. But, if *2value* were defined as

02 *2value* **pic** 9(9).99.

(i.e. with "." replacing "v" in the picture), then the value 12.48 would be represented by

000000012.48

If *2value* were defined as

02 *2value* **pic** z(8)9.99.

then 12.48 would be represented by

⎿⎤⎤⎤⎤⎤⎤⎤⎤⎦12.48

and if *2value* were defined as

02 *2value* **pic** $(9)9.99.

then 12.48 would be represented by

⎿⎤⎤⎤⎤⎤⎤⎤⎤⎦$12.48

Similarly, if *2quantity* were defined as

02 *2quantity* **pic** zzzz9.

then 24 would be represented by

⎿⎤⎤⎤⎦24

The effects of the picture characters "z", "$", and "." will be explored in a moment, but first an answer should be given to a question which students naturally ask when they are first introduced to editing pictures: if such convenient representations of numbers are possible in Cobol, why don't we use them all the time? The answer is quite simply that edited data items cannot be used in arithmetic expressions, nor can they be used as 'source' operands in the statements **add**, **subtract**, **multiply**, and **divide** — only **numeric** data items, as described in Chapter 7, can be so used. Edited items can, however, be 'destination' operands in any of the arithmetic statements.

For example, if *n* and *e* are defined

    n **pic** 9(3)v9
    e **pic** 9(4).99

then *n* is a **numeric** data item of the kind we have already met, and *e*, because its picture includes an editing character ("."), is an **edited** data item. The statements

```
compute n = n + e
subtract e from n
compute e = e + 1.5
add 1 to e
```

are all illegal because in every case *e* acts as a 'source' of a number. But all the following statements are legal because *e* acts *only* as a *destination* (i.e. a variable to which the result is assigned):

> **compute** *e* = 74.25
> **compute** *e* = *n*
> **compute** *e* = *n* + 1.5

It is normal practice, therefore, for programs which handle numbers to work throughout with ordinary numeric data items and to assign a value to an edited data item only when that value is to be output.

Like assignment to a numeric item, assignment to an edited item may involve the generation of zeros in excess digit positions or the truncation of digits which cannot be accommodated (see Chapter 7). Assignment to edited items is usually effected by a **move** or a **compute** statement. When the **compute** statement is used, size errors can be detected in the usual way, and rounding may be specified.

Given the above definitions of *n* and *e*, and given that *n* contains the character string

> 1234

then execution of either

> **move** *n* **to** *e*

or

> **compute** *e* = *n*

will assign to *e* the character string

> 0123.40

Truncation or zero-filling may also occur in a 'de-editing' **move**. If *e* contains the character string

> 1234.56

then execution of

> **move** *e* **to** *n*

will assign to *n* the character string

> 2345

The statement

> **compute** *n* = *e*

is, of course, illegal because *e* is not an arithmetic expression.

9.3 EXAMPLES OF NUMERIC EDITING

Figures 9.2 to 9.4 show the effects of various editing pictures; numbers in brackets in the following text refer to the examples. In the figures, pictures are shown in

No.	Value assigned	Picture	Result of assignment
1	10.17	9.9	0.1
2	10.17	9999.999	0010.170
3	10.17	zzz9.999	__10.170
4	10.17	zzzz.zzz	__10.170
5	0.02	zzzz.zzz	_____.020
6	0	zzzz.zzz	_____
7	12345	zzzzz	12345
8	345	zzzz9	__345
9	0	zzzzz	_____
10	0	zzzz9	_____0
11	20.34	$9999.99	$0020.34
12	20.34	$zzz9.99	$__20.34

Figure 9.2: Examples of editing (underlining denotes space characters)

No.	Value assigned	Picture	Result of assignment
13	12345	****9	12345
14	345	****9	**345
15	0	****9	****0
16	0	*****	*****
17	23	*****	***23
18	10.17	***9.999	**10.170
19	20.34	$***9.99	$**20.34
20	20.34	$$$$9.99	__$20.34
21	0	$$$$9.99	___$0.00
22	1234.56	$$$$9.99	$1234.56
23	12345.67	$$$$9.99	$2345.67

Figure 9.3: More examples of editing

their expanded forms; in a program the picture of (2) could be specified as 9(4).9(3) and that of (3) as z(3)9.9(3).

Assignment to an edited item resembles assignment to an ordinary numeric item in that the value assigned is aligned with respect to the decimal point position denoted by the picture, and truncation (1) or zero-filling (2) may occur. If z's appear in a picture they must precede any 9's. The effect of a z is the same as that of a 9, except that in the integer part of the number every leading zero in a position corresponding to a z is replaced by a space (3, 4); z is equivalent to 9 after the decimal point position (5), except when the value is zero, in which case the zero digits and the decimal point itself are replaced by spaces (6). It is common practice to specify 9 rather than z for the 'units' position (7, 8) in order to obtain non-blank output when the value assigned is zero (9, 10).

A *single* currency symbol ($) at the start of the picture (it may in fact be preceded by + or −, considered later) results in the appearance of that character in the corresponding position in the data (11, 12). For countries where the dollar is not the unit of currency, an implementor may choose to provide another graphic character which is used generally in place of $; in Britain the sterling symbol may be provided. In the absence of such provision, the program can specify in the environment division that, in pictures and in edited data, another

No.	Value assigned	Picture	Result of assignment
24	66682	99,999	66,682
25	1234.56	99,999.99	01,234.56
26	1234.56	zz,zz9.99	_1,234.56
27	25	zz,zz9.99	_____25.00
28	25	**,**9.99	****25.00
29	1234.56	$$$,$$9.99	_$1,234.56
30	525	$$$,$$9.99	____$525.00
31	211134	99/99/99	21/11/34
32	211134	999b9b99	211_1_34
33	525	009909	005205
34	-1234.5	zzz9	1234
35	-1234.5	+9999	-1234
36	6789	+9999	+6789
37	-1234	-9999	-1234
38	6789	-9999	_6789
39	-8	+zzz9	-____8
40	-8	zzz9+	____8-
41	-8	----9	____-8
42	-8	++++9	____-8
43	1234.5	----9.9	_1234.5
44	-1234.5	----9.9	-1234.5
45	1234.5	+++,++9.9	_+1,234.5
46	-234.5	+++,++9.9	____-234.5
47	67.89	$$$9.99CR	_$67.89__
48	-90.12	$$$9.99CR	_$90.12CR
49	67.89	$$$9.99DB	_$67.89__
50	-90.12	$$$9.99DB	_$90.12DB

Figure 9.4: More examples of editing

character will be used in place of $ (though, due to the syntax of pictures, the choice of character is limited). In Britain, the appropriate environment division clause is

currency sign is "£"

but, before using this facility, you should consult your implementor's document-ation.

In order to prevent fraudulent insertion of high-order digits on computer output, the 'check protect' character * may be used in a picture. Its effect is the same as that of z except that leading zeros are replaced by "*" characters instead of spaces (13 to 19).

On many documents the output of values representing sums of money appear with leading zeros suppressed and the currency symbol ($ or other) in the position immediately preceding that of the first printed digit. This form of output is achieved by the use of the 'floating currency symbol'. If the currency symbol appears *more than once* (as a string) in a picture, then the effect is like that of a string of z's except that the *rightmost* leading zero is replaced not by a space but by the currency symbol character (20 to 22). In the resulting data, one currency symbol will always precede the first digit, *even if this results in left truncation of the number* (23). So, for example, the range of values which can be assigned to x, defined as

02 x **pic** \$\$9.

is 0 to 99.

One or more commas (,) in a picture indicate that the corresponding positions in the data are to contain commas (24 to 26, 29). If the digit position preceding the comma position had a leading zero replaced by a space or an "*" then the comma position is treated as though it too contained a leading zero (27, 28), perhaps the last leading zero (30). Other 'insertion' characters are '/', zero and space (denoted by B in a picture), and they follow the same rules as the comma (31 to 33).

Up to this point we have considered only zero and positive (or absolute) values. If a negative number is assigned to a data item described by any of the pictures so far considered, then the normal numeric **move** rule is applied, and it is the absolute (i.e. unsigned) value which is edited (34). The picture symbols +, −, CR, and DB can be used to include a sign representation in edited data. A single plus sign (+) at the beginning or end of a picture results in the corresponding position in the data containing "+" if the value assigned is positive or zero, or "−" if it is negative (35, 36, 39, 40). A single minus sign (−) at the beginning or end of a picture results in the corresponding position in the data containing a *space* if the value assigned is positive or zero, or "−" if it is negative (37, 38).

A string of sign characters (+ or −) may appear in a picture (41 to 46). The effect is the same as that of a string of z's except that the last leading zero — or an insertion character following the last leading zero (46) — is replaced by the sign indication. The sign indication is as described in the preceding paragraph (always "−" for negative values, either "+" or *space* for positive values). One sign position will always exist in the data, and care must be taken to avoid truncation of a leading digit; see the earlier discussion of the floating currency symbol.

If either of the character pairs CR and DB appears at the end of a picture, then the corresponding positions in the data contain these characters when the value assigned is negative or two spaces if the value assigned is positive or zero (47 to 50). CR and DB are conventional abbreviations for 'credit' and 'debit' respectively. Cobol students are sometimes puzzled by the fact that both are used for negative values — surely credit is the opposite of debit and if one is negative the other must be positive? But the point is that *they are not both used for the same data item*. One data item in this context may represent a debit amount when its value is positive, in which case a negative value is a credit; another data item may, when positive, represent a credit, in which case a negative value is a debit.

The edited items described so far are properly described as **numeric edited** data items; there is another class of edited items called **alphanumeric edited** data items.

9.4 ALPHANUMERIC EDITING

If an item x is defined

x **pic** xx/bxx0

and the statement

> **move** "AB12" **to** x

is executed, then x will contain

> AB/⎵120

Item x is an example of an **alphanumeric edited** data item, in whose picture, otherwise alphanumeric, any of the insertion characters /, 0, or b may appear. (As in numeric editing, b in the picture results in a space in the data.) This is *not* an example of a general insertion facility — the *only* characters which can be inserted in the data are "/", "0" and the space character. The characters from the source data item are assigned to the positions corresponding to x's in the picture according to the normal rules for an alphanumeric **move**, as given in Chapter 2. Thus, if y is defined

> y **pic** xxx/x/

and the statement

> **move** "ABCDE" **to** y

is executed, then right truncation will occur and y will contain

> ABC/D/

9.5 INITIALIZATION OF EDITED DATA ITEMS

A **value** clause may be included in the description of an edited item, but the initial value is specified as an edited character string, because no editing will be applied to an initial value. Any editing characters required must therefore be present in the literal itself, as in

> 03 *unit-price* **pic** **9.99, **value** "*11.50".

10. Mixing data types

10.1 TYPES OF DATA

We have now met all the major kinds of Cobol data items. (There are others, which are of limited usefulness.) They are:

(a) **group items** (concatenations of other data items), treated for many purposes like elementary alphanumeric items; and
(b) **elementary items** (described by pictures):
  (i) **alphanumeric** (picture character x), as described in Chapter 2;
  (ii) **numeric** (picture characters 9, etc.), as described in Chapter 7;
  (iii) **alphanumeric edited**, as described in Chapter 9;
  (iv) **numeric edited**, as described in Chapter 9.

Procedure division statements may also make use of literals, of which there are two kinds:

(a) **non-numeric literals**: character strings enclosed in quotation marks, as introduced in Chapter 2;
(b) **numeric literals**: numbers not enclosed in quotation marks, as introduced in Chapter 7.

We now consider the effects of combining data items and literals of different kinds in **move** statements and in comparisons.

10.2 MOVE STATEMENTS

Cobol is not a 'strongly typed' language; a given value may be assigned to a data item of nearly any kind. The possibilities for a **move** statement are summarized in Figure 10.1, from which it will be seen that the only prohibition is a **move** from an alphanumeric edited item (or, incidentally, a **move** of the figurative constant **space** or **spaces**) to a numeric or a numeric edited item. (There is also, as we shall see in **7** below, a limitation applied to a **move** from a numeric item or literal to an alphanumeric or an alphanumeric edited item.) Many of the cases in Figure 10.1 will rarely be included intentionally in a real program; they are detailed here not merely for completeness but also to aid error detection during program debugging. The numbers in Figure 10.1 refer to the following rules.

1. All cases marked "1" are simple alphanumeric moves (involving left justification and perhaps either right truncation or space-filling) as described in

FROM	TO data item of type:				
	Group	**Alpha-numeric**	**Alpha-numeric edited**	**Numeric**	**Numeric edited**
Group item	1	1	1	1	1
Alphanumeric item or non-numeric literal	1	1	2	5	6
Alphanumeric edited item	1	1	2	X	X
Numeric item or numeric literal	1	7	8	3	4
Numeric edited item	1	1	2	9	10

*Figure 10.1: Possible operands of **move** statements. 'x' indicates an illegal move. Numbers refer to the rules given in the text*

Chapter 2. Notice particularly that these cases include *all* moves in which *either* of the operands is a group item. Thus, given the definition

   b **pic** xx/xxx

and an operand *a* whose content is the character string "ABCDE", then execution of

   move *a* **to** *b*

will assign to *b* the character string "AB/CDE" (by rule 2) if *a* is defined

   02 *a* **pic** x(5).

but will assign to *b* the character string "ABCDE⎵" (note the trailing space) if *a* is defined

   02 *a*.
      03 *c* **pic** xx.
      03 *d* **pic** xxx.

because in the latter case *a* is a group item, and so rule 1 applies.

   2. Alphanumeric *to* alphanumeric edited: An alphanumeric move as above, but with insertion of editing characters at positions indicated by the picture of the edited item, as explained in Chapter 9. The unlikely move from a **numeric edited** item to an **alphanumeric edited** item is treated in the same way.

   3. Numeric *to* numeric: A numeric move, involving alignment at the decimal point position and possibly zero-filling or truncation at either end, as described in Chapter 7.

   4. Numeric *to* numeric edited: A numeric move as above, but with numeric editing applied as described in Chapter 9.

5. Alphanumeric *to* numeric: A numeric move, with the alphanumeric item regarded as an unsigned integer item. Thus, given the definitions and content

   e   **pic** x(4)   1234
   f   **pic** s9(5)v9   **sign leading, separate**

execution of

   move *e* **to** *f*

proceeds as though *e*'s picture were 9(4) instead of x(4), and the result in *f* is

   +012340

If *e*'s content were

   A∗B?

then *f* would contain

   +0A∗B?0

and it is the programmer's responsibility to ensure that such assignments do not take place. The implementor may choose to abort execution when something like this happens. As we shall see, a potential error of this kind is easy to detect.

6. Alphanumeric *to* numeric edited: As in **5** above, the alphanumeric item is regarded as an unsigned integer item, and the case is treated as **4** above.

7. Numeric *to* alphanumeric: *The numeric operand must be an integer literal or a data item with an integer picture.* (Adherence to this rule can of course be checked at compile time.) Thus, given

   h **pic** x(4)

the statement

   move 11.5 **to** *h*

is illegal, as is

   move *g* **to** *h*

if *g*'s picture is 99v9. If, however, *g* has the definition and content

   g **pic** 9(3)   123

then execution of

   move *g* **to** *h*

results in *h* containing

   123⊔

The move proceeds as though *g*'s picture were x(3) rather than 9(3).
   If the numeric item is signed, *the sign is never moved.* So if *g* is defined

   g **pic** s99

with or without a **sign . . . separate** clause, and if *g*'s value is −78, then execution of

    move *g* **to** *h*

results in *h* containing

    78⌊⌊⌋

8. Numeric *to* **alphanumeric edited**: Treated as in **7** above, with insertion of editing characters.

9. Numeric edited *to* **numeric**: The edited item is 'de-edited' and the resulting value is assigned to the numeric item as in **3** above. For example, given the definition and content

    i **pic** +(4)9.99   ⌊⌊⌋−23.50
    j **pic** s9(4)v99 **sign leading, separate**
    k **pic** 9(6)v9

execution of

    move *i* **to** *j*

and

    move *i* **to** *k*

results in *j* and *k* respectively containing

    −002350

and

    0000235

10. Numeric edited *to* **numeric edited**: The value obtained from the 'de-editing' process is assigned as in **4** above.

10.3 TESTING FOR INCOMPATIBLE DATA

The insecurities which can result from all this automatic 'type conversion' have been known for a long time. (By contrast, the practical inconvenience of over-strong typing has still to be fully recognized.) Perhaps the worst danger arises from the possibility that a numeric move may truncate significant leading digits or lose a negative sign. A previous test in the program to ensure that the value is in a suitable range:

    n **pic** s9(4).

    ——

    ——

    ——

—

if *m* **not** < −9999 **and** *m* **not** > 9999
then move *m* **to** *n*
else . . .

is not altogether satisfactory since we may later change 'the picture of *n* without remembering to change the **if** statement. A comment with the definition of *n* can help, but it is preferable to use

compute *n* = *m*; **size error** . . .

because the **size error** phrase provides an error trap which is independent of the size of *n*.

Another problem arises from the fact that we can very easily assign non-numeric characters to a numeric data item, as illustrated in **5** above. The effect of the assignment or of a subsequent attempt to use the value of that item as an arithmetic operand, or as a subscript, is undefined in the Cobol standard. (Indeed, the effect of inconsistency between an item's picture and its content is undefined generally in the standard.) An implementor may choose to terminate program execution, or he may choose to allow execution to continue (e.g. by using only the four low-order bits of each character) and yield nonsensical results. This situation is an example of what the Cobol standard calls 'incompatible data' — inconsistency between an item's picture and its content. Incompatible data may also arise from the input of data which does not match the pictures defining the record area associated with the input file, and from keying errors associated with an **accept** statement. Most operational Cobol programs do a thorough validation of all raw input data.

10.4 CLASS CONDITIONS

Fortunately, it is an easy matter for a program to test whether the value of a numeric data item agrees with its picture. It is also easy, in a case where the value of an alphanumeric item is to be assigned to a numeric item, to test whether all the characters in that value are numeric digits. The condition

p **is numeric**

(the word **is** may be omitted) may validly be tested for any numeric item *p*. It takes into account the sign representation as defined for *p*. The above condition will be *true* for the following combinations of picture and content:

p	**pic** 99v9	012
p	**pic** s99v9 **sign leading, separate**	−665

and will be *false* for these combinations:

p	**pic** 99v9	⎵12
p	**pic** 99	−8
p	**pic** s999 **sign leading, separate**	*123
p	**pic** s999 **sign trailing, separate**	00Y+

Applied to a group item or an elementary alphanumeric item, the condition

> p is **numeric**

is true only if every character position of p contains a numeric digit. Thus the condition is *true* for the following combinations of picture and content:

```
                  p pic x(4)      0000
    01 p.                         1905
         02 q  pic x.
         02 r  pic 9(3).
```

and *false* for these combinations:

```
                  p pic x(4)      −665
    01 p.                         1⎵12345
         02 q  pic xx.
         02 r  pic x(5).
```

The Cobol standard prohibits the testing of this condition if p is a group item which includes any elementary *signed* numeric items.

The condition

> p is **not numeric**

may also be used.

The following tests may be applied to data items which are not numeric data items. In all cases the word **is** is optional and the word **not** may be used to reverse the truth value:

> p is **alphabetic**: true if every character in p is an upper-case letter, a lower-case letter, or a space;
>
> p is **alphabetic-lower**: true if every character in p is a lower-case letter or a space;
>
> p is **alphabetic-upper**: true if every character in p is an upper-case letter or a space.

Additional classes of characters may be defined in the **special-names** paragraph of the environment division. For instance, the definition

> **class** *direction* **is** "NESW"

enables the procedure division to include the condition

> p **is** *direction*

which tests whether every character in p is one of the four letters N, E, S, or W.

The conditions described in this section are referred to as **class conditions**. They may be combined with other conditions in conditional expressions (i.e. boolean expressions — Algol programmers please note) with the operators **and** and **or**. Conditional expressions are used mainly in **if, evaluate**, and **perform until** statements.

10.5 COMPARISONS

The other form of condition we have met is the **relation condition**, which uses one of the operators $<$, $=$, $>$, $<=$, and $>=$. We have seen in Chapter 2 how alphanumeric values are compared (character by character, left to right) and in Chapter 7 that two numeric values are compared in the obvious way. Other kinds of comparison are rare in real programs, but the programmer sometimes finds it useful during program debugging to know how comparisons between unlike kinds of data are carried out.

The rules, in fact, are simple. A *non-integer* numeric item or literal can be compared *only* with another numeric item. All valid comparisons except those between two numeric items (or one numeric item and one numeric literal) are carried out on a character-by-character, left-to-right basis as described in Chapter 2. If one of the operands is a numeric item, then:

(a) if the other item is an *elementary* item or a non-numeric literal, the numeric operand is treated as though it were first moved (according to **move** rule **7**, earlier in this chapter) to an elementary alphanumeric item of the same size as itself. Thus given the definitions and contents

> s **pic** x(5) $-123\sqcup$
> t **pic** s9(3) **sign leading, separate** -123

the condition

> $s = t$

is *false*, since the stages in the comparison are:
   (i) regard t as being moved to a temporary variable with picture x(4), i.e. $123\sqcup$
   (ii) regard the shorter operand as being extended by spaces to the length of the longer.
   The values actually compared are therefore

> $-123\sqcup$

and

> $123\sqcup\sqcup$

(b) if the other item is a *group* item, the numeric operand is treated as though it were first moved (according to **move** rule **1**, earlier in this chapter) to a group item of the same size as itself. Thus, given the definitions and contents,

> 01 s. $-123\sqcup$
>   02 u **pic** xx.
>   02 v **pic** x(3).
> 01 t **pic** s9(3) **sign leading, separate**. -123

the condition

$$s = t$$

is *true* since:

  (i) t is regarded as being moved to a group item 4 characters in length (in this case the sign is not lost);

 (ii) the shorter operand is regarded as being extended by spaces to the length of the longer. The character strings thus obtained are compared and found to be equal.

11. Indexed files — alternate record keys

(This chapter describes an alternative method of retrieving records from an indexed file. You should read the first few pages, which present the general picture; unless you are particularly interested in the topic, the detail which follows may safely be skipped on your first read-through.)

11.1 REFERENCE NUMBERS

The file *mailing-list* used as an illustration in earlier chapters was, as we noted, quite unrealistic. In particular, the choice of a person's surname as the identifying key for a record meant that no two people represented on the file could have the same surname. If we included the person's initials in the key, we would find that there would be other problems, and the possibility of key duplication, though reduced, would not be removed.

In commercial and administrative environments, computer programs and data files exist only to serve the organization which owns them and are part, often only a minor part, of a 'total system'. From the point of view of the total system, as well as from that of the program, it is usually expedient to use special identifying codes which are assigned by the organization to individual entities like persons, products, or transactions. These identifying codes are often called *reference numbers*, though they may well include characters other than numeric digits. Reference numbers are distinguished from other data *by having the single function of identifying individual entities.*

It has sometimes been the practice to construct a reference number for an entity in such a way that the reference number includes an indication of some attribute of that entity. For example, a customer reference number might be assigned so that it indicates the sales territory in which the customer's premises are situated, or a product reference number might include an indication of the product group to which the product belongs. The uses made of these reference numbers become a problem when the boundaries of sales territories change, or when a more useful product grouping is evolved. In most cases this kind of key is better avoided.

The following advantages are offered by a reference number which is free of any use except the unique identification of an entity:

(a) The value does not change. A given entity is identified by the same reference number value throughout its life in the system. This avoids the confusion which can arise around the time when a 'natural' key value is changed, some people using the old value and some the new. It also aids auditing, and it simplifies the analysis of past performance; for example, when we want to analyse sales to particular customers over the last few years, we know that a customer is always identified by the same key value.

(b) The value is unique. A given reference number value cannot identify more than one entity. 'Natural' keys very often cannot guarantee unique values. Reference numbers can be allocated by computer to avoid unintentional duplication of values.

(c) Reference numbers are shorter than natural keys and reduce the possibility of errors in transcription, spelling, punctuation, and keying.

(d) Such errors can be detected by appending one or more check digits to a reference number. Much of the advantage claimed for natural keys is lost if check digits are appended to them.

The disadvantage of using a reference number is, of course, that it is *not* 'natural'. If a customer comes into a branch office to enquire about his account, he is not likely to know his reference number. How is the enquiry clerk to enter the enquiry on a terminal? Well, we can arrange the program so that the clerk enters, say, the customer's surname, and the computer system responds by displaying the reference numbers, names, and addresses of customers who have that surname; the clerk asks the customer for his address and responds to the computer system by selecting the appropriate reference number, after which details from the record are displayed.

Now, if the customer file is a Cobol indexed file and reference number is the record key, how is the program to find all the records for people called Smith? One way would be use to use sequential access and examine in turn every record in the file to see whether it was for a customer named Smith; but, for files of a realistic size, the response time would be measured in minutes — indeed, it would probably be *many* minutes, rather than a few seconds. A more useful method is to design the file in such a way that the set of records for any given surname can be retrieved without a scan of the complete file.

11.2 ALTERNATE RECORD KEYS

The data item in a record format which the machine's file management software uses as the means of identifying a particular record — the **record key** in a Cobol indexed file — is referred to generally as a *prime key* or *primary key*. Other data items, on the basis of whose values reasonably fast retrieval of a record (or a set of records) is possible, are referred to as *secondary keys* — in Cobol terminology, these are **alternate record keys**. Usually retrieval of records on the basis of secondary keys is achieved by the use of indices or lists associated with the file. In our example, the data item representing the customer's surname could be defined as a secondary key. In the remainder of this chapter we examine the

alternate record key facility of Cobol, and we end by noting, from a practical viewpoint, a major deficiency of the Cobol provisions.

11.3 THE MAILING LIST AGAIN

Returning to the mailing list example, let us suppose now that the persons on our mailing list are identified by a reference number which is simply a four-digit integer, complete with leading zeros where appropriate. Let us also suppose, to make the example more interesting, that the organization is a charity and that our record for each person includes the amount of the person's total donations to date. (For clarity, textbook examples have to be unrealistically simple.) If records are also to be retrieved efficiently by surname and also by total donations amount, the file may be defined as in Figure 11.1.

A number of features of this file require some explanation. Firstly, each of the two alternate record keys is defined as being **with duplicates**. This means simply that any value of *surname*, and likewise any value of *donations*, may be duplicated in the file, i.e. a given value may occur in more than one record. For any alternate record key it is possible to omit the **with duplicates** phrase, in which case the system raises an invalid key condition when a **write** or **rewrite** statement would result in duplicate values of that key. The **record key** itself cannot, of course, be described as being **with duplicates**, since its function is unique identification of a record. It is always the value of the (primary) record key data item in the record

---

```
        -
        -
environment division.
   input-output section.
   file-control.
      select mailing-list   assign to xyz
            organization indexed
            access   ...
            record key ref-no
            alternate record key surname with duplicates
            alternate record key donations with duplicates.
        -
        -
data division.
   file section.
   fd   mailing-list.
   01   donor.
         02   ref-no          pic x(4).
         02   name.
               03   initials   pic x(6).
               03   surname    pic x(20).
         02   address-line-1 pic x(30).
         02   address-line-2 pic x(30).
         02   post-code      pic x(9).
         02   donations      pic x(7).
         02   dons   redefines donations   pic 9(5)v99.
```

Figure 11.1:   Description of an indexed file with two alternate record keys

area which determines the record to be removed by a **delete** statement or replaced by a **rewrite** statement.

Secondly, the record key data item in Figure 11.1, *ref-no*, is described by the picture x(4), even though 9(4) may seem more natural since we intend the value to be a four-digit integer. A value of *ref-no*, however, is not really a number — we do not add reference numbers together, or do any other kind of arithmetic on them. In this context they are simply strings of characters used to identify records. Describing *ref-no* as alphanumeric raises no possibility of error which could not just as easily arise if it were described as numeric; and, as we have seen in Chapter 10, it is an easy matter to ensure that any character string assigned to *ref-no* consists only of numeric digits.

Thirdly, the picture of *donations* is x(7). A value of *donations*, unlike a value of *ref-no*, really *is* a number. Presumably there will be a program which adds the amount of each new donation to *donations*, and the value will be output in numeric edited form. Why then the picture x(7)? The answer is that in indexed organization all keys must be alphanumeric; so, if we want to use *donations* as a key, we have to define it in this way. But we also want to use the value of *donations* in arithmetic and, as we saw in Chapter 7, arithmetic operations can be applied only to **numeric** data items. This is the reason for including the data item *dons* which follows *donations* in the record description. When we say

> *dons* **redefines** *donations*

what we are saying is that *both names refer to (or 'map') the same area of store*. In other words, character positions 100 to 106 of the record area can be referred to:

either (a) as *donations*, in which case the content is regarded as a string of seven characters (as when we refer to these characters as a key value);

or (b) as *dons*, in which case the content is regarded as an unsigned number with the implied decimal point between character positions 104 and 105 (as when we perform arithmetic using these characters).

Redefinition will be discussed in greater detail in a later chapter.

As with the record key, the positions in a record of all alternate record key data items are determined at the time when the file is created and cannot be changed by any program which subsequently uses the file.

11.4 RANDOM ACCESS

In general, *the only statements which can make use of alternate record key values to identify records are the* **read** *and* **start** *statements*. Since the **start** statement is not available in random access mode, the only relevant statement is **read**. We have already seen how the statements

> **move** "1234" **to** *ref-no*
> **read** *mailing-list*; **invalid key** . . .

will, if successfully executed, retrieve the record whose *ref-no* value is "1234". An equivalent pair of statements would be

> **move** "1234" **to** *ref-no*
> **read** *mailing-list*; **key is** *ref-no*; **invalid key** . . .

The record key, in other words, is the *default* key in a random **read** statement. But the **key** phrase enables us to say

> **move** "Inglis" **to** *surname*
> **read** *mailing-list*; **key is** *surname*; **invalid key** . . .

and

> **move** 2000 **to** *dons*
> **read** *mailing-list*; **key is** *donations*; **invalid key** . . .

in which cases respectively a record with *surname* value "Inglis" and a record with *donations* value "0200000" (i.e. *dons* value 2000.00) will be retrieved. (The invalid key condition will arise if there is no appropriate record in the file.) Only a data item defined as the **record key** or as an **alternate record key** can be named in the **key** phrase of a **read** statement.

But what happens when there is more than one "Inglis" record or 2000 record in the file? Which do we get? And does it matter which we get, when what we actually want is not *one* record but a *set* of records? There is a real problem here, for the Cobol file-handling philosophy is based on record-by-record access. To see how the problem is solved we must look at sequential access.

11.5 SEQUENTIAL ACCESS

An indexed file has the property that several logical *orderings* of the records can exist simultaneously. One ordering corresponds to each key designated in the file description. Figure 11.2 shows an instance of the file *mailing-list* described in Figure 11.1; the ordering shown is that appropriate to the record key, i.e. on ascending value of *ref-no*. Figures 11.3 and 11.4 show respectively the orderings appropriate to *surname* and *donations*. (Notice that, since *dons* is unsigned, the character-based ordering on *donations* is identical to the numeric ordering on *dons*.) A program may at any time make use of any of these orderings by establishing *ref-no* or *surname* or *donations* as the current **key of reference**.

It is important to recognize that these three logical orderings exist *simultaneously* throughout the life of the file, and are maintained by the system software. There is no implication of three different files existing, nor of the file being sorted when a program switches from one key of reference to another.

No matter how many logical orderings a file has, there is still the concept of a *single* file position 'pointer', and the "next record" in sequential access is the next within the ordering appropriate to the key of reference. *In sequential access mode, a key of reference is established (i.e. a particular ordering of the records becomes current) as a result of successful execution of an* **open** *or a* **start** *statement.* No other statement can change the key of reference.

```
ref-no  ...  surname    ...  dons
0002    ...  Westland   ...  1000
0005    ...  Maclure    ...    21
0107    ...  Macnaught  ...   360
0366    ...  Till       ...    45
0812    ...  Young      ...  3200
1653    ...  Brady      ...    92
1998    ...  Stockdale  ...  582.75
2821    ...  Maule      ...    45
3301    ...  Penman     ...     0
3516    ...  Ellis      ...     1.50
3800    ...  Penman     ...   900
3864    ...  Young      ...    45
4020    ...  Joyner     ...  1625.50
```

Figure 11.2:   A small indexed file corresponding to the description in Figure 11.1. Rows represent records and columns represent data items. Values are shown for the key data items only. Ordering is based on the record key (ref-no) and is assumed to be the order in which the records were written when the file was created. Record key ordering will probably be reflected to some extent in the physical disposition of the records on the file storage device. The value of dons is shown above in conventional numeric notation. As stored in the file, the value in the first record, for example, will be the character string '0100000'

```
ref-no  ...  surname    ...  dons
1653    ...  Brady      ...    92
3516    ...  Ellis      ...     1.50
4020    ...  Joyner     ...  1625.50
0005    ...  Maclure    ...    21
0107    ...  Macnaught  ...   360
2821    ...  Maule      ...    45
3301    ...  Penman     ...     0
3800    ...  Penman     ...   900
1998    ...  Stockdale  ...  582.75
0366    ...  Till       ...    45
0002    ...  Westland   ...  1000
0812    ...  Young      ...  3200
3864    ...  Young      ...    45
```

Figure 11.3:   The file shown in Figure 11.2, ordered on the alternate record key surname. (Ordering within one value of surname reflects the order in which the records were placed in the file.) This ordering will probably be implemented by an indexing technique

An **open** statement establishes the record key (prime key) as the key of reference. The program in Figure 11.5 therefore — since it contains no **start** statement — simply progresses through the records in the order shown in Figure 11.2. (In Figures 11.5 and 11.6 it is assumed that the file *mailing-list* has indexed organization and is defined by the program description given in Figure 11.1, with **access** specified as **sequential**.)

The program in Figure 11.6 demonstrates how Cobol solves the problem of retrieving a set of records. In this example, all records for people called Penman

```
ref-no  ...  surname     ...  dons
3301    ...  Penman      ...       0
3516    ...  Ellis       ...       1.50
0005    ...  Maclure     ...      21
0366    ...  Till        ...      45
2821    ...  Maule       ...      45
3864    ...  Young       ...      45
1653    ...  Brady       ...      92
0107    ...  Macnaught   ...     360
1998    ...  Stockdale   ...     582.75
3800    ...  Penman      ...     900
0002    ...  Westland    ...    1000
4020    ...  Joyner      ...    1625.50
0812    ...  Young       ...    3200
```

Figure 11.4:   The file shown in Figure 11.2, ordered on the alternate record key donations. *(Ordering within one value of* donations *reflects the order in which the records were placed in the file.) This ordering will probably be implemented by an indexing technique*

```
    -
    -
    -
    fd   mailing-list   ...   [as in figure 11.1]
    -
    -
    working-storage section.
    01   eof               pic x.
    01   total-donations   pic 9(9)v99.
    01   out-dons          pic $(9)9.99.
    -
    -
    -
procedure division.
main.
     open input mailing-list
     move 0 to total-donations
     perform, with test after, until  eof = "t"
          read mailing-list next;
          at end        move "t" to eof
          not at end    move "f" to eof
                        add dons to total-donations
          end-read
     end-perform
     move total-donations to out-dons
     display "Total donated:", out-dons
     stop run.
```

Figure 11.5:   Calculating the total donations for all persons on the mailing list. The file is accessed sequentially in ref-no *order*

are retrieved. (Of course in Figure 11.6 the literal "Penman" is used in order to · make the program easier to read; a real program would obtain the value of the surname from a data item. A similar observation applies to later examples in this chapter. Figures 11.5 and 11.6 depart from the conventions so far employed in the layout of **invalid key** and **at end** phrases — this is done purely to demonstrate possibilities, and a programmer would do well to adopt his own layout conventions, or those of his installation, and apply them consistently.)

```
    -
    -
    -
fd   mailing-list   ...   [as in figure 11.1]
    -
    -
    -
working-storage section.
01   eof   pic x.
    -
    -
procedure division.
 1  main. open input mailing-list
 2      move "Penman" to surname
 3      start mailing-list, key = surname;
 4      invalid key   perform empty-set
 5      not invalid key
 6          read mailing-list next;
 7          at end     move "t" to eof
 8          not at end move "f" to eof
 9          end-read
10          perform until  eof = "t"  or  surname not = "Penman"
11              perform process-record
12              read mailing-list next
13              at end        move "t" to eof
14              not at end  move "f" to eof
15              end-read
16          end-perform
17      end-start
18      stop run.
```

Figure 11.6: *Retrieving the set of records with a given value of an alternate record key (sequential access). The procedure* process-record *is called to do whatever is necessary with each record retrieved, and the procedure* empty-set *is called if no records satisfy the retrieval criterion*

We now examine the program in Figure 11.6 in some detail. The **open** statement at line 1 establishes *ref-no* as the key of reference, but before any **read next** is executed, the **start** statement at line 3 has the following effects:

(a) Since *surname* is named in the statement's **key** condition, *surname* is established as the new key of reference, and therefore the record ordering shown in Figure 11.3 will apply until another **start** is executed. None is, so the ordering applies during execution of the remainder of the program.

(b) The *first* record (in this newly established ordering) which satisfies the **key** condition is found and is established as the "next record", so that subsequent executions of **read next** statements will progress forward from this point. The "next record" at this stage is the record with reference number 3301. (For brevity, we will call this record simply "record 3301".)

The **read next** at line 6 retrieves record 3301 and, because *surname* is the key of reference, record 3800 becomes the new "next record". Record 3301 is processed at line 11, record 3800 is read at line 12 and is processed at line 11 on the next iteration, then record 1998 is read at line 12. At this stage the terminating condition at line 10 is true and the program terminates at the **stop run** statement. The *eof* test in the terminating condition is necessary because in general the

surname used for retrieval may be the last *surname* value in the ordering —
consider what would happen if records for persons called Young were to be
retrieved. Notice again that when in a program the word **perform** is followed by
a procedure name there is no corresponding **end-perform**.

Some of the clumsiness of this program can be avoided if dynamic, rather than
sequential, access is used. With dynamic access available, there is little point in
using sequential access for an input file.

11.6 DYNAMIC ACCESS

It will be recalled from Chapter 6 that dynamic access makes the random **read**
statement available in addition to the **start** and **read next** which were available
in sequential access mode. Like the **start** statement, the random **read** establishes
the key which is named in its key phrase as the key of reference.

The program in Figure 11.7 is functionally equivalent to that in Figure 11.6,
but uses dynamic access. The **read** statement at line 3 has the following effects:

(a) since *surname* is named in the **key** phrase, *surname* is established as the new
key of reference, and therefore the record ordering shown in Figure 11.3 will
apply until either a **start** or another random **read** is executed;
(b) the first record (in this newly established ordering) whose value of *surname*
matches that in the record area (i.e. record 3301) is read into the record
area, and record 3800 becomes the "next record".

Otherwise the program is straightforward.

```
        -
        -
      [file described as in figure 11.1]
        -
        -
      working-storage section.
      01   eof   pic x.
        -
        -
      procedure division.
  1   main.  open input mailing-list
  2         move "Penman" to surname
  3         read mailing-list; key is surname
  4         invalid key    perform empty-set
  5         not invalid key
  6             move "f" to eof
  7             perform until  eof = "t"  or  surname not = "Penman"
  8                 perform process-record
  9                 read mailing-list next;
 10                 at end        move "t" to eof
 11                 not at end    move "f" to eof
 12                 end-read
 13             end-perform
 14         end-read
 15         stop run.
```

*Figure 11.7:   Retrieving the set of records with a given value of an alternate
record key (dynamic access)*

The same technique is used in the program in Figure 11.8 which prints the reference number, surname, and donations for all persons whose total donations are in the range 50 to 1500 dollars (or pounds). On this occasion the complete program is shown, but initially we need concern ourselves only with the procedure *main* (lines 1 to 20). The key *donations* is established as the key of reference by the **start** statement at line 4 and, since no further **start** or random **read** statements occur, the record ordering of Figure 11.4 is used throughout the program. As we have seen, the name *donations* (since it is alphanumeric) must be used when we want to refer to the total donations value as a *key*, but in other contexts we can use the name *dons*, which enables us to specify numeric values in a more natural way, e.g. 50 rather than "0005000". Ascending order of the character-strings called *donations* is the same as ascending order of the unsigned numbers called *dons*.

At line 4, a **start** is used rather than a random **read** because use of the latter would require us to specify the precise value of the key in the first record to be accessed. The record identified by the **start** is record 1653; this record is retrieved by the **read next** at line 7. Thereafter, the **read next** at line 13 retrieves in turn records 0107, 1998, 3800, 0002, and 4020. All but the last of these records are printed; retrieval of record 4020 results in the terminating condition of the **perform** loop being satisfied.

This program provides a good opportunity to demonstrate, by using a printed output file, a very simple use of some features described in Chapter 8. *Readers who would prefer not to be distracted from the topic of alternate record keys can*

```
identification division.
  program-id.   print-donations.

environment division.
  input-output section.
    file-control.   select mailing-list   assign to abc
                      organization indexed
                      access dynamic
                      record key ref-no
                      alternate record key surname
                              with duplicates
                      alternate record key donations
                              with duplicates.
                    select print-file   assign to op
                      organization sequential
                      access sequential.

data division.
  file section.
  fd  mailing-list.
  01  donor.
        02  ref-no            pic x(4).
        02  name.
            03  initials      pic x(6).
            03  surname       pic x(20).
        02  address-line-1    pic x(30).
        02  address-line-2    pic x(30).
        02  post-code         pic x(9).
        02  donations         pic x(7).
        02  dons   redefines donations   pic 9(5)v99.
```

```
     fd   print-file,   linage 40, footing 39.
     01   2print-rec.
          02   2ref-no    pic x(6).
          02   2name      pic x(28).
          02   2dons      pic $(5)9.99.
          02   2end       pic x(17).

     working-storage section.
     01   eof        pic x.
     01   page-no    pic 99.
     01   out-heading.
          02   out-text       pic x(54).
          02   out-page-no    pic zz9.
     procedure division.
 1   main. open input mailing-list, output print-file
 2        perform start-printing
 3        move 50 to dons
 4        start mailing-list, key >= donations;
 5        invalid key   perform print-list-empty
 6        not invalid key
 7            read mailing-list next;
 8            at end        move "t" to eof
 9            not at end  move "f" to eof
10            end-read
11            perform until  eof = "t"  or  dons > 1500
12                perform print-this-record
13                read mailing-list next;
14                at end        move "t" to eof
15                not at end  move "f" to eof
16                end-read
17            end-perform
18            perform print-end-of-list
19        end-start
20        stop run.
21   start-printing.
22        move "List of donations between $50 and $1500    page"
23            to out-text
24        move 0 to page-no
25        perform new-page.
26   new-page.
27        add 1 to page-no
28        move page-no to out-page-no
29        move out-heading to 2print-rec
30        write 2print-rec after page.
31   print-this-record.
32        move ref-no to 2ref-no
33        move name to 2name
34        move dons to 2dons
35        move spaces to 2end
36        write 2print-rec; eop   perform new-page
37        end-write.
38   print-end-of-list.
39        move "End of list" to 2print-rec
40        write 2print-rec.
41   print-list-empty.
42        move "There are no donation totals in this range"
43            to 2print-rec
44        write 2print-rec.
```

Figure 11.8:   Retrieving the set of records in which the value of an alternate record key lies in a given range, and printing selected data items from the retrieved records

*limit their reading of the procedure division of Figure 11.8 to the procedure main
and can ignore the other procedures, which are concerned only with printing. These
readers may also skip the next two paragraphs here, but should return to them
after reading to the end of the chapter.*

Looking at the definition of *print-file* in the data division, we see that there
are 40 lines per page on the output, and the **footing** phrase means that an **eop**
(end-of-page) condition will occur when the current line number in a page exceeds
38. The description of *2print-rec* specifies the layout of one normal line of output.
The items *2ref-no* and *2name* are each two characters longer than the corresponding
items in records of the *mailing-list* file in order to ensure that two spaces will be
at the end of each on an output line. The length of an output line is extended
to 60 characters by the item *2end*, which will contain spaces on normal lines. The
item *2end* is included so that an output record will be long enough to accommodate
strings of text like page headings. (Since the name *2end* is never used in the
procedure division, it was not in fact necessary to give this item a name at all.)

Notice that there are several assignments to *2print-rec* of character strings
which do not match the definition of *2print-rec*. For example, if immediately after
execution of the **move** in line 39 any of the subordinate items of *2print-rec* were
used as a source of data, they would make no sense. The content of *2ref-no*
would be "End of", the content of *2name* would be "⎵list" followed by 23
spaces, and *2dons* would be all spaces. *Assignment to a group item takes no
account of the definitions of subordinate data items* (subject to an exception noted
in Chapter 14) — in lines 29, 39, and 43, *2print-rec* is simply an area of store to
which a character string is assigned. Notice also that lines 22 and 23 are initializing
the value of *out-text*, which thereafter remains constant; an alternative would be to
use a **value** clause.

11.7 INPUT–OUTPUT FILES

We have seen earlier that, unlike **open**, **read**, and **start** statements, the **delete**,
rewrite, and **write** statements neither change nor make use of the current
sequential position in a file. Similarly, **delete**, **rewrite**, and **write** statements neither
change nor make use of the current key of reference. Figure 11.9 summarizes
the position.

When a record is deleted, of course, it immediately disappears from every key
ordering, and when a new record is written it immediately and automatically
takes its appropriate place in every ordering. Thus, when a **write** statement places
in the file *mailing-list* a new record with reference number 1108, surname
"Colville", and donations 92, the record is inserted:

(a) between 0812 and 1653 in the *ref-no* ordering (Figure 11.2);
(b) between 1653 and 3516 in the *surname* ordering (Figure 11.3); and
(c) between 1653 and 0107 in the *donations* ordering (Figure 11.4).

In (c), the position is *after* 1653, not before it, because *any insertion into an
ordering is in the position following any records already present with the same
value of the key* on which the ordering is based.

Statement	Establishes key of reference?	Uses previously established key of reference?
open	yes	no
start	yes	no
(random) read	yes	no
read next	no	yes
delete	no	no
rewrite	no	no
write	no	no

Figure 11.9:   How a key of reference is established and used

---

When a record is replaced (or, more accurately, *updated*) by a **rewrite** statement, the changes may cause it to occupy a new position in one or more key orderings. Suppose that Miss Ellis (reference number 3516) marries a Mr Penman and wants to have her change of name recorded. The change is effected by program code on the lines:

> **move** "3516" **to** *ref-no*
> **read** *mailing-list*; **invalid key** . . .
* Record key *ref-no* is assumed when no **key** phrase
* appears in a **read**
> **move** "Penman" **to** *surname*
> **rewrite** *donor*; **invalid key** . . .

As a result of the **rewrite**, key values in the record become

3516 . . . Penman . . . 1.50

and, though the record retains its position in the *ref-no* and *donations* orderings, its position in the *surname* ordering is automatically changed from the second position to the end of the "Penman" sequence, i.e. between records 3800 and 1998.

The programmer needs to be careful when writing programs which update files with alternate record keys. Suppose that a trainee programmer is given the following requirements for changes to the file *mailing-list*:

(a) to make the above change of name from "Ellis" to "Penman";
(b) to 'gross up' the donations amount in every record to account for recovery of tax — for simplicity, let us assume that donations amounts are to be increased by 40 per cent; and

(c) to perform certain other processing on every record, involving the printing of selected records in order of surname.

For efficiency, the programmer decides to write one program which will meet all three requirements. Since all the records must be accessed, the obvious choice of access mode is sequential, and requirement (c) suggests that the file is best accessed in *surname* order. On this basis, the programmer produces a program whose main logic is shown in Figure 11.10. (The procedures *file-is-empty* and *other-processing* are not relevant to our discussion, nor is the action taken in the 'impossible' case of the **rewrite** producing the invalid key condition.)

The word **low-values** in the second line of Figure 11.10 is, like **spaces**, a figurative constant, i.e. a reserved word equivalent to a literal. The literal denoted by **low-values** is a suitably long string of characters, each of which is the lowest character in the collating sequence. As well as establishing *surname* as the key of reference, the **start** statement therefore identifies the first record in the *surname* ordering as the "next record". The **read next** statements in the program then progress through the records in the sequence shown in Figure 11.3 until the end of the file is reached.

The program in Figure 11.10 is incorrect. Before reading further, you should examine it in detail and try to spot the error.

Consider what this program does when the second record is read. The donations amount is increased from 1.50 to 2.10, the 'other processing' is performed, and, since the value of *ref-no* is 3516, the value of *surname* is changed from "Ellis" to "Penman" before the record is rewritten. The next record (record 4020) is

```
main.
        open i-o mailing-list
        move low-values to surname
        start mailing-list, key >= surname; invalid key
            perform file-is-empty
            stop run
        end-start
        perform, with test after, until  eof = "t"
            read mailing-list next;
            at end        move "t" to eof
            not at end
                move "f" to eof
                compute dons rounded = dons + .4 * dons
                perform other-processing
                if ref-no = "3516"
                then   move "Penman" to surname
                end-if
                rewrite donor;  invalid key   ...
                end-rewrite
            end-read
        end-perform
        stop run.
    file-is-empty.   ...
            -
            -
    other-processing.   ...
            -
            -
```

Figure 11.10:   A procedure containing a programming error

then read and processed and the program continues through the rest of the file. What the programmer has forgotten is that the **rewrite** of record 3516 has changed that record's position in the *surname* ordering. So, when the program reaches the point where record 3800 has been processed and rewritten, record 3516 is read *again*, this time from its *new* position, the donations amount is unintentionally increased from 2.10 to 2.94 and the 'other processing' unintentionally performed a second time.

Such errors do not often occur in quite this form in real programs since prime key ordering is normally used for a sequential updating pass through a file, and **rewrite** statements cannot alter the prime key ordering. Accessing records in prime key sequence also gives faster retrieval.

11.8 ALTERNATE RECORD KEYS — A GENERAL OBSERVATION

The facilities provided by the existence of alternate record keys in Cobol fall short of those often required in real applications. Alternate record keys enable a Cobol program to access records on the basis of a value, or a range of values, of *one* of a number of keys. Very often, however, what is required is access on the basis of values of *several* keys.

Consider for example a requirement to retrieve from the personnel file of a large organization the records corresponding to all programmers over 45 years of age working in the London branch of the organization. Even if the data items *job-title*, *year-of-birth*, and *branch* are all designated as alternate record keys, a Cobol program must choose one of these keys, read every record having the appropriate value (or a value within the appropriate range) of that key, then examine the values of the other keys in each record retrieved in order to determine whether that record meets the overall retrieval criterion. All records with *branch* = "London" might be read, each record being examined to establish whether the record corresponds to a programmer born more than 45 years ago. This particular approach would be a bad one if the organization had 600 employees in London, 100 employees who were programmers, and 500 employees over the age of 45 — it would clearly be better to read 100 records than to read 600. Though Cobol allows access through only one alternate record key at a time, it has no provision for determining in advance how many records will be read; the searching strategy adopted thus depends on the programmer's knowledge of the file content.

What makes the situation worse is the possibility that, since programmers still tend to be youngish, there may in fact be only three programmers at the London branch who are over the age of 45. Then, even with the optimum strategy, 97 per cent of the records read will not meet the overall retrieval criterion.

Such inefficiency is often unacceptable, particularly when critical response times are involved, and users sometimes have to use commercially supplied software packages in applications which include multi-term retrieval. Yet the very name 'indexed' implies that key-based retrieval is implemented by the use of indices. This almost certainly means that, stored with the above personnel file, there will be a list of identifications (usually prime key values) of all records with *job-title* = "Programmer", another list identifying all records with *branch* = "London", and lists identifying records in which *year-of-birth* = "1940", *year-of-birth* = "1941", etc. A resourceful assembly-language programmer who is conversant with the file-management facilities of the operating system will have no difficulty in accessing these lists and manipulating them to identify records which satisfy the original criterion. As a result, only records which actually satisfy the criterion are read from the personnel file.

It is a matter for regret that Cobol itself does not provide a means of accessing these lists or, better still, the ability to specify retrieval criteria in the form of boolean expressions.

12. Relative files

(Later chapters do not assume knowledge of the material presented in this chapter.)

12.1 INTRODUCTION

A file which has relative organization may be visualized as being stored in a number of cells or 'slots', each of which:

(a) is uniquely identifiable by an integer in the range 1 to n;
(b) either contains one record or is empty.

The number of slots (n) assigned to a given file is determined outside the Cobol program, possibly by operating system control statements.

A relative file has many features in common with an indexed file. Records can be accessed randomly on the basis of a primary key value (in this case, the 'slot' number); the same access modes (random, sequential, dynamic) and open modes (input, output, i–o, extend) are available; and the actions of the individual file-accessing statements are essentially the same as when applied to an indexed file. The major differences between indexed and relative organization are:

(a) in **indexed** organization, a record's primary key value is a character string embedded in the record; in **relative** organization, a record's primary key value is an integer which denotes the record's *position* in the file.
(b) **relative** organization provides no alternate record key facilities.
(c) the file storage space occupied by an indexed file is determined by the number of records in the file; implementations of relative file organization are usually (but need not be) such that the space requirement is determined by the range of slot numbers, regardless of the number of records present.

Relative organization is therefore simpler, but less immediately useful, than indexed organization. The programmer may decide that the relationship between the slot numbers in a file and the natural keys of records is to be a simple linear one. For instance, the days of a year may be allocated slot numbers 1–366 with 1 January as day 1 and 31 December as day 366, slot 60 being empty if the year is not a leap year. Alternatively, natural keys may be hashed to yield slot numbers in a given range, and each slot may contain a number of 'records' which, taken together, form a single record in the file. The latter strategy involves the program manipulating several 'records' in the file's record area. This, however, is a matter of application design and will not be pursued here.

This chapter presents a summary of the use of a relative file first of all as an **output** file, then as an **extend** file, then as an **input** file, and finally as an **i–o** file.

12.2 CREATING A RELATIVE FILE

A relative file may be created (i.e. opened in **output** mode) using either random or sequential access; in either case, the only statement available for accessing the file is the **write** statement. In relation to an output file, dynamic access is equivalent to random access.

12.2.1 RANDOM ACCESS

Consider the file called *sample* described in the program fragments of Figure 12.1. Notice particularly that the item defined as the **relative key** data item, *sample-key*, conforms to these general rules:

(a) its picture describes it as an unsigned integer;
(b) it is not subordinate to a record type which is associated with *sample* (i.e. it is not within the record area for the file; it may be in working-storage or in a record area associated with another file).

With random access there is no constraint on the order in which records are placed in the file. After execution of the statement

    open output *sample*

a program may write a record to any required slot in the file by:

```
    -
    -
environment division.
  input-output section.
  file-control.
    select sample  assign to efg
        organization relative
        access random
        relative key sample-key.
    -
    -
data division.
  file section.
  fd  sample.
  01  sample-rec.
      02 ...
    -
    -
  working-storage section.
    -
    -
  01  sample-key  pic 9(4).
    -
    -
```

Figure 12.1: An example of environment division and data division entries for a relative file which is to be accessed randomly

(a) ensuring that the record to be written is in the record area (*sample-rec*);
(b) ensuring that the value of *sample-key* is the number of the slot to which the record is to be written;
(c) then writing the record by the statement

       write *sample-rec;* **invalid key** . . .

The invalid key condition will arise if the value of *sample-key* identifies a slot to which a record has been written by earlier execution of a **write** statement, or if the value of *sample-key* is zero or greater than the highest slot number available for the file.

12.2.2 SEQUENTIAL ACCESS

Figure 12.2 illustrates how a relative file is created using sequential access. The process is the same as that for creating an indexed file (as in Figure 5.2) or for creating a sequential file (as in Figure 8.1), except that in the latter case there is no **invalid key** phrase. In the case of a relative file, the record written by the first execution of a **write** statement is placed in slot 1, that written by the second execution of a **write** statement is placed in slot 2, and so on; in general, the *r*th record written is placed in slot *r*. If *n* slots are provided for the file, the invalid key condition arises if and when an (*n*+1)th **write** is attempted.

   Notice that the **select** sentence in Figure 12.2 does not include a **relative key** phrase, but the **select** sentence in Figure 12.1 does. This is because there is no

```
        -
        -
environment division.
    input-output section.
    file-control.
        select sample   assign to hij
              organization relative
              access sequential.
        -
        -
data division.
    file section.
    fd   sample.
    01   sample-rec.
         02 ...
        -
        -
procedure division.
        -
        -
              open output sample
        -
        -
*     repeated execution of:
              write sample-rec;   invalid key ...
        -
        -
```

Figure 12.2:   Creation of a relative file, using sequential access

need to use a relative key data item when accessing a file sequentially, unless it is an **input** or an **i–o** file and a **start** statement is to be used. However, it is sometimes useful to know the numbers of the slots to which particular records are written, and this information can be obtained by adding to the **select** sentence a **relative key** phrase such as

   relative key *x*

where *x* is the name of a data item which is not within the record area for the file and which is described by its picture as an unsigned integer item. The effect of including this phrase is that, after each successful execution of a **write** statement for the file, the value of *x* will automatically be the number of the slot into which the **write** statement placed the record.

12.3 EXTENDING A RELATIVE FILE (SEQUENTIAL ACCESS ONLY)

Records may be added sequentially to the end of a relative file called *a* by opening the file with the statement

   open extend *a*

after which successive records are written by successive executions of **write** statements which have **invalid key** phrases (in case the file space is overrun). If the highest key already allocated at the time of opening is *k*, then the new records are written to slots *k*+1, *k*+2, etc. As in the case of a file opened for output, a **relative key** phrase may be included in the file description so that the program can identify the slot to which any particular record is written.

12.4 READING A RELATIVE FILE

When a relative file is opened in **input** mode, the statements available for accessing are:

   random access: **read**.
   sequential access: **read next, start**.
   dynamic access: **read, read next, start**.

12.4.1 RANDOM ACCESS

   Consider again the file called *sample* described in Figure 12.1. After execution of the statement

   open input *sample*

a program may retrieve the record stored in any slot in the file by:

(a) ensuring that the value of the relative key data item (*sample-key*) is the number of the slot to be accessed; then

(b) reading the record into the record area (*sample-rec*) by the statement

  read *sample*; **invalid key** . . .

The invalid key condition arises if the slot is empty or if the value of *sample-key* is zero or greater than the highest slot number available for the file.

12.4.2 SEQUENTIAL ACCESS

Suppose that *sample* is the unrealistically small file depicted in Figure 12.3. After the statement

  open input *sample*

has been executed, the first execution of a statement

  read *sample* **next**; **at end** . . .

will retrieve the record from slot 2. The next seven executions of a **read next** statement will retrieve, in order, the records from slots 3, 5, 6, 7, 8, 11, and 14. Thereafter, the next execution of a **read next** statement will result in the "at end" condition. When sequential access is used, records are retrieved in ascending order of slot number.

It is often important to know, after reading a record, the number of the slot from which it came. This information can be obtained by specifying, in the file description, the name of a **relative key** data item; every successful execution of a **read next** statement will then automatically set the slot number as the value of the relative key data item.

If a **start** statement is to be used, a **relative key** data item *must* be specified in the file description. The following examples of **start** statements assume that the file being accessed is that shown in Figure 12.3, that the file is named *sample*, and that the relative key data item is named *rk*. (In the case of a relative file, the only name which can be used in the **key** phrase of a **start** statement is the name of the relative key data item, and, if the **key** phrase is omitted, the operator "=" is implied.)

(a) Suppose that the value 8 is assigned to *rk* and the statement

  start *sample*; **key** = *rk*; **invalid key** . . .

is executed. The first **read next** statement executed thereafter will retrieve the record from slot 8, after which, if further **read next** statements are

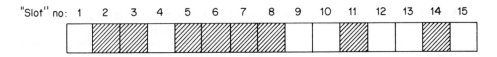

"Slot" no: 1   2   3   4   5   6   7   8   9   10   11   12   13   14   15

Figure 12.3: A small relative file with fifteen 'slots' and eight records. Hatching indicates the presence of a record

executed, they will retrieve the records from slots 11 and 14. The fourth execution of a **read next** will raise the "at end" condition.

(b) Suppose that the value 9 is assigned to *rk* and the statement

> **start** *sample*; **key** = *rk*; **invalid key** . . .

is executed. The result is the invalid key condition, since no record in the file satisfies the **key** criterion in the **start** statement. The identity of the "next record" becomes undefined and will normally be reset by another **start** before a **read next** is executed.

(c) Suppose that the value 9 is assigned to *rk* and the statement

> **start** *sample*; **key not** < *rk*; **invalid key** . . .

is executed. Since slot 11 contains the first record in the file which satisfies the **key** criterion, a subsequent **read next** statement will retrieve the record from slot 11.

(d) Suppose that the value 14 is assigned to *rk* and the statement

> **start** *sample*; **key** > *rk*; **invalid key** . . .

is executed. The invalid key condition is raised since no record in the file satisfies the **key** criterion. The identity of the "next record" becomes undefined and will normally be reset by another **start** before a **read next** is executed.

12.4.3 DYNAMIC ACCESS

As with an indexed file (see Chapter 6), dynamic access to a relative file opened for input simply combines the facilities of random and sequential access. Each of the statements available (random **read**, **read next**, and **start**) redefines the current position in the file. The effects of successful execution of these statements are summarized in Figure 12.4.

Statement	Accessed record is	"Next" record becomes
open	(None)	First record in file
start	(None)	Record identified by **start**
(random) **read**	Record in the slot whose number is specified by **relative key** data item.	Record following accessed record
read next	"Next" record	Record following accessed record

Figure 12.4: Statements in dynamic access to an input file—effects of successful execution

12.5 *UPDATING A RELATIVE FILE*

When a relative file is open in **i–o** mode, the statements available for accessing are:

random access:	**read, write, rewrite, delete.**
sequential access:	**read next, start, rewrite, delete.**
dynamic access:	**read, read next, start, write, rewrite, delete.**

12.5.1 RANDOM ACCESS

Consider again the file description in Figure 12.1. Section 12.4.1 describes the use of a **read** statement to retrieve a record from a given slot.

To write a new record to this file, a program ensures that a record is present in the record area *sample-rec* and that the value of *sample-key* is the number of the slot to which the record is to be written. The record is then written by the statement

write *sample-rec*; **invalid key** . . .

The invalid key condition arises if the slot does not exist in the file or if there is already a record in the slot.

To write a record to the file in such a way that it replaces an existing record a program ensures that *sample-rec* and *sample-key* are set up as above; the record is then placed in the file by the statement

rewrite *sample-rec*; **invalid key** . . .

The invalid key condition arises if the slot does not exist in the file or if the slot is empty. The following statements are the outline of a procedure to amend the record in slot 6 by changing the value of one of its data items, *abc*, to "JIM":

move 6 **to** *sample-key*
read *sample*; **invalid key** . . .
move "JIM" **to** *abc*
rewrite *sample-rec*; **invalid key** . . .

To delete the record in a given slot, a program ensures that the value of *sample-key* is the number of the slot; the record is then deleted (i.e. the slot becomes empty) by the statement

delete *sample*; **invalid key** . . .

The invalid key condition arises if the slot does not exist in the file or if the slot is already empty.

12.5.2 SEQUENTIAL ACCESS

When a relative file is accessed sequentially and is opened in **i–o** mode, the following facilities are available:

(a) All the facilities which would be available as a result of opening in **input** mode (see Section 12.4.2).
(b) The ability, by use of a **rewrite** statement, to update a record after it has been read.
(c) The ability to delete a record after it has been read.

Notice that these facilities exclude the **write** statement.

A **rewrite** or **delete** statement may validly be executed only when the last access statement executed for the file was a successful **read next**. In effect, after a record has been read, that record may be either deleted or rewritten once. Thus a record may be read and updated:

> **read** *sample* **next**; **at end** . . .
> **move** "JIM" **to** *abc*
> **rewrite** *sample-rec*

In the context of sequential access, no **invalid key** phrase is specified in the **rewrite** statement or the **delete** statement. The slot operated on is that accessed by the preceding execution of a **read next** statement.

12.5.3 DYNAMIC ACCESS

When the description of a relative file includes the words **access dynamic** and the file is opened in **i–o** mode, then the file may be accessed by any statements from (a) and (b) below:

(a) **read next**, (random) **read**, and **start** statements. These are used in exactly the same way as in dynamic access to an input file (see Section 12.4.3). Execution of any of these statements determines a new current position in the file and, after execution of a **read next** statement, the value of the relative key data item is the number of the accessed slot.
(b) **write**, **rewrite**, and **delete** statements. These normally include **invalid key** phrases and are used in exactly the same way as in random access to an i–o file (see Section 12.5.1). Thus before execution of any of these three statements, the value of the relative key data item must first be set to the appropriate slot number.

These facilities are in essence the same as those for dynamic access to an indexed file when no alternate record keys are involved. The effects of the various statements are summarized in Figure 12.5.

12.6 SUMMARY

Relative organization is useful and efficient for any file whose primary key values can conveniently be mapped on to a range of integers and in which most of the key values correspond to actual records. Relative files present no difficulty to anyone who understands the use of indexed files. The accessing capabilities are

Statement	Accessed record is	"Next" record will be that in the lowest-numbered slot whose slot number satisfies the condition:
open	(None)	≥1
start	(None)	≥slot number of record identified by **start**
(random) **read**	Record in the slot whose number is specified by **relative key** data item	>slot number of accessed record
read next	"Next" record	>slot number of accessed record
delete	Record in the slot whose number is specified by **relative key** data item	(Not affected)
rewrite	Record in the slot whose number is specified by **relative key** data item	(Not affected)
write	(New record written to slot whose number is specified by **relative key** data item)	(Not affected)

Figure 12.5: Statements in dynamic access to an i–o file—effects of successful execution

the same as those provided for indexed files without alternate record keys, the only important difference being that a **relative key** value identifies a record by its position in the file, whereas a **record key** value identifies a record by the content of a key field in the record itself. In both cases, sequential access is according to ascending order of key value. Figure 6.3 presents a useful summary of the accessing statements which are available for each combination of access mode and open mode; the table shown there applies to both indexed and relative files.

13. Arrays and the perform statement

13.1 ARRAYS OF ONE DIMENSION

Like most other programming languages, Cobol provides facilities for the definition and manipulation of arrays. Arrays are called **tables** in Cobol, but we will use the more generally accepted term. Different elements of an array have the same name and the elements are distinguished from each other by **subscripts** following the name. The definition

   02 *a* **pic** 9(5) **occurs** 4.

says that

(a) there are four data items called *a*, each of which represents a five-digit unsigned integer;
(b) they occupy 20 consecutive character positions in store; and
(c) the four data items are referred to as *a*(1), *a*(2), *a*(3), and *a*(4).

The first item of an array is always identified by subscript value 1, and the amount of storage allocated to the array is fixed at compile time—it is *not* possible to define an array as

   02 *b* **pic** 9(5) **occurs** *n*.

Arrays of group items may be defined, as in

   04 *e* **occurs** 3.
      05 *f* **pic** xx.
      05 *g* **pic** x(4).

Each occurrence of *e* occupies six character positions, and any reference to *e*, *f*, or *g* in the procedure division must be subscripted, since there are three occurrences of each. The storage mapping is

A complete array can be given a name, as in

03 *d*.
  04 *e* **occurs** 3.
    05 *f* **pic** xx.
    05 *g* **pic** x(4).

where the data item *d* is the whole array of eighteen characters and is treated like any other group item. It is possible therefore to fill the array with space characters by the single statement

move spaces to *d*

or to fill it with asterisks:

move all "*" **to** *d*

When the word **all** precedes a non-numeric literal as here, the literal is repeated as many times as are necessary to match the length of the data item with which it is associated in the program. So, if *h* is defined

h **pic** x(5)

then execution of

move all "*–" **to** *h*

gives *h* the value

––*

Without the word **all** the normal **move** rule applies, so that execution of

move "*–" **to** *h*

gives *h* the value

*–␣␣␣

This facility is useful in generating a line across a printed page by statements like

move all "–" **to** *print-line*
write *print-line*

A literal preceded by **all** cannot be used in association with a numeric or a numeric edited data item, but this rule does not preclude the statement

move all "0" **to** *i*

where *i* is defined

03 *i*.
  04 *j* **pic** 9(4).
  04 *k* **pic** 9(3).

because *i*, being a group item, is treated as alphanumeric.

So every *f* in array *d* above can be set to the value "A1" and every *g* there to the value "****" by execution of

move all "A1****"**to** *d*

The content of the array may be tested for uniform values or repeated patterns by statements like

    if d = **spaces** . . .

and

    if d = **all** "A1****" . . .

13.2 ARRAYS AND RECORDS

An array, like any other data item, may be a record, as in

```
01   m.
     02   n   occurs 20.
          03   p   pic s9(7)v99.
          03   q   pic s9(5).
          03   r   pic x.
```

in which case m consists of 300 character positions; or an array may be part of a record, as in

```
01   s.
     02  t  pic x(5).
     02 u  pic 9(6)   occurs 5.
     02  v  pic s9(10).
     02 w  occurs 10.
          03 x pic x(5).
          03 y pic x(5).
```

in which case the record s includes two arrays and occupies 145 character positions. It is *not* possible, however, to define an array of records. A definition like

```
01  z  pic  x(50)  occurs  6.
```

is not allowed, but the definition of z could simply be moved down to level 2, as in

```
01 z-array.
     02 z pic x(50) occurs 6.
```

13.3 SUBSCRIPTS

For some unexplained reason, the committees which develop the Cobol standards have always set their faces against allowing the use of a general arithmetic expression as a subscript. Disregarding Cobol's 'indexing' facility for the moment, the following are the *only* forms which a subscript can assume:

(a) a numeric literal which is a positive integer, as in

    $a(2)$

(b) an *unsubscripted* data name which identifies a numeric item represensuting an integer, as in

   $a(n)$

where *n* has a picture like 999

(c) an unsubscripted data name as in (b) above, but with the addition or subtraction of an integer literal, as in

   $a(n + 20)$ and
   $a(n - 1)$

All the following are illegal (the first not unreasonably so):

   $a(0)$
   $a(n(m))$
   $a(n + m - 1)$
   $a(n * 2)$

To achieve the effect of the last of these statements, the programmer must resort to such code as

   compute $p = n * 2$

followed by a reference to $a(p)$.

13.4 THE PERFORM STATEMENT

Because a variant of the **perform** statement is much used in referencing arrays, this is a suitable point at which to summarize some of the attributes of the **perform** statement generally. In the next chapter we return to the topic of arrays.

A **perform** statement can be used as a simple procedure call, as in

   perform *print-stars*

or it can be used to call a procedure several times in succession. Thus, given suitable data definitions, the program fragment in Figure 13.1(a) would print three lines of asterisks. When a **perform** specifies a procedure to be executed, it is known as an *out-of-line* **perform**.

The **perform** in Figure 13.1(b) is functionally equivalent to that in Figure 13.1(a) but, instead of naming a procedure, the **perform** itself includes the statements which are to be executed repeatedly. This form is known as an *in-line* **perform**.

All variants of the **perform** *statement described in this section can be used in both out-of-line and in-line statements.*

If a data item *n* has a picture indicating that it represents an integer, then the value of *n* at execution time can be used to determine the number of iterations, as in

   perform *print-stars* *n* **times**

```
        perform print-stars 3 times
        -
        -
        -
print-stars.
        move all "*" to print-rec
        write print-rec.
        -
        -
```

(a) Out-of-line **perform**.

```
        perform 3 times
            move all "*" to print-rec
            write print-rec
        end-perform
```

(b) In-line **perform**.

Figure 13.1: *The two basic forms of the* **perform** *statement*

If the value of *n* is zero or negative, then *print-stars* will not be executed at all. (Notice that, unlike many languages, Cobol does not require the program to allocate a control variable and specify the range of values as being from 1 to *n*.)

Another variant of **perform**—the **perform until**—is heavily used both in the examples in this book and in real programs. Execution of

perform *p1* **until** *r* = "Fred"

causes repeated execution of procedure *p1* until the terminating condition (*r* = "Fred") is true. The terminating condition is tested *before* each execution of *p1* and so, if it is initially true, *p1* will not be executed at all. Cobol's **until** resembles Pascal's *while*; to obtain an effect similar to that of Pascal's *until*, we say

perform *p1*, **with test after**, **until** *r* = "Fred"

The words **with test after** result in the terminating condition being tested *after* each execution of *p1*, so that *p1* will be executed at least once. The normal **perform** resembles Pascal's *while* statement with the condition complemented, and **perform with test after** resembles Pascal's *repeat . . until* statement.

13.5 EVALUATION OF CONDITIONS

The **perform until** is only one of several statements which call for execution-time evaluation of a condition, and the following observations apply equally to conditions specified in other contexts.

A condition in Cobol may include the operators **not**, **and**, and **or**. The normal precedence rule of Boolean expressions is applied—**not** before **and** before **or**—and sub-expressions may be enclosed in parentheses. Thus

$a > b$ **or** $c =$ "Fred"   **and** d **is numeric**

is equivalent to

$a > b$ **or** $(c =$ "Fred"   **and** d **is numeric**$)$

The condition

$(a > b$ **or** $c =$ "Fred")   **and** d **is numeric**

means something quite different. Like arithmetic operators, the relational operators $<$, $=$, $>$, $<=$, and $>=$ must be preceded by, and followed by, at least one space.

An inconvenience often associated with the use of boolean expressions in programming languages (though *not* in Cobol) is exemplified by the expression

$(b = 0)$ **or** $(a / b > 3.5)$

(The parentheses here are purely for readability.) Since an implementor of a language is free to evaluate an expression by any method he chooses, there is a danger that the evaluation of the above expression will be effected in the following way:

evaluate $b = 0$
then evaluate $a / b > 3.5$
then apply the **or** operator to the resulting truth values.

The problem is of course that, if $b = 0$ is true, then the second evaluation will probably lead to abortion of program execution, accompanied by some operating system message about overflow or division by zero. The programmer may claim quite angrily that the whole point of including the $b = 0$ test was to avoid this very situation, but most languages do give the implementor the right to evaluate the expression in the above manner.

When the condition appears within an **if** statement, it can justifiably be claimed that the programmer who said

if $(b = 0)$ **or** $(a / b > 3.5)$
then perform *p1* . . .

should really have said

if $b = 0$
then perform *p1*
else if $a / b > 3.5$
    then perform *p1* . . .

But, when the condition appears in a language's *while* or *until* construct, the programmer has good cause for complaint. All the terminating conditions have to be stated in one expression; yet one of these conditions may not be safely evaluable unless some other has a particular truth value, and there is no facility for specifying the interdependence. The situation gives rise on occasion to some remarkably clumsy programming.

In Cobol the problem does not arise. The rule for evaluation is straightforward: an expression is evaluated from left to right, and *evaluation ceases as soon as the truth value of the expression can be determined*. This rule is applied recursively to sub-expressions implied by operator precedence or denoted by parentheses. (This method of evaluation was introduced into Cobol in the 1985 Standard, but it is by no means an innovation in programming languages generally—'sequential' operators have been known for many years and have been included in minority languages; because these operators are not commutative, some people believe that they should be distinguished from the normal **and** and **or** operators.)

Let us look at some examples. In Figure 11.8 there was a statement which began

perform until *eof* = "t" **or** *dons* > 1500

However reasonable that statement may have seemed in the context of Chapter 11, we now see that its correctness depends on the evaluation rule just given. We also see why the terms of the expression were specified in the order shown. Suppose that the end of file has been reached. When the terminating condition above is evaluated, the leftmost term (*eof* = "t") is evaluated first and found to be true. At this stage evaluation stops, for in general if x is true then

x **or** y

is true. There is no risk therefore that execution will be aborted because of inconsistent data in the item *dons*. (Remember that the unsuccessful **read**, which established the "at end" condition, left the content of the record area, of which *dons* is part, in an undefined state. Remember too that the implementor is free to deal as he chooses with inconsistencies between data and operation, the operation in this case being *numeric* comparison and the data possibly being non-numeric.)

Another example is the statement

perform *p1* **until** (*i* **is numeric**) **and**
$\quad\quad\quad\quad$ (*i* + 10 > *top-value*)

where evaluation stops if the first term (*i* **is numeric**) is evaluated as false, for in general if x is false then

x **and** y

is false. Again there is no risk that execution will be aborted, or a nonsensical result obtained, through inconsistent data when the arithmetic expression $i + 10$ is evaluated.

Finally, in the case of our earlier example,

(b = 0) **or** (a / b > 3.5)

when the value of b is zero, the second term is not evaluated and therefore no attempt is made to divide by zero.

We shall see another example of the usefulness of Cobol's evaluation rule when we consider the application of the **perform** statement to array-handling.

13.6 THE PERFORM STATEMENT AGAIN

Another variant of the **perform** statement is really an extension of **perform until**. Like the latter, it causes repeated execution until the terminating condition is true, but additionally it enables us to state that a specified data item, akin to what other languages call the loop *control variable*, is to be given certain values on successive iterations. This variant, the **perform varying**, is Cobol's typically verbose near-equivalent of a Fortran DO loop and an Algol/Pascal *for* statement.

Execution of the statement

     perform *p1* **varying** *j* **from** 15.6 **by** -0.2 **until** $j < 11.3$

causes *p1* to be executed repeatedly, successive executions being made with $j = 15.6, 15.4, 15.2 \ldots 11.6, 11.4$. If the values of k, l, and m are 15.6, -0.2, and 11.3 respectively, then a statement which is usually equivalent to the above is

     perform *p1* **varying** *j* **from** k **by** l **until** $j < m$

This is 'usually' equivalent because it is possible that procedure *p1* changes the value of l or m; in practice, few programmers today would construct such a procedure. The initial value of j (following **from**) and the increment (following **by**) must be either numeric literals or numeric data items; arithmetic expressions are not permitted.

It will be evident from the above example that

(a) the terminating condition is tested *before* each iteration; and
(b) the control variable is incremented *after* each iteration.

This is why *p1* is not executed with $j = 11.2$.

The application to arrays should be obvious. Given the definitions

     01 *a*.
           02 *b* **pic** s9(5) **occurs** 25.
     01 *asum* **pic** s9(7).
     01 *i* **pic** 99.

we can assign to *asum* the total of the 25 values in array *a* by the statements shown in Figure 13.2. *Before* each iteration the terminating condition ($i > 25$) is tested and, if it is true, no further iterations take place; *after* each iteration the control variable *i* is incremented by 1. Hence the terminating condition is $i > 25$, not $i = 25$.

In order to be sure of understanding this form of **perform**, you should study Figure 13.3, which shows also a program fragment having equivalent effects, but expressed in a more primitive style using **go to** statements. (Incidentally, notice that a Cobol paragraph-name can be used as a *label*—the destination of a **go**

```
move 0 to asum
perform varying i from 1 by 1 until i > 25
    add b (i) to asum
end-perform
```

Figure 13.2: Summing the elements of array a

```
perform varying i from m by n
                until  i > p
        add b (i) to asum
        move 0 to b (i)
    end-perform
```

(a) perform statement


```
        move m to i.
  x.    if not   i > p
        then    add b (i) to asum
                move 0 to b (i)
                add n to i
                go to x
        end-if
```

(b) Equivalent primitive code.

Figure 13.3: 'Normal' **perform**

---

to—as well as a procedure name.) It should be clear from a study of Figure 13.3 that:

(a) if the terminating condition is initially true, no iterations occur;
(b) if the final iteration is to be for $i = p$, then the terminating condition should be $i > p$ because i is incremented before the condition is tested;
(c) for the same reason, the value of i on exit from the **perform** is *not* the value used in the final iteration.

Like an ordinary **perform until**, a **perform varying** statement can include the words **with test after**. In this case, after each iteration the terminating condition is tested. If it is true, execution of the **perform** terminates; if it is false, the control variable is incremented. An equivalent program fragment in primitive style is given in Figure 13.4, from which it should be clear that:

(a) at least one iteration always occurs;
(b) if the final iteration is to be for $i = p$, then the terminating condition is $i = p$;
(c) the value of i on exit is the value used in the final iteration.

The normal **perform** (i.e. the one which tests *before* each iteration) is adequate for most purposes, and its use is advisable in most cases where the number of iterations is variable—it is usually good practice to allow for the possibility of no iterations being required. To avoid confusion, the best strategy is to use the

```
perform with test after
     varying i from m by n until  i = p
          add b (i) to asum
          move 0 to b (i)
   end-perform
```

(a) perform statement.


```
     move m to i.
x.   add b (i) to asum
     move 0 to b (i)
     if not  i = p
     then  add n to i
             go to x
     end-if
```

(b) Equivalent primitive code.

Figure 13.4: **Perform with test after**

---

normal **perform** in all situations except those which clearly call for the **with test after** version.

Suppose that a program is to examine an array to determine whether a given value is present, and if so to ascertain its position in the array. Suppose also that all values in the array are unique, and that the number of values in the array varies from time to time, but never exceeds 20. Given the definitions in Figure 13.5, the program fragment in Figure 13.6, if it finds the value, calls the procedure *found*, having set i to indicate the position (subscript) of the value in the array.

The **continue** statement, which is used in Figure 13.6, is Cobol's 'no operation' statement—it has no effect at all, and is included in a program when, as here,

---

```
01   list-of-names.
     02  name  pic x(25)  occurs 20.
01   no-of-names  pic 99.
*no-of-names indicates how many names are currently in the
*list. n names occupy the first n positions in the array.
01   given-name  pic x(25).
*given-name is the name to be sought in the array.
01   i  pic 99.
```

Figure 13.5:   *Data division entries used in Figures 13.6, 13.7, and 13.8*

```
perform  varying i from 1 by 1 until
           i > no-of-names  or  name (i) = given-name
     continue
end-perform
if  i > no-of-names
then  perform not-found
else  perform found
end-if
```

Figure 13.6:   *Finding a value in an array*

the language syntax requires a statement (we may well wonder why) but the
program logic does not. The **perform varying** in Figure 13.6 requires no iterated
statements because the test of the terminating condition does all that is necessary
with each value of *name*.

The versions shown in Figures 13.7 and 13.8 are attractive, but both are wrong.
Figure 13.7, which is simply Figure 13.6 with the terms of the terminating
condition interchanged, can fail when *no-of-names* = 20, since the array can then
be accessed with subscript value 21. The Cobol standard prohibits such accesses.

```
perform   varying i from 1 by 1 until
              name (i) = given-name   or   i > no-of-names
      continue
end-perform
if   i > no-of-names
then   perform not-found
else   perform found
end-if
```

Figure 13.7:   Finding a value in an array—a program containing an error

```
perform, with test after, varying i from 1 by 1 until
              i = no-of-names   or   name (i) = given-name
      continue
end-perform
if   name (i) = given-name
then   perform found
else   perform not-found
end-if
```

Figure 13.8:   Finding a value in an array—another erroneous program

```
main. open input f
      move "f" to eof
      perform varying n from 0 by 1 until   eof = "t"
          read f next; at end   move "t" to eof
          end-read
      end-perform
      compute   n-out = n - 1
      display "There are ", n-out, " records in the file"
      stop run.
```

Figure 13.9:   Counting the number of records in a file

```
main. open input f
      move "f" to eof
      perform with test after
                  varying n from 0 by 1 until   eof = "t"
          read f next; at end   move "t" to eof
          end-read
      end-perform
      move n to n-out
      display "There are ", n-out, " records in the file"
      stop run.
```

*Figure 13.10:   Counting the number of records in a file, using **perform with
test after***

In many implementations of Cobol—those which do not check subscripts—we would get away with it, but the program would not be portable to an environment where the compiler generated subscript checks. The version in Figure 13.8, which uses a **perform with test after**, fails when *no-of-names* = 0.

The terminating condition need not involve the control variable at all. Figures 13.9 and 13.10 show the procedure divisions of two possible programs to count how many records there are in a sequentially accessed file *f*. The **compute** statement in Figure 13.9 is necessary because the **perform** has counted the number of **reads** executed and the final **read** did not retrieve a record. The use of **perform with test after** in Figure 13.10 is reasonable because, even if the file is empty, one iteration (i.e. one **read**) must be performed to establish the fact. Both programs assume that *n* has a picture like 9(4) and *n-out* a picture like zzz9.

14.   More about arrays

14.1 ARRAYS OF MORE THAN ONE DIMENSION

Cobol's hierarchical view of data makes the definition of multi-dimensioned arrays very straightforward. A three-by-two matrix can be defined as in Figure 14.1(a); Figure 14.1(b) shows the resulting storage structure. There, a consists of three occurrences of b, and each occurrence of b consists of two occurrences of c. Thus the data-name a requires no subscripts, b requires one subscript, and c requires two subscripts. We can refer to the complete array, as in

> **move spaces to** a

or to an individual 'row', as in

> **if** $b(2)$ = **all** "done" . . .

or to an individual element, as in

> **move** x **to** $c(3, 1)$

Notice that the comma between the subscripts is followed by a space. The space is, in fact, the separator between the subscripts; one or more spaces must be present, but the comma may be omitted, and the above statement could have been written as

> **move** x **to** $c(3\ 1)$

This is unusual in practice; much more common is the omission of the spaces following a comma, allowed by some non-standard compilers.

Of course, if we never want to refer to the matrix as a whole, or to individual rows, we can simply define the matrix as

> 02 **occurs** 3.
>   03 c **pic** x(4) **occurs** 2.

in which case we have a view of an array which is familiar to users of Fortran and other languages. Then the only references we can make are to c, every reference including two subscripts.

The extension of these ideas to arrays of three and more dimensions is obvious. The definition of a three-dimensional array in Figure 14.2 allows us to operate on the complete array d (20 000 character positions) or on particular elements, e.g. $e(7, 1, 48)$, $e(f, g, h)$. Each subscript should be in one of the forms listed in Chapter 13. The maximum number of dimensions allowed is seven.

```
02   a.
    03   b   occurs 3.
        04   c   pic x(4)   occurs 2.
```

(a) Definition of a three-by-two matrix.

(b) Resulting storage structure.

Figure 14.1:   A two-dimensional array

```
01   d.
    02   occurs 10.
        03   occurs 5.
            04   e   pic s9(4)   occurs 100.
```

Figure 14.2:   Definition of a three-dimensional array

Like nested DO loops and nested *for*s in other languages, nested in-line **perform**s can be used to access systematically all the elements of a multi-dimensional array. The program fragment in Figure 14.3 shows how the values of the elements of a matrix are summed. There would be little point in using an out-of-line **perform** in simply summing a matrix, but a summation program is a useful example for illustration. Figures 14.4 and 14.5 show program fragments

```
    -
    -
    02   occurs 10.
        03   k   pic s9v9(4)   occurs 15.
01   ksum   pic s9(3)v9(4).
01   i      pic 99.
01   j      pic 99.
    -
    -
    -

    move 0 to ksum
    perform   varying i from 1 by 1 until   i > 10
        perform   varying j from 1 by 1 until   j > 15
            add k (i, j) to ksum
        end-perform
    end-perform
    -
    -
```

*Figure 14.3:   Summing the elements of a matrix—nested in-line **perform***

```
         -
         -
      move 0 to ksum
      perform adding varying i from 1 by 1 until  i > 10
                      after   j from 1 by 1 until  j > 15
         -
         -
         -
 adding.   add k (i, j) to ksum.
         -
         -
```

Figure 14.4:   Summing the elements of a matrix—out-of-line **perform**

```
         -
         -
      move 0 to ksum
      perform one-row varying i from 1 by 1 until  i > 10
         -
         -
 one-row.
         perform adding varying j from 1 by 1 until  j > 15.
 adding.   add k (i, j) to ksum.
         -
         -
```

Figure 14.5:   Summing the elements of a matrix—nested out-of-line **perform**

which are equivalent to the procedure division statements of Figure 14.3. As many **after** phrases as required may be included in an out-of-line **perform**.

The elementary items included in an array need not be homogeneous. For example, a table may be constructed in which the performance of 20 sales representatives over a year is summarized. Each row of the table contains a representative's name, twelve figures representing his sales in the months January to December, and a figure representing his total sales for the year. The table may be defined as shown in Figure 14.6.

The complete table *sales-analysis* might be moved to another record area, at least 1840 characters in length, and written to a file, as in

    move *sales-analysis* **to** *s-rec*
    write *s-rec.* . . .

Alternatively, individual rows, reps' names, and annual totals can be accessed by use of one of the names *one-rep*, *rep-name*, and *rep-total*, with *one* subscript. The value of a rep's sales in a particular month can be accessed by use of the name *month-sales* with *two* subscripts, the first identifying the representative, the second the month.

```
 01   sales-analysis.
      02   one-rep   occurs 20.
           03   rep-name    pic x(25).
           03   month-sales pic 9(5)   occurs 12.
           03   rep-total   pic 9(7).
```

Figure 14.6:   Definition of a table representing salesmen's performance over a year

Suppose now that representatives' names and the sales figures for the twelve months have all been inserted in the table. The program fragment in Figure 14.7 calculates and inserts the rep-total values.

Figure 14.8 shows how the table can be printed on a page. In line 5, the last character of "July" is assumed to coincide with the last character position of the program line. The literal is continued in the usual way in line 6. Notice also that the assignments to *print-line* (line 2) and to *p-month-and-total* (line 7), because these are group items, take no account of the data descriptions which are subordinate to them.

14.2 VARIABLE NUMBERS OF OCCURRENCES

Refer back to Figure 13.5. The relationship there between *list-of-names* and *no-of-names*, which is stated in the comment, can be explicitly stated in the definition of *name*:

> 02 *name* **pic** x(25)
>   **occurs** 0 **to** 20 **depending on** *no-of-names*.

Then statements referring to *list-of-names* will take into account the current value of *no-of-names* (which must be in the range 0 to 20). For example, if the value of *no-of-names* is 4, then execution of

> **move** *list-of-names* **to** *z*

will move only items *name*(1) to *name*(4), rather than *name*(1) to *name*(20); that is, the length of *list-of-names* is taken as being 100 characters rather than 500. Similarly, execution of

> **move** *z* **to** *list-of-names*

will be a move to the first 100 character positions of the storage space allocated to *list-of-names*, the content of the remaining 400 being unchanged. It remains the responsibility of the program to ensure that *no-of-names* has at all times the appropriate value, as for example the program fragment of Figure 14.9 does on

---

```
    -
    -
 01   i   pic 99.
 01   j   pic 99.
    -
    -

      perform  varying i from 1 by 1 until i > 20
         move 0 to rep-total (i)
         perform  varying j from 1 by 1 until  j > 12
            add month-sales (i, j) to rep-total (i)
         end-perform
      end-perform
    -
    -
```

Figure 14.7: Inserting rep-total *values into the table defined in Figure 14.6*

```
        -
        -
        file section.
        fd   print-file.
        01   print-line.
             02   p-rep  pic x(25).
             02   p-month-and-total.
                  03   p-month  pic $(6)9  occurs 12.
                  03   p-total  pic $(8)9.
             -

             -
        working-storage section.
        01   i  pic 99.
        01   j  pic 99.
        01   sales-analysis.
             02   one-rep  occurs 20.
                  03   rep-name    pic x(25).
                  03   month-sales pic 9(5)  occurs 12.
                  03   rep-total   pic 9(7).
             -
             -

        procedure division.
             -
             -
1            open output print-file
2            move "Sales Analysis 1986" to print-line
3            write print-line after page
4            move "Name" to p-rep
5            move "....Jan....Feb....Mar....Apr....May...June...July
6 -               "....Aug...Sept....Oct....Nov....Dec....Total"
7                 to p-month-and-total
8            write print-line after 3
9            perform  varying i from 1 by 1 until  i > 20
10               move rep-name (i) to p-rep
11               perform  varying j from 1 by 1 until  j > 12
12                   move month-sales (i, j) to p-month (j)
13               end-perform
14               move rep-total (i) to p-total
15               write print-line after 2
16           end-perform
             -
```

Figure 14.8: Printing the table

```
if   no-of-names < 20
then add 1 to no-of-names
     move given-name to name (no-of-names)
else perform name-space-full
end-if
```

Figure 14.9: Adding a new name to the end of the list

---

adding a new name to the end of the list. The amount of storage allocated to *list-of-names* remains constant at 500 character positions.

Commonly, as in the examples in Figure 14.10, the data item which specifies the number of occurrences is part of a record which includes the array itself. In Figure 14.10, the storage space allocated to *a* is 206 character positions in length $(4+2+(20\times10))$, but the actual size of a record which is stored there may be 6

```
01   a.
     02   b   pic x(4).
     02   c   pic 99.
     02   d   occurs 0 to 20 depending on c.
          03   e   pic xx   occurs 3.
          03   f   pic 9(4).

01   m.
     02   n   pic x(4).
     02   p   pic 99.
     02   q   pic x(10), occurs 0 to 20 depending on p.
```

Figure 14.10:   Two record descriptions which include arrays with variable numbers of occurrences

---

character positions, or 16, or 26, or any number ending in 6 up to 206. If $c=2$, then, when the statement

> **move** *a* **to** *z*

is executed, only the first 26 characters of the area act as the source operand in the move. However, when the statement

> **move** *z* **to** *a*

is executed, the destination of the move is the complete storage area allocated to *a*. The general rule is that, when a *destination* item is a group item (e.g. *a*) which includes both an array (e.g. $d(1)$, etc.) *and* the data item specifying its number of occurrences (e.g. *c*), then *the number of occurrences is disregarded* and the *maximum* number of occurrences (e.g. 20) determines the size of the destination area. The need for this rule becomes apparent when we consider, in relation to Figure 14.10, what happens when the statement

> **move** *m* **to** *a*

is executed, with $p=3$. Because $p=3$, the size of the source item, *m*, is 36; the size of the destination item, *a*, however, is the maximum, 206. The effects of the move are therefore that the leftmost 36 characters of *a* become a copy of *n*, *p*, $q(1)$, $q(2)$, and $q(3)$, and that the rightmost 170 characters of *a* are space-filled.

14.3 OCCURS DEPENDING—RESTRICTIONS

Within any record description, there can be at most *one* data item whose description includes the words **occurs depending**, and this data item must be at the end of the record area. In other words, it cannot be followed, in the same record, by another data item. Further, an **occurs depending** data item cannot be part of another array. Thus the uses in Figure 14.10 are both correct—in the case of record *a*, item *d* is at the end of the record (since *e* and *f* are subordinate to *d*)—and the uses in Figure 14.11 are both illegal—in (i), item *c* is not at the end of the record and, in (ii), item *h* is subordinate to another **occurs** (i.e. is part of another array).

```
(i)        01   a.
                02   b   pic 99.
                02   c   pic x, occurs 1 to 5 depending on b.
                02   d   pic x(5).

(ii)       01   e.
                02   f   pic 9.
                02   g   occurs 6.
                     03   h   pic xx, occurs 1 to 5 depending on f.
```

*Figure 14.11:   Illegal uses of **occurs depending***

14.4 INITIALIZATION OF ARRAYS

When a **value** clause is included in an item description which also includes, or is
subordinate to, an **occurs** clause, all occurrences of the item are initialized to the
value specified. Thus, in Figure 14.12, example (i) is equivalent to example (ii),
and example (iii) is equivalent to example (iv).

```
(i)        01   a.
                02   b   pic x(5)   occurs 30
                                    value spaces.


(ii)       01   a   value spaces.
                02   b   pic x(5)   occurs 30.


(iii)      01   c.
                02   d   occurs 6.
                     03   e   pic 999   value 1.
                     03   f   pic xx    value "AB".


(iv)       01   c   value all "001AB".
                02   d   occurs 6.
                     03   e   pic 999.
                     03   f   pic xx.


(v)
       01   days-of-week   value
            "Monday    Tuesday   WednesdayThursday Friday".
       02   dayofweek  pic x(9)   occurs 5.
```

Figure 14.12:   Examples of array initialization

When an array is to be initialized with non-uniform values, the **value** clause
must be specified for the array as a whole, as in example (v). (Another way of
achieving the same effect will be met in Chapter 16.)

When a **value** clause is included in the description of an item having a variable
number of occurrences (**occurs depending**), the initial value is assigned to the
maximum number of occurrences.

15. Records with varying format and varying length

The records in a file need not all be the same length, nor need they all have the same format. They may differ from one another in length or in format or both.

15.1 FIXED LENGTH, FIXED FORMAT

All the examples so far have assumed that all records in a file have the same format and the same length. In this case, a program contains one record description (i.e. 01 entry) for the file, and that description includes no **occurs depending** data items (see Chapter 14) and no redefinitions. (Redefinitions were mentioned briefly in Chapter 11; they are described further in this chapter and the next chapter.)

15.2 VARIABLE LENGTH, FIXED FORMAT

When an **fd** sentence includes the words **record varying**, the records stored in the file may be of different lengths. Consider, for example, the file described in Figure 15.1, which contains grossly oversimplified records representing financial accounts. As we have seen, the record area associated with this file will be of the appropriate size to accommodate the maximum-sized record, i.e. 183 character positions. The *fixed* part of the record (the first three data items at level 02) is 15 character positions in length, and the maximum length of the *variable* part is $12 \times 14 = 168$ character positions. A **write** or a **rewrite** statement, like a **move** statement, will take account of the value of *no-of-adjustments*. Thus, if the record area *account* contained the character-string shown in Figure 15.2, the number of characters written to the file by a **write** or **rewrite** statement would be $15 + (14 \times 2) = 43$. The file *accounts* may therefore contain records whose lengths vary between 15 and 183 characters.

When the record shown in Figure 15.2 is read back from the file, the **read** operation places it in the leftmost 43 character positions of the record area, leaving the content of the remaining 140 character positions undefined. The program may then add a further *adjustment* to the account record by code such as that shown in Figure 15.3. The effects will be that the value of *new-adjustment* will be assigned to *adjustment*(3) in the record area, and that the new version of

```
fd   accounts; record varying.
01   account.
     02   ac-no                pic x(6).
     02   balance              pic s9(5)v99.
     02   no-of-adjustments pic 99.
     02   adjustment occurs 0 to 12 depending on no-of-adjustments.
          03   dated  pic 9(6).
          03   amount pic s9(5)v99, sign leading separate.
```

Figure 15.1: Description of a file containing variable-length fixed format records

---

```
ZX1194004850002871122-0001200871208+0012475
```

Figure 15.2: Possible content of the first 43 character positions of the record area account. *The fourteenth and fifteenth characters (02) establish the length of the record as 43 characters*

```
     -
     -
     -
read accounts   ...   end-read
if no-of-adjustments = 12
then   perform record-overflow
else   add new-amount to balance
              size error   ...   end-add
       add 1 to no-of-adjustments
       move new-adjustment to adjustment (no-of-adjustments)
       rewrite account   ...   end-rewrite
end-if
     -
     -
```

Figure 15.3: Changing the length of a record in the accounts *file, where* accounts *is an* **indexed** *file or a* **relative** *file*

---

the record (57 characters in length) will replace in the file the original, smaller, record. A record in a file may be replaced by a record of different length only if the file's organization is **indexed** or **relative**. A **rewrite** to a sequential file must not change the record length.

15.3 FIXED LENGTH, VARIABLE FORMAT

It is sometimes convenient to keep records with different formats in the same file, and just occasionally the records may all be the same length. Figure 15.4 describes a file called *assets*, in which any record may be either a *vehicle* record or a *building* record. This characteristic is denoted in a program by the appearance following the **fd** sentence of two record descriptions rather than one. (The Cobol standard places no restriction on the number of record descriptions which can be associated with a file.)

Recall from Chapter 3 that every file has precisely *one* associated record area; that any successful **read** operation presents a record in the record area associated

```
fd    assets.
01    building.
      02   record-type pic x.
*[value of first character is "B"]
      02   list-no      pic x(4).
      02   district     pic x(5).
      02   floor-area   pic 9(6)v99.

01    vehicle.
      02                     pic x.
*[value of first character is "V"]
      02   regn-mark    pic x(7).
      02   capacity     pic 9(4).
      02   date-acquired pic 9(6).
```

Figure 15.4:   A file with fixed-length records of different formats

with the file; and that any **write** or **rewrite** statement writes from that record area to the file. It does not matter how many record descriptions are specified for a file—*there is still only one record area*. It follows that, when a program specifies multiple record descriptions for a file, all the record descriptions apply to the file's associated record area; i.e. *all map on to a single area of store*. Figure 15.5 shows the two mappings of the record area associated with the file *assets*.

If a program were placing a new record in *assets*, it might for example assign values to *list-no*, *district*, and *floor-area*, then continue:

> **move** "B" **to** *record-type*
> **write** *building*

(Since *building* and *vehicle* both identify the same area of store and since both are group items, the statement "**write** *vehicle*" would have the same effect here as "**write** *building*", but its presence would cause unnecessary difficulty for anyone reading the program.) Alternatively, the program might assign values to *regn-mark*, *capacity*, and *date-acquired*, then continue:

> **move** "V" **to** *record-type*
> **write** *vehicle*

It must be stressed that the data item *record-type* in this example is entirely the invention of the application programmer. As far as Cobol is concerned, there is no need for the formats to be distinguished at all; Cobol has no mechanism by

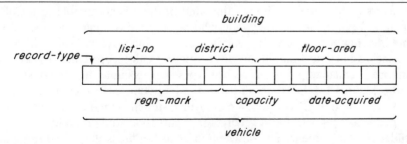

Figure 15.5:   The two mappings applied to the record area associated with the assets *file*

which the record "types" *vehicle* and *building* are recognized or distinguished from each other. The Cobol system simply sends an eighteen-character record to the file when a **write** or **rewrite** statement is executed, and simply reads an eighteen-character record from the file when a **read** statement is executed. The mapping applied to the record area is the responsibility of the procedure division statements alone; it is up to the programmer to decide how the program is to interpret a record read from the file.

So, in relation to the foregoing example, execution of the statements

> **read** *assets* . . .
> **move** *regn-mark* **to** . . .

would *not* give rise to a run-time error if the record read happened to be a *building* record (to which the use of *regn-mark* is inappropriate)—the **move** statement would simply take as its source data the content of character positions 2 to 8 of the record area (the value of *list-no*, followed by the first three characters of *district*). The effect presumably intended would more usually be achieved by statements such as

> **read** *assets* . . .
> **if** *record-type* = "V"
> **then move** *regn-mark* **to** . . .

There is therefore complete freedom to use any data-name which refers to any part of the record area at any time while the file is open. This freedom explains why there is no need to name the first character position of the record area in the description of *vehicle* in Figure 15.4; the data-name *record-type* can be used, regardless of what has been read from, or what is to be written to, the file. Notice the useful convention adopted in Figure 15.4 of including a comment to indicate the relationship between the record format and the value of *record-type*.

Incidentally, one may reasonably assume from Figure 15.4 that the organization of *assets* is sequential or relative. An indexed file would require the presence of the **record key** data item in the same position in all records of the file. Since, apart from the first character position, no two data items in *building* and *vehicle* map on to identical character positions, it is unlikely that an indexed file would contain these two record types. The possibility is not, however, completely ruled out. It would be possible for, say, *list-no* to be defined as the record key, in which case the record key value of a *vehicle* record would be taken as the first four characters of *regn-mark*. Though this kind of thing is acceptable to a Cobol compiler, it is certainly *not* so to anyone who has to read or maintain a program.

It sometimes happens that a file contains records which are in *nearly* the same format as each other; most data items are common to all record types, but certain data items are peculiar to particular record types. For example, in a file of student records, the records for full-time and part-time students may contain the same data items, except that a record for a full-time student contains details of the student's financial support, and a record for a part-time student contains details of the student's employment. The description of such a file is illustrated in Figure 15.6, and the corresponding record area mapping in Figure 15.7. A specification

> *y* **redefines** *x*

```
fd    students.
01    student.
      02   matriculation-no pic x(6).
      02   s-type               pic x.
   *[f=full-time; p=part-time]
      02   surname          pic x(20).
      02   pre-names        pic x(20).
      02   ft-details.
   *[where s-type = "f"]
           03   grant-awarding-authority pic x(30).
           03   duration-of-grant        pic 9.
      02   pt-details, redefines ft-details.
   *[where s-type = "p"]
           03   employment   pic x(15).
           03   employer     pic x(16).
      02   faculty          pic x.
      -
      -
```

Figure 15.6: Redefinition of part of a record

```
1-6     matriculation-no
7       s-type
8-27    surname
28-47   pre-names
48-78   ft-details                         or    pt-details
        48-77  grant-awarding-authority          48-62  employment
        78           duration-of-grant            63-78  employer
79      faculty
```

Figure 15.7: Partial storage mapping (positions 1–79) of the record described in Figure 15.6

---

means that the data item *y* is to be mapped on to the same area of store as the previously defined data item *x*. Any program writing or rewriting a record to the *students* file must first ensure that the data placed in character positions 48 to 78 are appropriate to the type of the student as indicated by the value of character position 7; similarly, any program which reads a record from the file will normally test the value of *s-type* before referring to character positions 48 to 78.

Provided that, as here, the number of characters is the same in all definitions of an area of store, there is no difference in principle between the use of different record descriptions, as in Figure 15.4, and the use of *redefinition*, as in Figure 15.6. In both cases two or more different data structures are mapped on to a common area of storage. Redefinition is explained in greater detail in the next chapter.

15.4 VARIABLE LENGTH, VARIABLE FORMAT

Figure 15.8 shows the data and procedure divisions of a program which makes a copy of a file. The file being copied (*infile*) contains records of two different lengths—some records (*inlarge*) are 100 characters in length, and others (*insmall*) are 85 characters in length. The longer records contain the character "L" in the eighth character position; the shorter records contain "S" in that position. The

```
data division.
file section.
fd  infile, record varying.
01  inlarge.
    02               pic x(7).
    02  rec-type pic x.
    02               pic x(92).

01  insmall       pic x(85).


fd outfile, record varying.
01  outlarge  pic x(100).
01  outsmall  pic x(85).

working-storage section.
01  file-end  pic x(5).

procedure division.
main.
    open input infile, output outfile
    perform, with test after, until  file-end = "true"
        read infile next;
        at end   move "true" to file-end
        not at end
            move "false" to file-end
            if  rec-type = "S"
            then   move insmall to outsmall
                   write outsmall
            else   move inlarge to outlarge
                   write outlarge
            end-if
        end-read
    end-perform
    stop run.
```

Figure 15.8:   Making a copy of a file which contains variable-length records

___

remaining character positions in the two record types are unnamed since the program is concerned only with copying the records and not with their content.

When a file contains records of different lengths, the length of the record area for that file is the length of the longest record which could legally be in the file. Record descriptions of records which are shorter than this maximum length are each mapped on to the record area, starting at the first (i.e. leftmost) character position. Thus the record area associated with *infile* in Figure 15.8 is 100 characters in length; the description of *inlarge* is mapped on to character positions 1 to 100; and the description of *insmall* is mapped on to character positions 1 to 85. These mappings accord with the action of a **read** statement, which always places the retrieved record in the record area with its first character occupying the first character position of the area (i.e. the record is left-justified in the record area). Thus the eighth character of any record read from *infile* will be in character position 8 of the record area; since *rec-type* is mapped on to this position, the name *rec-type* can be used regardless of whether a short or a long record is in the record area.

The record area associated with *outfile* too is 100 characters in length. The name *outlarge* is a reference to the whole record area, and *outsmall* is a reference to character positions 1–85 of that area. And it now becomes clear why, in general, **write** and **rewrite** statements must specify a *record-name* and not, as a **read** statement does, a file-name—if the **write** statements in Figure 15.8 were in the form "**write** *outfile*", then we would have no means of telling the system whether a large or a small record was to be written. Like the **read** statement, **write** and **rewrite** always treat the record as starting at character position 1 of the record area. Thus "**write** *outsmall*" sends to the file the content of character positions 1 to 85 of the record area, and "**write** *outlarge*" sends the content of the complete area.

At this point, students often ask how record lengths are represented inside a file; for, they point out, a record need not contain any indication of its length. The answer is that Cobol goes to some trouble to shield programmers from considering this question. All we need to know when we program in Cobol is that, if we write a record of a particular length, and then later read that record, we will receive back the same number of characters as we previously wrote. It is left to the Cobol implementor to determine precisely how records are represented on the file storage medium—record-marks may terminate all records; there may be a 'directory' at the start or end of every block in a file; or each record may be preceded by a field specifying its length—but the details are not seen by the Cobol program, which simply receives back, on reading, the record which it originally wrote to the file.

The program in Figure 15.8 is satisfactory enough for a file with only two different record lengths. But a file may contain records of many different lengths. Perhaps each record in a file might be a character string of any length from 85 to 100 characters; in such an event, the technique used in Figure 15.8 would demand sixteen different record descriptions and a means of identifying from the record content each of the sixteen different cases. It is even possible that a file contains records which are unformatted character strings containing no indication of their lengths (e.g. a file containing the successive records 'London', 'Edinburgh', 'New York', 'Ohio', etc.).

A method of handling such files is illustrated in Figure 15.9, which introduces two features not so far discussed. The first of these is the use of the word **into** in a **read** statement. A statement of the form

> **read** *filename* . . . **into** *identifier* . . .

is equivalent to the same statement without the words "into *identifier*" followed by a **move** statement which moves the content of the record area to the data item *identifier*. After execution, therefore, there will be in main store two copies of the record read—one in the file's record area, and one as the value of *identifier*. The latter value may of course be a truncated copy or a copy extended by spaces on the right. (An assumption here is that only group items or elementary alphanumeric items are involved.) There is a similar provision for **write** and **rewrite**. A statement in the form

> **write** *recordname* **from** *identifier* . . .

or the form

> **rewrite** *recordname* **from** *identifier* . . .

```
data division.
file section.
fd   infile, record varying from 85 to 100
                    depending on rec-size.
01   inrecord  pic x(100).

fd   outfile, record varying from 85 to 100
                    depending on rec-size.
01   outrecord pic x(100).

working-storage section.
01   file-end  pic x(5).
01   rec-size  pic 999.

procedure division.
main.
     open input infile, output outfile
     perform, with test after, until  file-end = "true"
         read infile next  into outrecord;
         at end  move "true" to file-end
         not at end
             move "false" to file-end
             write outrecord
         end-read
     end-perform
     stop run.
```

Figure 15.9:   Another program to copy a file which contains variable-length records

---

is equivalent to

    move *identifier* **to** *recordname*

followed by

    write (or **rewrite**) *recordname*

The second new feature introduced in Figure 15.9 is the use of the words **depending on** in an **fd** sentence. The data-name which follows these words must be the name of an unsigned integer data item in the working-storage or the linkage section (see Chapter 18). The effects are: (a) when a record is read from the file, the value of the data item becomes the number of characters in the record; (b) when a **write** or **rewrite** statement is executed, the number of characters written is determined by the value of the data item. In Figure 15.9, since the same data item, *rec-size*, is specified for both files, the value of *rec-size* is set by each **read** statement executed and used by the subsequent execution of a **write** statement. Each of the two record areas *inrecord* and *outrecord* is, of course, large enough to hold the longest possible record.

In a typical Cobol application, however, a file containing variable-length variable-format records is more likely to be of the kind illustrated in Figure 15.10, which is intended to typify a file of changes to be applied to a 'master' file. Each record in the *changes* file will be 31, 7, 96, or 15 characters in length, and has as its first 5 characters a key identifiying the master record to be changed, and

```
fd   changes,  record varying.

*[type = "N"]
  01   ch-name.
       02   c-ac-no    pic x(5).
       02   c-type     pic x.
       02   new-name   pic x(25).

*[type = "S"]
  01   ch-status.
       02              pic x(6).
       02   new-status pic x.

*[type = "A"]
  01   ch-address.
       02              pic x(6).
       02   new-address.
            03   new-address-line pic x(30),  occurs 3.

*[type = "B"]
  01   ch-balance.
       02              pic x(6).
       02   authority  pic xx.
       02   new-balance pic s9(4)v99,  sign leading,  separate.
```

Figure 15.10: A file with variable-length records of varying formats

---

```
read changes   ...
evaluate c-type
    when "N"    perform name-change-proc
    when "A"    perform address-change-proc
    when "B"    perform balance-change-proc
    when "S"    perform status-change-proc
    when other perform report-invalid-code
end-evaluate
```

Figure 15.11: Typical processing of the file described in Figure 15.10

---

as its sixth character an indicator of the type of change, as shown by the comment lines. When used as input, this file would be processed by a program which deals with each record in the way indicated by Figure 15.11. The procedure *balance-change-proc*, for example, would make use of the items *authority* and *new-balance*; it would not, in any sensible approach, refer to the data-names, such as *new-name*, which are appropriate only to other types of record.

16. String handling and redefinitions

16.1 STRING HANDLING

Cobol usually views data as a collection of records each of which contains fixed-length elementary data items. The size of a data item has to be large enough to accommodate the longest value, measured in character positions, which could possibly be allocated to it; when a value is shorter, the excess positions are space-filled or zero-filled, depending on the item's picture.

But it is often convenient to present data to a computer system in a somewhat freer format. For example, one might present a person's name and address in such a way that the various 'fields' of the input data are separated by colons, as in:

J. Inglis:28, Gas Street:Leith::

If we assume that the maximum number of characters in the name is 15, and the maximum number in each of three lines of the address is 20, then the maximum length of such a string is 79 characters (75 plus 4 colons). A file whose records are in this format might be defined as in the data division of Figure 16.1, where the record area *person* is large enough to contain the maximum size record. But any program which needs to refer to the various fields of a record must first convert the record into conventional internal Cobol format, like the record area *expanded-person* in the working-storage section of Figure 16.1. The conversion can be achieved very easily by use of an **unstring** statement.

The execution of the **unstring** statement in Figure 16.1 proceeds as follows. Starting at the first character position of *person*, a search is made for the first occurrence of a **delimiter** (colon). All characters passed over during the search are then assigned to the first item listed after the word **into**, i.e. *name*, according to normal **move** rules (i.e. left-justified; space-filling or truncation on the right). The next colon in *person* is then searched for, and the characters passed over in the search are assigned in the same way to the second item named in the list, i.e. *address-line*(1); the same then happens for the third item in the list, *address-line*(2), then for the fourth item, *address-line*(3). When the end of the list is reached, the process terminates. An example of the resulting value of *expanded-person* is shown in Figure 16.2. Notice that, when two consecutive delimiters occur in *person*, the appropriate item (e.g. *address-line*(3)) is space-filled. Had the item been a numeric one, it would have been zero-filled.

```
data division.
file section.
fd   people; record varying from 4 to 79 characters
                depending on rec-size.
01   person  pic x(79).
  -
  -
  -

working-storage section.
01   rec-size  pic 99.
01   expanded-person.
     0?  name           pic x(15).
     02  address-line pic x(20)   occurs 3.
  -
  -

procedure division.
  -
  -

     read people ...
     unstring person   delimited by ":"
         into name, address-line (1), address-line (2),
             address-line (3)
  -
  -
```

*Figure 16.1: A simple use of the **unstring** statement*

```
J.⊔Inglis⎸⎸⎸⎸⎸⎸28, Gas Street⎸⎸⎸⎸⎸⎸Leith⎸⎸⎸⎸⎸⎸⎸⎸⎸⎸⎸⎸⎸⎸⎸


⎸⎸⎸⎸⎸⎸⎸⎸⎸⎸⎸⎸⎸⎸⎸⎸⎸⎸⎸⎸⎸⎸⎸
```

Figure 16.2:   The content of expanded-person *after execution of the **unstring** statement of Figure 16.1. The record read by the **read** statement is assumed to have been the character-string:*
"J. Inglis:28, Gas Street:Leith::"

Figure 16.3 illustrates the use of alternative delimiters. If the **accept** statement placed the character string

$$22-518=$$

in *inarea*, then the effect of the **unstring** statement would be to assign the following values

x:	0022
y:	05180
op1:	−
op2:	=

since the values of *x* and *y*, which are numeric data items, are set according to the rules for moving data from an alphanumeric item to a numeric item. In practice, of course, a program to handle input strings such as the above would be more complex. We would, for instance, have to check that the operands contained only numeric characters, using Cobol features like reference modification (Section 16.3) and **inspect** (Chapter 19).

```
data division.
    -
    -
working-storage section.
01   inarea  pic x(20).
01   x       pic 9(4).
01   y       pic 9(4)v9.
01   op1     pic x.
01   op2     pic x.
    -
    -
procedure division.
    -
    -
    accept inarea
    unstring inarea  delimited by  "+" or "-" or "="
        into x,   delimiter in op1
             y,   delimiter in op2
    if   op1 = "+"
    then  ...
```

*Figure 16.3: Another example of a use of the **unstring** statement*

Detailed discussion of the facilities offered by the **unstring** statement is beyond the scope of this book, but the following summary should furnish some idea of the capabilities. A search for a delimiter never proceeds beyond the end of the data item containing the input string (i.e. the data item whose name appears after the word **unstring**)—the end of the data item is itself regarded as a delimiter, and the substring preceding it is assigned to the appropriate data item. It is possible to check for missing delimiters by use of a **tallying** option, which counts the number of substrings. The number of characters in any substring can be made available by use of a **count** option. Failure to examine all characters in the input data item, as, for example, when an extra delimiter is accidentally present, can in certain circumstances be detected by use of an **overflow** option.

16.2 COMPRESSION AND EXPANSION OF RECORDS

As noted earlier, internal processing of data in Cobol requires that each record consist of fixed-length data items, the length of a data item being the maximum expected size of any value which that data item will assume. Consider the customer record *expanded-customer* in the working-storage section of Figure 16.4. It is a reasonable assumption that not many customers have names or lines in their addresses which are as long as 30 characters; indeed, the average length of a name or an address line may be as low as about 15. In a file containing several thousand of these records, the large number of redundant spaces stored may have some impact on storage and retrieval costs. It can therefore be worth while to compress each record before writing it to a file.

Before looking at the compression process in relation to Figure 16.4, we note three assumptions being made about the data involved:

(a) When the data entered the computer system, all *embedded* strings of spaces within names and addresses were replaced by a single space. (Look, for

```
data division.
file section.
-
-

fd   customer-file; record varying from 29 to 207 characters
            depending on c-size.
01   filed-customer.
     02  f-cust-no pic x(7).
     02            pic x(200).
-
-

working-storage section.
01   c-size   pic 999.
01   expanded-customer.
     02  e-cust-no       pic x(7).  | ABC1234
     02  name            pic x(30). | J. Smith
     02  address-line-1 pic x(30). | 4 High St
     02  address-line-2 pic x(30). | York
     02  address-line-3 pic x(30). |
     02  tax-class       pic x(5).  | AS251
     02  carriage        pic x(35). | Rail(KX).
     02  sales pic 9(6), occurs 4. | 000000058211000056000000
     02  discount-date   pic 9(6). | 870308
-
-

procedure division.
-
-

     move e-cust-no to f-cust-no
     move 8 to c-size
     string tax-class  delimited by size,
            name, "+", address-line-1, "+",
            address-line-2, "+", address-line-3, "+"
               delimited by "  "
            sales (1), "+", sales (2), "+", sales (3), "+",
            sales (4), "+"
               delimited by "000000"
            discount-date  delimited by size,
            carriage  delimited by ".",
            ".*"  delimited by size
     into filed-customer  with pointer c-size;
     on overflow  perform notify-control
     end-string
     subtract 1 from c-size
     write filed-customer  ...
-
-
```

*Figure 16.4: Use of a **string** statement to compress a record before writing to a file. An example of the content of* expanded-customer *is shown on the right of the program*

---

example, at the specimen content of *address-line-1* shown on the right in Figure 16.4—there are only single spaces between "4" and "*High*" and between "High" and "St").

(b) The last significant character in the data item *carriage* is always a period (.), and no other periods are present there. These conditions were checked when the data entered the computer system.

(c) There are no "+" characters in names and addresses; this condition too was checked during data entry.

The length of *expanded-customer* is 197 characters. Mr Smith's record, shown on the right in Figure 16.4, need not make such demands on file space; in fact, the procedure division statements shown reduce its length to 69 characters before writing it to *customer-file*.

The main statement used to effect this compression is **string**, the complementary statement of **unstring**. Taking Mr Smith's record as an example, we will examine how the output record is constructed in *filed-customer*. The basic form of a **string** statement is

string list-of-items **into** destination

The list-of-items may include both literals and the identifiers of data items, and the action of the **string** statement is to arrange their values one after the other in the destination area. The list-of-items may be subdivided, as here, into sub-lists, each of which has a common delimiter (or a common set of delimiters) specified. Notice that in this example the destination is *filed-customer* (i.e. the record area associated with *customer-file*), and that the words

with pointer *c-size*

are added. The result of this pointer specification is that the data item *c-size* always points to the next available character position in *filed-customer*. It is the responsibility of the program to set *c-size* to a suitable value before the **string** statement is executed. To illustrate this point, the portion of the procedure division shown in Figure 16.4 first places the customer number in *f-cust-no*, the first seven character positions of *filed-customer*. The second statement therefore sets *c-size* to indicate that the next available position in the destination area *filed-customer* is position 8.

We now examine step by step the action of the **string** statement in Figure 16.4. During this examination, you may find it useful to refer to Figure 16.5, which shows the content of *filed-customer* as it will be at the end of the operation.

(1) The first sub-list in the **string** statement consists of the single item *tax-class*. The words **delimited by size** mean that no delimiter is to be sought in that item—the complete content is to be placed in the next available space in the destination area. Thus the character string "AS251" is placed in character positions 8 to 12 of *filed-customer*; thereafter the next available position is character position 13.

(2) The second sub-list consists of a number of items, all subject to the phrase **delimited by** "   ". What this means is that the value of each item is transferred character by character to the destination until *either* a pair of consecutive spaces is recognized *or* the end of the item is reached. If the transfer is terminated by a double space, the spaces themselves are not transferred. Thus, in the case of Mr Smith's record, "J. Smith" is transferred, the transfer being terminated by a double space in *name*; then the literal "+" is transferred; then "4 High St", then the literal "+", then "York", then the literal "+"; then, when an attempt is made to transfer the value of *address-line-3*, a double space is encountered immediately

```
ABC1234AS251J. Smith+4 High St+York+++058211+000056++870308Rail(KX).*
```

Figure 16.5:   The record written to customer-file *by the program of Figure 16.4, assuming the content of* expanded-customer *to be as shown there*

---

in the first two character positions of *address-line-3*, with the result that no characters are transferred; finally, the literal "+" is transferred.

(3) The third sub-list contains a number of items all subject to the phrase **delimited by** "000000". When an attempt is made to transfer the value of *sales*(1), the delimiter is encountered immediately, so no characters are transferred; the next item in the sub-list, "+" is transferred, followed by the value of *sales*(2), "+", the value of *sales*(3), and "+"; then (because on the attempted transfer of *sales*(4) the delimiter "000000" is found immediately) another "+".

(4) The fourth sub-list consists of the single item *discount-date*. This is specified as **delimited by size**, so the string "870308" is transferred.

(5) The fifth list also consists of a single item, this time *carriage*, delimited by ".". The first eight characters of *carriage* "Rail(KX)") are transferred, then the delimiter is found.

(6) The final list is simply the literal ".*" which, being **delimited by size**, is transferred as it stands.

While all this has been happening, the value of *c-size* has automatically kept pace with the transfers and its value indicates the next available character position in *filed-customer*. (If before the transfer of any character the value of *c-size* exceeds the number of character positions in *filed-customer*, no further transfer takes place and an **overflow** condition exists. An overflow condition also exists if the value of *c-size* is initially less than 1.) So the penultimate statement in Figure 16.4 (**subtract**) sets the value of *c-size* as the number of characters placed in *filed-customer*, i.e. the number of characters to be written to *customer-file*. Since *c-size* is in fact the 'depending on' data item specified in the **fd** sentence of *customer-file*, the statement

> **write** *filed-customer*

writes the correct number of characters, thus placing the compressed record in the file.

Of course, when such a record is read back from the file, it often has to be expanded back to its original form. Figure 16.6 shows an expansion program which is the counterpart of the compression program shown in Figure 16.4. In Figure 16.6 there are four **unstring** statements, each using the same pointer, *ptr*. If the phrase **with pointer** is used in an **unstring** statement, the pointer data item (which must be an unsigned integer item) indicates the next character position to be examined in the source data item. The statement

> **move** 1 **to** *ptr*

in Figure 16.6 results in the **unstring** statement which follows starting its examination of *filed-customer* at the first character position (which, incidentally, it would also have done had there been no **with pointer** phrase). Since the first

```
-
-
-
read customer-file   ...
move 1 to ptr
unstring filed-customer into e-cust-no, tax-class
    with pointer ptr
unstring filed-customer delimited by "+"
    into name, address-line-1, address-line-2,
         address-line-3,
         sales (1), sales (2), sales (3), sales (4)
    with pointer ptr
unstring filed-customer into discount-date
    with pointer ptr
unstring filed-customer delimited by "*"
    into carriage
    with pointer ptr
-
-
-
```

Figure 16.6:   Expanding a compressed record. (Assume that ptr *has picture 999.)*

unstring statement contains no **delimited by** phrase, characters are transferred one by one to each data item named in the list until all character positions in that data item have been filled. Thus the first seven characters of *filed-customer* are transferred to *e-cust-no*, and the next five to *tax-class*. After execution of this **unstring**, the value of *ptr* is 13. So, when the second **unstring** statement in the program is executed, examination of *filed-customer* begins at position 13. Thereafter the second **unstring** behaves as described earlier in this chapter, transferring each substring to the appropriate data item. If the content of *filed-customer* is that shown in Figure 16.5, then, when **unstring** encounters the three consecutive "+" delimiters, the null substring between the first and second "+" characters results in spaces in *address-line-3*, whereas the null substring between the second and third "+" characters results in "000000" in *sales*(1). This is because *address-line-3* is an alphanumeric item but *sales*(1) is a numeric item. After execution of the second **unstring** is complete, the value of *ptr* is again the ordinal number of the next character position to be examined. The third and fourth **unstring** statements in Figure 16.6 are straightforward.

16.3 REFERENCE MODIFICATION

For accessing substrings of characters within a data item, **reference modification** is a more flexible alternative to the use of **string** and **unstring** statements. Assume that the item *instring*,

    01 *instring* **pic** x(10).

has the value "abcdefghij". A reference to

    instring(2:3)

is a reference to that part of *instring* which starts at the second character position and is three characters in length, i.e. character positions 2, 3, and 4. Thus a statement beginning

    move *instring*(2:3) **to** . . .

would be regarded as having a source data item three characters in length, whose value is "bcd". Similarly, *instring*(1:6) would have the value "abcdef", and *instring*(9:1) the value "i". The expression

    instring(4:2) = "de"

would yield the value *true*, and the statement

    move *instring*(1:2) **to** *instring*(8:3)

would result in the value of *instring* becoming "abcdefgab " (note the trailing space). Readers who have met such facilities in other languages should note that the number after the colon is the *length* of the substring, *not* its final character position.

The substring positions specified are treated as though they constituted an alphanumeric data item. Subject to some restrictions which need not detain us here, reference modification on the above lines can be used in any context in which an alphanumeric data item can be used. But the data item containing the substring need not be alphanumeric—it may, for example, be an edited item or a numeric item. Thus given the descriptions

    01 *w* **pic** s9v999, **sign trailing separate**.
    01 *y* **pic** x(4).

and assuming that the value of *w* is 2.44, execution of

    move *w*(3:3) **to** *y*

would result in *y* containing the value "40+ ", because the storage representation of 2.44 as the value of *w* is the character string "2440+".

The starting position and length of the substring may each be specified in the form of an arithmetic expression, as in the arbitrarily chosen example

    instring(a(1, 7) + $p * 2 : q$)

where *a* is assumed to be an integer element of a two-dimensional array. It is left to the implementor to decide on the run-time action to be taken if the value of the first expression does not identify a character position in *instring* (i.e. is less than 1 or greater than 10) or if the sum of the values of the first and second expressions, minus one, is greater than the number of character positions in *instring*.

When reference modification is specified for a subscripted data-name, the substring specification follows the subscript specification, as in

    a(1, 2)(4:3)

which is a reference to character positions 4, 5, and 6 of item a(1, 2).

16.4 REDEFINITIONS

Chapter 15 explained how Cobol is capable of handling different kinds of files. One of the techniques used was redefinition of the whole or part of the record area associated with a file. The facility of redefining a storage area is not, however, limited to the file section; with some restrictions, it can be used generally throughout the data division. We close this chapter by looking at the main rules governing the use of redefinitions.

The description of a data item starts with its level-number, usually followed by its name. Then follow a number of optional clauses such as **pic**, **value**, and **occurs**, which may be specified in any order. If a **redefines** clause is present, however, the **redefines** clause must immediately follow the name of the data item (or, if the item is unnamed, the level-number), thus preceding all other optional clauses in the description.

A redefinition always *immediately follows a previous definition of the same storage area*, with no other data item descriptions intervening, except those subordinate to the previous definition. The level-number of the redefinition must be the same as that used in the previous definition. The name used after the word **redefines** is always that of the *first* definition of the storage area. So, in

03 *price-per-unit* **pic** 99v99.
03 *price-per-ten* **redefines** *price-per-unit* **pic** 999v9.
03 *price-per-hundred* **redefines** *price-per-unit* **pic** 9(4).

it would have been wrong to say

redefines *price-per-ten*

in the last line.

Each redefinition of a storage area remaps that area, starting at the first character position. A redefinition need not remap the whole of the original area; in other words, every redefining data item must be shorter than, or the same length as, the data item being redefined. In Figure 16.7, *b* is the same length as *a*, and *c* is shorter than *a*. This rule is relaxed in the case of redefinitions at level 01 (so long as the record area being redefined is not **external**—see Chapter

---

```
   -
   -
   02    a.
         03    a1    pic 9(5).
         03    a2    pic x(4).
   02    b, redefines a.
         03    b1    pic 99.
         03    b2    pic x(6).
         03    b3    pic x.
   02    c, redefines a, pic x(7).
   02    ...
   -
   -
```

Figure 16.7:   An example of redefinition

18), where descriptions may be specified in any order, and the size of the record area is the length of the longest "record type" described. Redefinition takes place *automatically* (i.e. without use of the word **redefines**) at level 01 in the file section.

An item whose description includes an **occurs** clause cannot be redefined; the redefinition in Figure 16.8 is illegal. But, since items subordinate to such an item *can* be redefined, the limitation is easily overcome, as shown in Figure 16.9. It is permissible to redefine a group item which has items with **occurs** clauses subordinate to it, and it is also permissible to nest redefinitions; Figure 16.10 illustrates both of these possibilities.

```
    -
    -
 02  array.
    03  char  pic xx,  occurs 10.
    03  int   redefines char,  pic 99.
 02  ...
    -
    -
```

Figure 16.8:   An illegal redefinition

```
    -
    -
 02  array.
    03  occurs 10.
       04  char pic xx.
       04  int  redefines char, pic 99.
 02  ...
    -
    -
```

Figure 16.9:   Redefining elements of an array

```
    -
    -
 02  array.
    03  occurs 10.
       04  char pic xx.
       04  int  redefines char, pic 99.
 02  redefines array.
    03  name       pic x(15).
    03  quantity   pic 9(5).
    03  percentage redefines quantity, pic 999v99.
 02  ...
    -
    -
```

Figure 16.10:   Redefinition of a complete array, and a nested redefinition

The last limitation worth noting is that a **value** clause cannot appear in the same data item description as a **redefines** clause, nor in the description of any subordinate data item within a redefinition. However, as shown in Figure 16.11, the description of the item *being* redefined, or of any of its subordinate items, may contain a **value** clause. Figure 16.11, in fact, shows a commonly used method of initializing an array (cf. Figure 14.12(v)).

```
01   days-of-week.
     02   pic x(9),    value "Monday".
     02   pic x(9),    value "Tuesday".
     02   pic x(9),    value "Wednesday".
     02   pic x(9),    value "Thursday".
     02   pic x(9),    value "Friday".
     02   pic x(9),    value "Saturday".
     02   pic x(9),    value "Sunday".
01   redefines days-of-week.
     02   dayofweek pic x(9),    occurs 7.
```

Figure 16.11:   Array initialization

17. Program modularization

17.1 PROCEDURES IN GENERAL

A standard technique of programming has always been the design and implementation of programs as sets of functional modules. The concept of 'procedure' or 'subroutine' is central to all programming activity, and may be used to extend the facilities of the conceptual machine by providing functions which are useful in a particular application area ('bottom-up design') or to 'step-wise refine' a program by concentrating design and programming activity initially at a high level, leaving the elaboration of lower-level functions to a later stage ('top-down design').

A procedure call causes execution of the procedure named or referenced in the call statement, after which (as is the case after statements generally) execution normally continues at the statement logically following the call statement. Programming languages vary widely in their provision of procedure facilities:

(1) Data may be communicated in either direction between a calling procedure and a called procedure by parameter-passing. The called procedure includes a specification of *formal parameter* names and types, representing data to be received from, or returned to, any calling procedure. A calling procedure specifies, for each call, the *actual parameters* which are to replace the formal parameters in the called procedure. Some languages do not provide for parameter-passing; communication of data is then achieved through global variables or through 'common' storage which is accessible to both procedures. Languages which do provide for parameter-passing may allow the specification of different forms of parameter (e.g. by value, by reference, by name).

(2) Some languages allow a procedure to be called *recursively* (i.e. to be called by itself or during execution of a procedure called directly or indirectly by itself); others do not. Another approach is to allow recursion only where a procedure is defined in the program as being potentially recursive.

(3) In most languages, local variables may be declared in a procedure. Such languages differ in what happens to these variables at the end of procedure execution. Possibilities are:
 (a) Values of all local variables are lost, so that on the next call these variables (and the procedure state generally) are as they were on every preceding call, i.e. in their initial state. Unless a language with this approach has a facility for specifying initial values of variables, all local variable values will be undefined on every call.

(b) Values of all local variables are lost, except for those variables specifically declared to be 'own' variables. An 'own' variable is in its initial state the first time the procedure is called, and on every subsequent call it has the value last assigned to it.

(c) All local variables behave as 'own' variables and, after its first call within a 'run-unit', the procedure is always in its 'last-used state', unless the language provides a feature which facilitates reinitialization.

(4) In languages with nested scoping rules for variables, procedures are usually subject to the same scoping rules; in other words, a procedure is callable only within the scope of another procedure in which it is defined. In other languages, any procedure may be called by any other (subject, in non-recursive languages, to obvious limitations); and some languages provide for both locally defined and globally defined procedures.

(5) Even in languages which provide parameter-passing facilities, it is often possible for procedures to interact with each other in ways other than by passing parameters. This happens when global or common variables exist, particularly in those languages in which a called procedure inherits the scope of a calling procedure. Interactions other than those specifically declared between pairs of procedures are nowadays generally regarded as undesirable.

17.2 PROCEDURES IN COBOL

Cobol has two quite distinct kinds of procedure call:

(a) the out-of-line **perform** statement (see Chapter 13), which causes execution of a paragraph, or a number of paragraphs, within the same program as the **perform** statement itself;

(b) the **call** statement, which causes execution of another program, which may have been compiled separately.

Throughout this book, the programs presented have necessarily been toy programs, unrealistically short and simple. In such programs it is often adequate to use the **perform** statement for all sub-processes. But a **perform**ed procedure is the most primitive kind of procedure possible; **perform**ed procedures cannot take us far in the construction of realistic maintainable programs. They have these characteristics:

(1) There is no parameter-passing facility.
(2) Recursive calls are not allowed.
(3) There is no facility for defining data local to the procedure.
(4) Procedures are local to the program in which they appear.
(5) All data interaction between the calling and the called procedure is through the data division of the program in which they both occur, or through files. Every procedure has access to every item defined in the data division.

Nothing more need be said about the **perform** statement, and the remainder of this chapter will concentrate on interaction between **programs**. The general picture is:

(1) A program calls another by use of the **call** statement. After execution of the called program, control returns to the statement logically following the **call**. A **call** statement usually has an associated parameter list. Parameters may be passed by **content** or by **reference**.
(2) Recursive calls are not allowed.
(3) A called program may be an **initial** program, in which case it is in its initial state every time it is called. If it is *not* an **initial** program, then, on each call after the first, the called program is in its 'last-used' state. A program can be returned to its initial state by a **cancel** statement.
(4) Programs may be textually nested within other programs or they may be independently written and compiled. When programs are nested, hierarchical scoping rules apply to program names, but there is a facility for defining **common** programs.
(5) If programs are nested within other programs, items at any program level may be defined as **global**, in which case they may be referenced by lower-level programs according to hierarchical name-scoping rules. Use can also be made of **external** items, which can be made available to any program in a run-unit. Otherwise a program can reference only its own local data.

Let us look first at the use of the **call** statement without any parameters, and at program nesting. A program calls another program, named *x*, by the statement

   call "x"

Notice that the name of the called program appears as a literal in the **call** statement. This is because a facility exists for identifying the called program dynamically at run-time. The following statements, for example, would also result in a call of program *x*:

   move "x" **to** *pname*

   ―

   ―

   ―

   call *pname*

A called program returns control to the calling program by use of the statement **exit program**.

17.3 NESTED PROGRAMS

In the terminology of the latest Standard (1985), a Cobol program may *contain* one or more other Cobol programs, which may themselves contain other programs, and so on. Whenever one program contains others, then each of the programs involved must end:

   end program *program-name*.

where *program-name* is the name specified in the **program-id** entry of the program's identification division. The word **end** must start in Area A of a line (see Appendix 1). All programs contained within a given program are positioned textually at the end of the containing program. Figure 17.1 shows the outline of a program *p1* which contains two programs, *p2* and *p3*. Figure 17.2 shows the same situation, but with *p2* containing another program *p4* which itself contains program *p5*. Notice that the requirements regarding Areas A and B of program lines make it impossible for the program text to make these relationships clear by indentation.

Every program must have an identification division, so that it can be given a name (**program-id**). Each of the other three divisions (environment, data, and procedure) need be present only if required. *A program can call either another program which has been separately compiled or a program which it itself directly contains.* For example, *p1* in Figure 17.2 can call *p2* or *p3*, but it cannot call *p4* or *p5*, which it contains only indirectly. Program *p1* can, however, call *p2*, which can call *p4*, which in turn can call *p5*. Program *p3* cannot call (or be called by) p2, p4, or *p5*.

17.4 COMMON PROGRAMS

Most of the time these rules are satisfactory, and they fit in well with strictly hierarchical methods of program design. Sometimes, however, we want a program to include a sub-process or a function which has to be available not just to one sub-program, but generally to the program and all its other sub-programs. In Cobol, a program which realizes such a sub-process is called a **common** program.

```
identification division.
   program-id.  p1.
   -
   -
   -
   --

procedure division.
   -
   -
   -
   identification division.
      program-id.  p2.
      -
      -
      -
      -
   end program  p2.
   identification division.
      program-id.  p3.
      -
      -
      -
      -
   end program  p3.
   end program  p1.
```

Figure 17.1: Program p1 *contains programs* p2 *and* p3

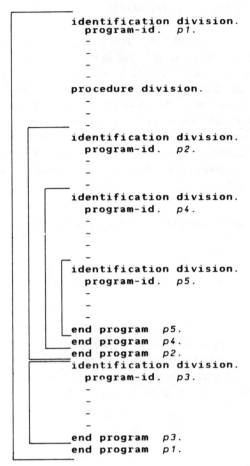

```
            identification division.
              program-id.   p1.
              -

              -
              -
              -
            procedure division.
              -

              -
              -
            identification division.
              program-id.   p2.
              -

              -
              -
            identification division.
              program-id.   p4.
              -

              -
              -
              -
            identification division.
              program-id.   p5.
              -

              -
              -
              -
            end program   p5.
            end program   p4.
            end program   p2.
            identification division.
              program-id.   p3.
              -

              -
              -
              -
            end program   p3.
            end program   p1.
```

Figure 17.2:   As Figure 17.1, but with p2 *containing* p4, *which contains* p5

A **common** program may occur at any hierarchical level except the highest; in other words, a **common** program must be contained in another program.

A **common** program is designated as such by including the word **common** after its name in its identification division, e.g.

   identification division.
   program-id. *tidy-up* **common.**

The effect of this specification is that the program *tidy-up* may be called, not only from the program which directly contains it, but also from all programs directly or indirectly contained in that containing program, except of course from *tidy-up* itself or from any programs which *tidy-up* contains. In Figure 17.2, program *p3* may be called only from *p1*; however, if the **program-id** entry for *p3* were changed to

   program-id. *p3* **common.**

then *p3* could be called from any of the programs *p1*, *p2*, *p4*, and *p5*.

17.5 *THE 'GLOBAL ATTRIBUTE'*

If you are accustomed to the name-scoping rules of Algol-based languages, you should be careful to note that a nested program in Cobol does *not* automatically inherit the name scope of a program which contains it. Automatic nesting of name scopes gives rise to certain difficulties and insecurities in program maintenance; Cobol therefore insists that any such inheritance be explicitly stated.

With one exception, the procedure division of program p can use only those data-names and file-names for which descriptions exist in its own data division. The single exception allowed is reference to data-names and file-names which are 'given the global attribute' in any program which directly or indirectly contains p. A program may describe as **global**:

(a) one or more files;
(b) one or more 01 level items in its file section or working-storage section.

Given the description

    fd *abc* **global** . . .
    01 *abc-rec.*
        02. . . .

in a program p, the file *abc* may be accessed by all programs directly or indirectly contained in p. The name *abc*, in other words, has the global attribute. So do the record-name *abc-rec*, all names subordinate to *abc-rec*, and all names used in any other record description for file *abc*. Therefore a program contained in p may access not only the file but also its record area. But given the description

    fd *def.*
    01 *def-rec,* **global**.
        02 . . .

in program p, the file *def* cannot be accessed by programs contained in p (e.g. these programs cannot read records from, or write records to, *def*); these programs, however, may access the record area using the name *def-rec* and all names subordinate to *def-rec*. If more than one record description is specified for a file, and if the file itself is not described as **global**, then only those descriptions explicitly stated to be **global** may be referenced in contained programs. The same rule applies to redefinitions of record areas in the working-storage section.

A global file or data item may be masked from a contained program *either* by another description of the same name within that contained program *or* by another description *which gives the name the* **global** *attribute* within an intermediate program. Consider the program *n0* in Figure 17.3, which has three data items *a*, *b*, and *c*, all of which are global. The procedure division of program *n1*, contained in *n0*, may use the names *a*, *b*, *c*, and *d* with the following significance:

a: The name refers to the global *a* described in its own working-storage section; this *a* masks out the *a* described in *n0*.
b: Since no *b* is described in *n1*, the reference is to the global *b* described in *n0*.

```
        identification division.
          program-id.  n0.

        data division.
        working-storage section.
        01   a pic xx   value "a0" global.
        01   b pic xx   value "b0" global.
        01   c pic xx   value "c0" global.

        procedure division.
        t1.  display "0", a, b, c
             call "n1"
             display "done".
             stop run.

          identification division.
            program-id.  n1.

          data division.
          working-storage section.
          01   a pic xx   value "a1" global.
          01   c pic xx   value "c1".
          01   d pic xx   value "d1".

          procedure division.
          t1.  display "1", a, b, c, d
               call "n2"
               exit program.

            identification division.
              program-id.  n2.

            data division.
            working-storage section.
            01   b pic xx   value "b2".

            procedure division.
            t1.  display "2", a, b, c
                 exit program.
          end program   n2.
          end program   n1.
        end program   n0.
```

Figure 17.3: A program to illustrate the scopes of global data-names

---

c: The reference is to the local item *c* described in *n1* itself, which masks out the global *c* described in *n0*.

d: The reference is to the local item *d* described in *n1*.

Program *n2*'s references to *a*, *b*, and *c* are as follows:

a: Program *n2* has no local *a*, but there are global *a*'s in *n0* and *n1*, both of which contain *n2*; because *n1* is the lower-level program of these two, the reference is to the global *a* described in *n1*.

b: The reference is to the local item *b* in *n2*, which masks out the global *b* described in *n0*.

c: Program *n2* has no local *c*; program *n1*'s local *c* is not accessible to *n2* since it is not global, but, by the same token, it does not mask out the global *c* described in *n0*; the reference is therefore to the global *c* described in *n0*.

Program *n2* cannot refer to the item *d* described in *n1*, since it is not specified as **global**. A Cobol program can thus protect its local variables against any corruption by other programs. Such protection is not possible in languages which provide only the form of name scoping traditionally associated with nested procedure declarations.

You can check your understanding of nested programs by confirming for yourself that the character strings displayed by program *n0* are, in the order shown:

0a0b0c0

1a1b0c1d1

2a1b2c0

done

Before you run programs which include calls of other programs which have been separately compiled, you should consult your implementor's manual for details of any prior 'linking' process which may be required.

18.   Parameter-passing, initial programs, and external data

18.1 PARAMETER-PASSING

Nested programs, as described in Chapter 17, were first introduced in the most recent Cobol standard. Previously, programs could call only other programs which had been separately compiled. Global items therefore did not exist and programs had disjoint name scopes. The only ways in which two programs could communicate data to each other were:

(a) by parameter-passing;
(b) by one program writing a file to be read by the other program.

This restriction served well over the years by enabling application programs to be modularized in such a way that interaction between modules was restricted to parameter-passing and file storage. All data interfaces were thus formally stated in the programs, and there was no danger of programs affecting each other by changing the values of global or common variables.

Regardless of whether it is nested or independently compiled, a program which is to be called by another usually has a formal parameter list. This appears in the procedure division heading, as in

> **procedure division using** *x, y, z*.

If you are familiar with the use of parameters in other languages, you will notice that, though the formal parameters (*x*, *y*, and *z*) have been named here, their types have not been stated. In fact, all formal parameters in Cobol are record-names, i.e. the names of data items defined at level 01. Each of the names *x*, *y*, and *z* is the name of a record area. Each of these record areas has to be described by a record description, but the descriptions are not written in the formal parameter list. Instead, a further section of the data division is introduced in addition to the file section and working-storage section. This new section is called the **linkage section** and is used solely for the purpose of describing the structures of records which act as parameters. Unlike the other two sections, the linkage section does not result in storage being allocated within the program. Instead, linkage section record descriptions are used as templates or mappings to be applied to the storage areas which contain the values of the actual parameters.

You may also have noticed that the method of passing the parameters (**by reference** or **by content**) has not been specified. In Cobol, the method of parameter-passing is determined, not in the formal parameter list, but in the *actual* parameter list of the **call** statement. *We will assume initially that all parameters are passed* **by reference**.

The example in Figure 18.1 illustrates the main features of inter-program relationships. The called program, *module2*, defines two formal parameters (*n* and *m*); the calling program shown, *module1*, names two actual parameters (*ar* and *b*) in a **call** statement—the number of actual parameters must be the same as the number of formal parameters. A formal parameter, as we have seen, must be a record-name; an actual parameter must name either a record or an elementary data item.

Formal and actual parameters are matched according to their positions in the parameter lists of the procedure division heading and the **call** statement. The first formal parameter (*n*) in Figure 18.1 corresponds to the first actual parameter (*ar*); similarly, *m* corresponds to *b*. When parameters are passed by reference, as here, there need be no similarity of description between a pair of corresponding parameters, beyond the requirement that both be the same length (i.e. number of character positions); both *n* and *ar* have a length of 9, and both *m* and *b* have a length of 7. Whereas *module1* sees the second parameter (*b*) as a four-digit unsigned integer followed by a three-digit unsigned integer, *module2* sees the corresponding parameter (*m*) as a string of seven characters; possibly *module2* simply writes the parameter value to a file and therefore needs to know nothing about its detailed structure. Of course, corresponding parameters can be (and very often are) described by identical record descriptions.

If parameters are passed by reference, then any reference to a formal parameter in the called program is interpreted as a reference to that record area in the calling program which is identified by the corresponding actual parameter of the current **call** statement. (In the case of a hierarchy of calls, the actual parameter may refer to the linkage section of the calling program, so that the actual record area referenced may be in another program.) Thus, in the example of Figure 18.1, any use in *module2* of the name *m* will be interpreted as a reference to record area *b* in *module1*, and any use of *q* will be interpreted as a reference to character positions 3 to 5 of data item *ar1*. By use of reference parameters, therefore, a calling program can pass data to the called program and also receive data from the called program. Literals cannot appear in the parameter list of a **call** statement.

As may be deduced from Figure 18.1, the parameters listed in a **call** statement are, by default, passed by reference. If a parameter, or a list of parameters, is to be passed by content, then the words **by content** must precede the parameter or list. Thus, if a program *report-error* were called by the statement

    call "report-error" **using by content** *error-code, id-no*

then both *error-code* and *id-no* would be passed by content. The statement

    call "assign-payment" **using**
        by content *customer-no, amount*
        by reference *response, new-balance*

passes two parameters by content and two by reference.

```
identification division.
  program-id.  module1.
  -
  -
data division.
  file section.
  fd  a.
  01  ar.
      02  ar1  pic x(5).
      02  ar2  pic x.
      02  ar3  pic 9(3).
  -
  -
  working-storage section.
  -
  -
  01  b.
      02  c  pic 9(4).
      02  d  pic 9(3).
  -
  -
procedure division.
  -
  -
  -
        call "module2" using ar, b
  -
  -
  -
**************************************************
identification division.
  program-id.  module2.
  -
  -
data division.
  file section.
  -
  -
  working-storage section.
  -
  -
  linkage section.
  01  m  pic x(7).
  01  n.
      02  p  pic xx.
      02  q  pic x(3).
      02     pic x(4).
  -
procedure division  using n, m.
  -
  -
  -
*        [references to m, n, p, q]
  -
  -
      exit program
  -
  -
```

Figure 18.1: An example of inter-program relationships

In the case of a parameter passed by content, the data descriptions of both parameters (the actual parameter named in the **call** and the formal parameter named in the procedure division heading of the called program) must be the same, 'meaning', in the words of the Standard, 'no conversion or extension or truncation'. 'The value of the item is moved when the **call** statement is executed and placed into a system-defined storage item possessing the attributes declared in the Linkage Section.' The called program may therefore assign values to the parameter item but this has no effect on the corresponding item in the calling program. Despite the affinity with "call by value" in other languages, Cobol's **by content** facility does not permit the actual parameter to be anything other than an identifier of a data item; literals and expressions cannot appear in parameter lists.

A very simple program to illustrate the difference between reference and content parameters is shown in Figure 18.2. In this case the called program, *cp2*, is a contained program. In the **call** statement, *b* is passed by reference and *c* by content. The character strings output by the two **display** statements are:

    003,003

and

    004,003

```
identification division.
   program-id.   cp1.

data division.
   working-storage section.
   01   a.
        02   b   pic 999   value 3.
        02   c   pic 999   value 3.

procedure division.
   l1.   display b, ",", c
         call "cp2"   using by reference b
                            by content c
         display b, ",", c
         stop run.

         identification division.
            program-id.   cp2.

         data division.
            linkage section.
            01   x   pic 999.
            01   y   pic 999.

         procedure division   using x, y.
         l1.   add 1 to x
               add 1 to y
               exit program.

         end program cp2.

   end program cp1.
```

Figure 18.2:   A simple illustration of reference and content parameters

since incrementing x in $cp2$ in fact increments b in $cp1$, but incrementing y in $cp2$ has no effect on c in $cp1$.

So, if a parameter is to be used as a means of transmitting data back *from* a called program, the parameter must be passed by reference. But, if the function of the parameter is purely to communicate data *to* the called program, it is usually preferable to pass the parameter by content. This practice improves program security by ensuring that the only data items in the calling program which can be affected by the called program are those through which information is intended to be transmitted to the calling program. The security is improved by the fact that the **call** statement, rather than the called program, determines the kind of parameter passing used.

Modular program design is based on the principle that modules are regarded from the outside as 'black boxes', accepting certain specified inputs and producing certain specified outputs. The design of any programming language should reflect this principle by making it possible for programs to be written in such a way that no module can affect the internal operations or data of another module except by defined inputs and outputs. In practice, this means that modules must be capable of retaining information between one call and the next. Any language which compels a module to lose all its internal 'memory' between invocations is unsuitable for the implementation of realistic programs—the 'memory' then has to be realized in global or common data space which is accessible to other modules. In this respect, Cobol has long been more secure than some highly praised languages.

18.2 INITIAL PROGRAMS

In Cobol, a program is in its 'initial state' when it is first called in a run unit. This means principally that any data items whose descriptions include **value** clauses have the specified initial values, that the values of non-valued data items are undefined, and that files are in the closed state. Thereafter, unless the program is defined as an **initial** program, a subsequent call of the same program will normally find the program in its 'last-used state'. This means that the values of its internal data items and the states and positions of its internal files are as they were when the program was last quitted by an **exit program** statement.

A non-initial program, p, may at any time be restored to its initial state by the statement

    cancel "p"

which may be used in any program context in which it would be valid to **call** p. Restoring p to its initial state includes the closing of any of p's internal files which are open. Any programs contained in program p are also restored to their initial states.

Sometimes we want to write a program, q, which does *not* retain any memory of earlier invocations. This is achieved by specifying in the identification division:

    program-id. q **initial.**

(An initial program may also be a common program, in which case the words **initial** and **common** may be written in either order.) The effect is that, when an **exit program** statement is executed in q, all q's internal data items are restored to their initial values (which may be undefined) and any open internal files are closed. If program q contains other programs, they too are restored to their initial states when an **exit program** statement is executed in q.

18.3 THE 'EXTERNAL ATTRIBUTE'

We have now seen two methods by which programs can communicate data to each other:

(a) By use of the **global** facility, a program may allow programs which it contains to access certain files or data items.
(b) By use of parameter-passing, a program may communicate data to any program which it calls, or which calls it, as a sub-process.

But it sometimes happens that several separately compiled programs which are used together in a run unit need to access a common file or perhaps a common body of data, such as a table of constant values. Data resources such as these are referred to as **external** data—data which can be made available to every program in a run unit.

Only two kinds of object can be described as external:

(a) a file;
(b) a record area which is not associated with a file. (A record area may, of course, be just an elementary item described at level 01.)

An external file can be accessed by a program when that program includes a description of the file in its file section; an external record area can be accessed by a program when that program includes a description of the record area in its working-storage section. In both cases the description includes the word **external**.

Suppose that programs $p1$ and $p2$ both include in their working-storage sections the record description:

```
01  r1, external.
    02  a pic xx.
    02  b pic x(4).
    02  c pic 9(4).
```

Since both $p1$ and $p2$ use the name $r1$ to describe an **external** record area, then there exists a single record area $r1$ which 'belongs to' the run unit rather than to any individual program. Other programs in the run unit may also access $r1$ so long as each program concerned includes the same record description, including the word **external**. Because $r1$ is an external object, its value is unaffected by execution of **exit program** and **cancel** statements.

An external object may or may not be described as global within a given program; the external and global attributes are quite distinct from each other. With this solitary exception, the record descriptions of $r1$ which are used in the various programs must be *identical*. Each of the level 02 descriptions therefore must be as shown above in all the programs concerned. If there were any redefinitions within the description, even these would have to be identical. However, any of the programs may redefine the complete record area to suit its own purposes. In other words, the record description above may be followed in any program by a redefinition beginning

> 01 *my-r1* **redefines** *r1*.
> 02 . . .

and the name of the redefinition (*my-r1*), as well as the structure described, may be different in each program. (The requirement that record descriptions be identical is not as tiresome as it at first sight appears to be—many Cobol users keep copies of data descriptions in program libraries in the computer system, enabling the descriptions to be copied into programs by use of the Cobol **copy** statement.)

An important restriction on the description of an external record area is that it is not possible to initialize the content of the record area or any part of it; **value** clauses must not be specified within the description of an external record, except in level 88 entries. (These will be introduced in a later chapter.) The suggestion was made earlier that an external record area might contain a table of constant values; when this is the case, one of the programs concerned must first assign the values to the record area.

When an **fd** sentence in a program includes the word **external**, then the file being described is an external file. If several programs in a run unit all contain a description in the form

> **fd** *f1* **external** . . .
> 01 . . . .

then all these programs are referring to a single file which 'belongs to' the run unit, rather than to any one program. The clauses in all these file descriptions must be 'functionally identical'—for example, the words **access sequential** might be present in one description but implied by default in another. Any data items whose names appear in these clauses must also be defined as external; for example, a data item designated as the **relative key** item, or a data item named in a **record varying depending on** clause, must be an external item. The 1985 Standard, which first introduced the **external** facility, appears to imply that the descriptions of the record area associated with an external file need not be identical in all the programs. This is an interpretation which is made by at least one advance implementation of the 1985 Standard language.

Figure 18.3 demonstrates, by a very simple example, the use of an external file (*names*) and an external record area (*eof*). It must be stressed that the use in Figure 18.3 is unrealistic—no sane programmer would modularize a solution in this way; but there would be little point in asking you to read your way through realistic programs merely in order to see an example of two programs sharing external data.

A bad programmer could obviously use external record areas and files in a way which would defeat the objectives of modularization. Used sensibly, however, they represent a useful addition to the language.

```
identification division.
 program-id.  use-record.

environment division.
  input-output section.
  file-control.
    select names,  assign to xyz.

data division.
  file section.
  fd  names  external.
  01  nrec.
      02  classn  pic x.
      02  name    pic x(9).

  working-storage section.
  01  eof  pic x  external.

procedure division.
n4. move "f" to eof
    open input names
    call "get-record"
    perform until  eof = "t"
       display name
       display classn
       call "get-record"
    end-perform
    stop run.
****************************************************

 identification division.
  program-id.  get-record.

environment division.
  input-output section.
  file-control.
        select names,  assign to xyz.

data division.
  file section.
  fd  names  external.
  01  nrec   pic x(10).

  working-storage section.
  01  eof  pic x  external.

procedure division.
g2. read names next;  at end
        move "t" to eof
    end-read
    exit program.
```

Figure 18.3: Use of an external file and an external record area by two programs in a run unit

19. The inspect and evaluate statements

These two statements are treated in some detail here because they introduce ideas which may be new to programmers coming to Cobol from other popular languages. The statements are easy to use in their simpler forms, though the detailed specification of their syntax and semantics is complex. It would take too long to give a full treatment of the facilities which these statements offer, but this chapter should give enough information to enable you to explore more complicated uses.

19.1 THE INSPECT STATEMENT

Throughout this description, the following data items will be used in examples:

01 x **pic** x(8).
01 i **pic** 99.
01 j **pic** 99.
01 k **pic** 99.

The item which is 'inspected' (x in the examples) may in general be a data item of any of the types introduced so far. The data items used for counting (i, j, k in the examples) must be elementary numeric items.

The simplest use of **inspect** is in counting the number of occurrences of a given character or character string within the value of a data item. Execution of

move 0 **to** i
inspect x **tallying** i **for all** "*"

will result in the value of i being the number of "*" characters in x. If there were a one-character data item called *astsk* with value "*", then

move 0 **to** i
inspect x **tallying** i **for all** *astsk*

would have the same effect. (In general, any literal in the examples may be replaced by an identifier of a data item, in which case the value of the data item is used in the same way as the literal.)

Execution of

move 0 **to** i
inspect x **tallying** i **for all** "a", "e", "i", "o", "u"

will result in the value of i being the number of lower-case vowels in x. Note that in these examples it is necessary to set the value of i to zero since the **inspect** statement *adds* the count to the value of i.

Execution of

> **move** 0 **to** i
> **inspect** x **tallying** i **for all** "ee"

will result in the value of i being the number of occurrences in x of the substring "ee". After an occurrence of "ee" has been found during left-to-right scanning of x, the scan resumes at the character position following "ee". Thus, if the value of x were "abcdeeef", then only one occurrence of "ee" would be counted.

More than one count may be obtained by a single **inspect** statement. If the value of x were "Aberdeen", then execution of

> **move** 0 **to** i, j
> **inspect** x **tallying** i **for all** "a", "A"
> j **for all** "e", "E"

would result in i being assigned the value 1 and j the value 3.

The **inspect** statement scans the value of x from left to right. Starting in turn at each character position in x, it attempts to match each of the values specified, *in the order* in which they are specified. When a value is matched, the scan resumes at the character position, if any, following the last character of the matched substring. So, if x has the value "jijimjji", then execution of

> **inspect** x **tallying** i **for all** "ji"
> j **for all** "jim"

would add 3 to i and 0 to j, because, after matching the second "ji", the scan is resumed at the character "m". However, given the same value of x, execution of

> **inspect** x **tallying** j **for all** "jim"
> i **for all** "ji"

would add 2 to i and 1 to j.

The reserved word **characters** is regarded as matching *any* single character; given the above value of x, execution of

> **inspect** x **tallying** j **for all** "jim"
> i **for all** "ji"
> k **for characters**

would add 2 to i, 1 to j and 1 to k, since the **characters** match occurs only when the "jim" and "ji" matches fail. Execution of the (pointless) statement

> **inspect** x **tallying** k **for characters**
> j **for all** "jim"
> i **for all** "ji"

would add 0 to i, 0 to j, and 8 to k, since each character position in turn of x would match **characters** and matches on "jim" and "ji" would never be attempted.

The word **leading** may be used if only those occurrences which precede all other characters are to be counted. Thus, if the value of x were "00001202", then execution of

> **inspect** x **tallying** i **for leading** "0"

would add 4 to i.

The area of x in which scanning occurs may be controlled by the use of reference modification (see Chapter 16) or by specifying some character or substring which can act as a delimiter. For example, if the value of x were "Aberdeen", then execution of

> **inspect** x **tallying** i **for all** "e" **after initial** "r"

would add 2 to i, and execution of

> **inspect** x **tallying** i **for all** "e" **before initial** "d"

would add 1 to i. Execution of

> **inspect** x **tallying** i **for characters before initial** "r"

would add 3 to i, and execution of

> **inspect** x **tallying** i **for characters after initial** "r"

would add 4 to i. Execution of

> **inspect** x **tallying** i **for characters after initial** "b",
> **before initial** "n"

would add 5 to i. Execution of

> **inspect** x **tallying** i **for leading** "r" **after initial** "b"

would leave i unchanged, but execution of

> **inspect** x **tallying** i **for leading** "e" **afer initial** "b"

would add 1 to i.

The statement acts as one would expect when a delimiting character or substring is not found. Thus, assuming the value of x to be "Aberdeen", execution of

> **inspect** x **tallying** i **for characters after initial** "y"

would leave i unchanged, and execution of

> **inspect** x **tallying** i **for characters after initial** "b"
> **before initial** "m"

would add 6 to i, since the delimiting "m" would never be found.

The **inspect** statement may be used in such a way that matched characters or substrings are replaced rather than tallied. In this kind of use, matching proceeds in the same way as it does for tallying. If the value of x were "Aberdeen", then execution of

> **inspect** x **replacing all** "e" **by** "∗"
> **leading** "A" **by** "+"

would result in x's value being "+b*rd**n"; and execution of

inspect x **replacing characters by** "$' **after initial** "d"

would result in x's value being "Aberd$$$. If the value of x were "0012304+",
then execution of

inspect   x   **replacing leading** "0" **by space**
                all "+" **by** "&"

would result in x's value being "⌴⌴⌴12304&".

It is also possible to replace only the *first* occurrence of a character or substring;
thus, if the value of x were "jjimbjim", then execution of

inspect x **replacing first** "jim" **by** "joe"

would result in x's value being "jjoebjim", but execution of

inspect   x   **replacing first** "jim" **by** "joe"
                after initial "b"

would result in x's value being "jjimbjoe". A substring can be replaced only by
a substring of the same length.

One use of the replacing facility is in transliteration, or the translation of single
characters, as exemplified in

inspect   x   **replacing all** "a" **by** "m"
                all "b" **by** "n"
                all "x" **by** "m"
                all "y" **by** "p"

but this can be tedious if many characters are to be specified, and especially so
if the same context (**after initial** . . **before initial** . .) has to be given for each. A
shorthand version, using the word **converting**, is available for these cases; a
shorter equivalent of the above statement is:

inspect x **converting** "abxy" **to** "mnmp"

and such a statement may also specify an **after initial** and/or a **before initial**
phrase.

The **inspect** statement can be used in more complex ways than those described
here, and the rules governing such uses can be found in the Cobol standard. For
most purposes, however, the uses exemplified above are likely to be adequate.

19.2 THE EVALUATE STATEMENT

The simplest uses of the **evaluate** statement have been exemplified in earlier
chapters. In one of these uses, we specify

evaluate true

followed by a number of **when** clauses. This form of **evaluate** is preferable to a
nest of **if** statements, to which it is equivalent. For example, the program
fragments in Figures 19.1(a) and 19.1(b) are equivalent.

```
evaluate true
    when    a < b
            move ar to cr
    when    a = b
            move ar to cr
            display cr
            move br to cr
    when    a > b
            move br to cr
end-evaluate
```

Figure 19.1(a):   A simple use of **evaluate**

```
if a < b
then move ar to cr
else if  a = b
     then move ar to cr
          display cr
          move br to cr
     else if  a > b
          then move br to cr
          end-if
     end-if
end-if
```

Figure 19.1(b):   Equivalent nested **if** *statements*

In another use of **evaluate**, the program determines which of several courses of action to take according to the value of a data item. This use closely resembles the *case* statements available in other languages, but allows more flexibility than some. The program fragments in Figures 19.2(a) and 19.2(b) are equivalent.

Regardless of the manner in which an **evaluate** statement is used, it is always possible to associate a single set of actions with more than one **when** clause. If a **when** clause specifies no actions, then the actions associated with that clause are those which appear in the next **when** clause which *does* specify actions. Thus the program fragment in Figure 19.3(a) is equivalent to that in Figure 19.3(b).

An **evaluate** statement may test the values of more than one data item, as in the example of Figure 19.4(a), which is equivalent to the code shown in Figure 19.4(b). In the latter, notice the departure from the usual indentation conventions; some programmers find it useful not to indent nested **if** statements when these are used, as here, to implement a selection of one condition from several alternatives.

In general, the items appearing between the word **evaluate** and the first **when**, and those following each **when**, may be expressions. This is illustrated by the statement in Figure 19.5(a), an equivalent of which is given in Figure 19.5(b).

The **evaluate** statement is useful for achieving a clean implementation of a limited-entry decision table, where the table is to be interpreted on a 'first rule satisfied' basis. (If you have not met decision tables before, look at the example in Figure 19.6. In the body of the table, "Y" means 'true', "N" means 'false', and a dash means 'irrelevant'. The first column is interpreted: '*if* S < 12000 is true *and* S > 8000 is true *and* e-code = "H" is false, *then* perform action A'. The last column means 'if S < 12000 is false, then perform action D'.) The

```
evaluate  name
    when  "Jim"
          add 1 to y (2)
          perform special-case
    when  "Tony"
          add 1 to y (1)
    when  "Mick"
          perform another
          add 1 to y (3)
    when  other
          add 1 to y (4)
end-evaluate
```

*Figure 19.2(a):   Another simple use of **evaluate**, illustrating the **when other** clause*

```
if    name = "Jim"
then add 1 to y (2)
     perform special-case
else if   name = "Tony"
     then add 1 to y (1)
     else if    name = "Mick"
          then perform another
               add 1 to y (3)
          else add 1 to y (4)
          end-if
     end-if
end-if
```

*Figure 19.2(b):   Equivalent nested **if** statements*

```
if    initial-letter = "J"
then evaluate name
          when "Jacques"
          when "Jean"
          when "Jean-Jacques"
               perform French-name
          when "Jurgen"
          when "Johann"
               perform German-name
          when "John"
          when "James"
               perform English-name
          when other
               perform unknown-nationality
     end-evaluate
end-if
```

Figure 19.3(a):   Multiple conditions leading to the same action

---

decision table of Figure 19.6 could be implemented with **if** statements, as in Figure 19.7(a), but is better implemented by the **evaluate** statement of Figure 19.7(b), and best of all by the **evaluate** statement of Figure 19.7(c).

The next example illustrates that *ranges* of values may be specified after the word **when**; it also shows a nested **evaluate** statement. The problem addressed is as follows. Data items m, s and c represent respectively a student's percentage marks in maths, statistics, and computing. The student passes the examination only if the three marks satisfy one of these conditions:

```
if    initial-letter = "J"
then if    name = "Jacques"   or   name = "Jean"
                        or   name = "Jean-Jacques"
    then perform French-name
    else if    name = "Jurgen"   or   name = "Johann"
        then perform German-name
        else if    name = "John"   or   name = "James"
            then perform English-name
            else perform unknown-nationality
            end-if
        end-if
    end-if
end-if
```

Figure 19.3(b):   Equivalent effect with nested **if**

```
evaluate h also i
    when 1 also j       perform w
    when 2 also j       perform x
    when 0 also any     perform y
    when other          perform z
end-evaluate
```

Figure 19.4(a):   Testing the values of two data items

```
if    h = 1   and   i = j
then perform w
else if   h = 2   and   i = j
then perform x
else if   h = 0
then perform y
else perform z
end-if end-if end-if
```

Figure 19.4(b):   Equivalent effect with nested **if**

```
evaluate h + i also "yes"
    when e + f also signal1     perform a
    when 4 * e also signal2     perform b
    when other                  perform c
end-evaluate
```

Figure 19.5(a):   Use of expressions in **evaluate**

```
if    h + i   =   e + f   and   "yes" = signal1
then perform a
else if    h + i   =   4 * e   and   "yes" = signal2
then perform b
else perform c
end-if end-if
```

Figure 19.5(b):   Equivalent effect using **if**

(a) all three marks 50 or over;
(b) two marks (one of which must be maths) 60 or over, and the remaining mark
    40 or over;
(c) maths mark 75 or over, and the other two marks each 40 or over.

```
S <  12000      | Y  -  Y  N
S >   8000      | Y  N  -  -
e-code =  "H"   | N  N  Y  -
                |_____
perform         | A  B  C  D
```

Figure 19.6:   A simple decision table

```
if    S <  12000   and   S >  8000   and   not (e-code =  "H")
then  perform A
else if    not (S >  8000)   and   not (e-code =  "H")
then  perform B
else if    S <  12000   and   e-code =  "H"
then  perform C
else if    not (S <  12000)
then  perform D
end-if end-if end-if end-if
```

Figure 19.7(a):   A Cobol implementation of the decision table of Figure 19.6

```
evaluate true
    when S <  12000   and   S >  8000   and   not (e-code =  "H")
            perform A
    when not (S >  8000)   and   not (e-code =  "H")
            perform B
    when S <  12000   and   e-code =  "H"
            perform C
    when not (S <  12000)
            perform D
end-evaluate
```

Figure 19.7(b):   Another implementation of the decision table

```
evaluate
        S <  12000    also   S >  8000    also   e-code =  "H"
    when    true      also   true      also   false       perform A
    when    any       also   false     also   false       perform B
    when    true      also   any       also   true        perform C
    when    false     also   any       also   any         perform D
end-evaluate
```

Figure 19.7(c):   Another implementation

```
evaluate         m            also         s           also          c
    when 50 thru 100    also   50 thru 100   also   50 thru 100
    when 60 thru 100    also   60 thru 100   also   40 thru 100
    when 60 thru 100    also   40 thru 100   also   60 thru 100
    when 75 thru 100    also   40 thru 100   also   40 thru 100
    evaluate         m            also         s           also          c
        when 75 thru 100    also   75 thru 100   also       any
        when 75 thru 100    also       any       also   75 thru 100
        when     any        also   75 thru 100   also   75 thru 100
                perform distinction
    when other
            perform pass
    end-evaluate
    when other
        perform fail
end-evaluate
```

*Figure 19.8:   Nested **evaluate** statements and the use of **evaluate** for range tests*

```
identification division.
  program-id.  get-integer.

data division.
  working-storage section.
  01  correct    pic x.
  01  given      pic x(80).
  01  init-posn  pic 9.
  01  p          pic 99.
  01  m          pic 99.
  01  d          pic 99.

  linkage section.
  01  i          pic s9(5).

procedure division  using by reference i.
1.  display "number?"
    perform, with test after, until  correct = "t"
      move spaces to given
      accept given
      move 0 to p, m, d
      inspect given tallying
          p for leading "+"
          m for leading "-"
          d for characters before space
      evaluate
              p also m also        d       also         true
        when 1 also 0 also   1 thru 5  also   given(2:d) numeric
        when 0 also 1 also   1 thru 5  also   given(2:d) numeric
            move 2 to init-posn
            move "t" to correct
        when 0 also 0 also   1 thru 5  also   given(1:d) numeric
            move 1 to init-posn
            move "t" to correct
        when other
            display "?"
            move "f" to correct
      end-evaluate
    end-perform
    move  given (init-posn:d)   to i
    if    m = 1
    then compute  i = - i
    end-if
    exit program.
```

*Figure 19.9: Validating an input number using **inspect** and **evaluate***

A student who passes the examination is awarded a distinction if any two marks
are 75 or over. (A consequence of these rules is that marks of 75, 75, and 39
would fail, whereas 75, 75, and 40 would give a distinction; but we are not
concerned here with the iniquities of the examination system.)

The program to determine a student's final result has three procedures—*fail*,
pass (dealing with passes which do not qualify for distinction), and *distinction*.
Figure 19.8 shows nested **evaluate** statements which determine which of the three
procedures to call. The outer **evaluate** statement determines the student's pass/
fail status; for those who pass, the inner **evaluate** determines whether a distinction
is awarded.

Figure 19.9 shows the use of **inspect** and **evaluate** together in a program which
accepts an integer from a terminal, validates it, and returns it to the calling

program as the value of parameter i. To be valid, the integer must be input as a string of one through five numeric digits, optionally preceded by a "+" or a "–".

20. Other general facilities

In this chapter we look at some general facilities of the language. Some of these have been introduced briefly in earlier chapters and are now treated in greater detail; others are introduced here for the first time.

20.1 FIGURATIVE CONSTANTS

A **figurative constant** is a word which can be used in place of a literal. For example, in Figure 11.10 the word **low-values** was a figurative constant, and the statement

    move low-values to *surname*

had the effect of assigning, to every character position of *surname*, the character which is lowest in the collating sequence. Similarly, in Figure 8.8 the statement

    move spaces to *left-margin*

placed a space character in every character position of *left-margin*. The full list of figurative constants is:

    zero, zeros, zeroes
    space, spaces
    high-value, high-values
    low-value, low-values
    quote, quotes

In each of these cases, the singular word and the plural word are equivalent. So, if the data item x is three characters in length, either

    $x =$ **quote**

or

    $x =$ **quotes**

can be used to test whether the value of x is a string of three quotation characters. (The quotation character is the double quote.)

    According to context, the word **zero** (or **zeros** or **zeroes**) can represent *either* a string of characters each of which is "0" *or* the numeric value zero. Thus, given the definitions

    a **pic** x(3).
    b **pic** s9(5) **sign leading separate.**

the condition

  a = **zero**

tests whether every character position of a contains the character "0", but the condition

  b = **zero**

tests whether b contains a representation of the numeric value zero (e.g. "+00000"). The condition

  a = **high-values**

tests whether every character position of a contains the highest character in the collating sequence. The word **all**, followed by a literal, is also regarded as a figurative constant (see Chapter 13).

A figurative constant may be used in a program wherever a literal may be used; if the context allows the use of a *numeric* literal only, then the only appropriate figurative constant is **zero**.

20.2 SYMBOLIC CHARACTERS

Most computers today use eight binary digits to represent a character and thus provide 256 possible binary encodings for characters. But, if you look at the list of the encodings in your computer's character set, you will probably see that the number of characters which have a graphic representation is well under 100. In other words, under 100 of the 256 bit-patterns represent characters, like "A", "b", "5", "∗", for which graphic symbols exist. Some of the remaining bit-patterns are allocated to characters which are used for purposes like communications and which have names like ACK and BELL, and some bit-patterns are unallocated.

There is no straightforward way in which a program can refer to these non-graphic characters using the facilities described so far. But it is possible to specify names for these characters (or any others) in a paragraph of the environment division called **special-names**. For example, the environment division extract in Figure 20.1 equates the name *ack* with the encoding 00000110 (binary 6), the name *bel* with the encoding 00000111 (binary 7), and the name *end-symbol* with the encoding 00100100 (binary 36). The numbers are each one less than the corresponding number in the program because the latter specifies the ordinal position in the collating sequence, and the first character in that sequence is the one represented by binary zero. Thus, given the definitions

  p **pic** x
  q **pic** x(3)

a procedure division statement

  move *ack* **to** p

results in p containing the bit-string 00000110, and a statement beginning

  if q = **all** *end-symbol*

tests whether every character position of q has the binary value 00100100.

```
environment division.
  configuration section.
    -
    -
    -
  special-names.
    symbolic characters   ack 7, bel 8, end-symbol 37.
    -
    -
```

Figure 20.1:   The definition of symbolic characters

20.3 NATIONAL NOTATIONS

Those editing facilities described in Chapter 9 which involve the use of the dollar sign ($) are of limited usefulness in countries where the dollar is not the unit of currency. In Britain the sterling sign (£) can be substituted for the dollar sign by specifying in the **special-names** paragraph:

   currency sign is "£"

The role of "$" in an editing picture is then taken instead by "£". For example, given the definition

   val **pic** £(4)9

execution of the statement

   move 1234 **to** *val*

would result in the value of *val* being the string "£1234".

   The literal which follows the words **currency sign is** must be a single-character non-numeric literal. It cannot be a digit, nor can it be a space or any character which has some other syntactic significance. A full list of prohibited characters can be found in your implementor's manual.

   Another national difference is in the use of commas and periods in numbers. In some countries the number which we write as 1,234.5 is written instead as 1.234,5. This difference also is catered for in the **special-names** paragraph, where the clause

   decimal point is comma

may be specified. Its effect is that the functions of comma and period are interchanged in numeric literals and in pictures. (A period, however, retains its normal significance outside these contexts.) For example, given the definition

   g **pic** 9.999,99

execution of the statement

   move 1234,5 **to** *g*

results in *g* containing the character string "1.234,50".

20.4 SCALING OF NUMERIC DATA ITEMS

Numeric data items, as we have seen them so far, must be such that at least one of the digits stored is adjacent to the decimal point position. Taking the example of a three-digit representation, the only possible scalings are those shown in Figure 20.2. As will be seen from Figure 20.3, the character "p" may be used in a picture to indicate the scaling of a number in which no digit position is adjacent to the decimal point position. The number of "p"s in the picture indicates the distance of the decimal point from the leftmost or rightmost digit stored. This scaling is taken into account during execution of statements which reference the data item. For example, given the definitions

    m **pic** 9ppp
    n **pic** 9(5)v9

execution of either

    move 2000 **to** *m*

or

    move 2900 **to** *m*

will result in *m* containing the character "2", which represents the value 2000; truncation occurs in the usual way. After either of these statements, execution of

Picture	Content	Value represented	Scaling
999	"123"	123	0
99v9	"123"	12.3	-1
9v99	"123"	1.23	-2
v999	"123"	.123	-3

Figure 20.2:   All possible scalings of a three-digit numeric data item, when the picture character p is not used. (The 'scaling' column indicates the power of 10 of the least significant digit.)

Picture	Content	Value represented	Scaling
999p or 9(3)p	"123"	1230	1
999pp or 9(3)p(2)	"123"	12300	2
p999 or p9(3)	"123"	.0123	-4
pp999 or p(2)9(3)	"123"	.00123	-5

Figure 20.3:   Some possible scalings of a three-digit numeric data item, using the picture character 'p'

compute $n = m + 75$

will result in n containing the character-string "020750", representing the number 2075.

20.5 RIGHT JUSTIFICATION OF CHARACTERS

It is sometimes useful for printing purposes to be able to align a string of characters at a right-hand, rather than a left-hand, margin. Such alignment can be achieved by describing an elementary alphanumeric data item as **justified right**, or simply **justified**, or even **just**, or (my personal preference) the happy-sounding **just right**. These descriptions are equivalent.

When the data item is a destination item (i.e. an item to which a value is assigned), they result where appropriate in truncation or space-filling *on the left*. The first **move** statement in Figure 20.4 assigns to *jl* the string "Jim⎵⎵⎵" and to *jr* the string "⎵⎵⎵Jim", and the second **move** statement assigns "Winte" to *jl* and "ottom" to *jr*.

20.6 CONDITION-NAMES

Suppose that an input file contains records representing objects which are coloured. One single-character data item in the record format indicates the colour, colours being coded perhaps "R" for red, "B" for blue, "G" for green, "A" for black, etc. If the data item is named *colour*, then a program might include tests of the kind

    if *colour* = "R" . . .

Such tests have two disadvantages. Firstly, for someone reading the program, the meanings of the tests are not clear unless the encodings are known. Secondly, if

```
-
data division.
    -
    -
    02   jl   pic x(5).
    02   jr   pic x(5) just right.
    -
    -
    -
procedure division.
    -
    -
    -
    move "Jim" to jl, jr
    -
    move "Winterbottom" to jl, jr
    -
    -
```

Figure 20.4: Assignment to left-justified and right-justified data items

the code letters used for the colours are to be changed, the procedure division must be searched for all uses of these code letters so that the changes can be carried out; there are then the dangers that some uses will be missed and that some literal in the program which has nothing to do with colour will be changed in error.

If the language provided for constants, we could define a constant called *red* whose value was "R", and so on. One unsatisfactory answer to Cobol's lack of a constant-defining facility is to define data items called *red, blue*, etc., and use the **value** clause to assign them values of "R", "G", etc. Then tests like

>   **if** *colour* = *red* . . .

could be used.

But the designers of Cobol felt that a general constant-defining facility (which Cobol at that time included) was not appropriate for such cases. The code letters were associated with a particular data item in a record area, and their definition should really be part of the definition of that item. So the **condition-name** was introduced. An example is shown in Figure 20.5. The special "level-number" 88 is not a hierarchical level number at all (the maximum such number permitted is 49), but an indication that the name that follows is a condition-name. Thus *red, blue*, etc., are condition-names. The condition-names in Figure 20.5 are all associated with the data item *colour* because their definitions follow that of *colour* with no intervening data item definitions. Every condition-name must be associated with some data item in this way.

A condition-name may be used in the procedure division wherever a conditional expression is appropriate, as in an **if, evaluate**, or **perform** statement. So, given the definitions in Figure 20.5, the procedure division could include a statement beginning

>   **if** *red*
>   **then** . . .

or

>   **perform until** *yellow* . . .

which are respectively equivalent to

>   **if** (*colour* = "R")
>   **then** . . .

and

>   **perform until** (*colour* = "Y") . . .

```
02   colour   pic x.
     88   red                 value  "R".
     88   blue                value  "B".
     88   yellow              value  "Y".
     88   green               value  "G".
     88   black               value  "A".
     88   primary-colour values  "R",  "B",  "Y".
```

Figure 20.5:   Condition-names

The condition-name *primary-colour* is equivalent to the expression

    (*colour* = "R" **or** *colour* = "B" **or** *colour* = "Y")

The condition

    not *green*

is equivalent to

    (**not** (*colour* = "G"))

and the condition

    not *primary-colour*

is equivalent to

    (**not** (*colour* = "R" **or** *colour* = "B" **or** *colour* = "Y"))

If a further definition

    88 *special-letter*, **values** "A" **thru** "F", "M" **thru** "P", "Z".

were added to those in Figure 20.5, then a statement beginning

    if *special-letter* . . .

would be equivalent to

    if ((*colour*   **not**   <   "A"   **and**   *colour*   **not**   >   "F")
    or (*colour*   **not**   <   "M"   **and**   *colour*   **not**   >   "P")
    or (*colour*   = "Z")) . . .

A more realistic use of ranges of values is shown by the definitions in Figure 20.6, which result in the condition-name *fail* being equivalent to

    (*mark* **not** < 0 **and** *mark* **not** > 39)

pass being equivalent to

    (*mark* **not** < 40 **and** *mark* **not** > 100)

and *distinction* being equivalent to

    (*mark* **not** < 75 **and** *mark* **not** > 100)

These definitions enable us to write procedure division statements like

    if *pass*
    then . . .

and to adjust the pass and distinction boundaries by changing only the level 88 entries in the data division.

```
03 mark    pic 999.
   88 fail    values 0 thru 39.
   88 pass    values 40 thru 100.
   88 distinction    values 75 thru 100.
```

Figure 20.6:   Condition-names defined in terms of range

Like boolean variables in other languages, condition-names may be freely mixed with other kinds of condition in conditional expressions, as in

if *distinction* **and** (*maths-mark* > *stats-mark*) . . .

But, unlike boolean variables, condition-names cannot act as source or destination items in an assignment statement. Except in one context, it is best to think of a condition-name as a macro (though this does not quite work with unnamed data items). In other words, imagine that your Cobol compiler actually substitutes for the condition-name the appropriate expression as shown in the examples above. For instance, the prohibited statement

move *fail* **to** *red*

is equivalent to

move (*mark* **not** < 0 **and** *mark* **not** > 39)
　　to (*colour* = "R")

which, in Cobol terms, is nonsense.

There is one case in which a condition-name does not act as a macro. The 1985 Standard has introduced a use of the **set** statement which allows any named condition to be set as true. For example, the statement

set *yellow* **to true**

makes the condition *yellow* true by setting the associated data item *colour* to the appropriate value ("Y"). If the condition-name signifies more than one value, then the associated data item is set equal to the first literal to appear in the condition-name definition. Thus the statement

set *primary-colour* **to true**

sets *colour* to "R", and

set *pass* **to true**

sets *mark* to 40. These are not, of course, sensible uses of the **set** statement, since it would be better to assign the required values explicitly to the data items. But this facility has some justification in allowing 'flags' to be set in a program in such a way that their representation is not made explicit in the procedure division. As we have seen, use of flags is occasionally unavoidable; using condition-names and the **set** statement can make them appear slightly more respectable than they do in the examples in this book. Consider the program fragment of Figure 7.1(a), which is shown again as Figure 20.7(a). The code shown as Figure 20.7(b), which implements the flag by condition-names, may at first sight seem obtuse. Why define *not-ok*? It is not immediately clear to a reader of the procedure division that setting *not-ok* true automatically sets *ok* false. Instead, why not, in the event of a size error, just set *ok* false? This would give a reader a complete picture of what was happening without requiring him to consult the data division. Undoubtedly these changes would make the whole thing more intelligible; but the problem is that, while Cobol allows us to **set** a condition-name to true, it provides no facility for setting it to false! There is some

```
-
-
data division.
-
-
u1  ok  pic x.
-
-
procedure division.
    -
    -
    compute credit rounded = credit + capital * .083
        size error       move "f" to ok
        not size error move "t" to ok
    end-compute
    -
    -
    if  ok = "t"
    then  ...
```

Figure 20.7(a): A 'flag' (ok) with its representation made explicit in the procedure division

```
-
-
data division.
-
-
01.
    88 ok       value "t".
    88 not-ok value "f".
    -
    -
procedure division.
    -
    -
    compute credit rounded = credit + capital * .083;
        size error       set not-ok to true
        not size error set ok to true
    end-compute
    -
    -
    if  ok
    then  ...
```

Figure 20.7(b): A 'flag' implemented by use of condition-names

---

justification, which we need not go into here, for this anomaly, but its existence means that the use of condition-names for flags is perhaps less satisfactory than the more primitive technique shown in Figure 20.7(a).

20.7 ABBREVIATED CONDITIONS

Various options are available for specifying conditions in a shorter form. For example, a statement beginning

    if $a < b$ **and** 5

is equivalent to one beginning

    if $a < b$ **and** $a < 5$

and the expression

    $a < b$ **and** > 5

is equivalent to

    $a < b$ **and** $a > 5$

The commonest use of this facility is in testing a data item for one of several values:

    if $x =$ "C" **or** "P" **or** "S"
    then perform y

is equivalent to

    if $x =$ "C" **or** $x =$ "P" **or** $x =$ "S"
    then perform y

The facility can be dangerous. For example,

    if x **not** $=$ "C" **or** "P" **or** "S"
    then perform y

will always result in execution of y, since the expanded form is

    if x **not** $=$ "C" **or** x **not** $=$ "P" **or** x **not** $=$ "S"
    then perform y

To obtain the effect presumably intended, the statement should begin

    if x **not** $=$ "C" **and** "P" **and** "S"

which expands to

    if x **not** $=$ "C" **and** x **not** $=$ "P" **and** x **not** $=$ "S"

but does not reflect normal English language usage.

20.8 QUALIFICATION OF DATA-NAMES

A data-name may be qualified by the name of a higher-level item. Figure 20.8 shows various ways in which data items may be referenced in the procedure division. For example, it is possible to say

    move spaces to b **in** a

rather than just

    move spaces to b

though programmers do not usually do this. It is also possible to qualify a record-name (or the name of a data item within a record area) by a file-name to which it is subordinate.

```
Definitions              Qualified references

01   a.
     02  b  ...          b  in  a
     02  c.              c  in  a
          03  d  ...     d  in  c  in  a;  d  in  c;  d  in  a
          03  e  ...     e  in  c  in  a;  e  in  c;  e  in  a
     02  f.              f  in  a
```

Figure 20.8:   Qualification of names

Because data-names may be qualified, different data items may be given the same name. If two or more data items have the same name, then that name *must* be qualified every time it is used and the qualification must be sufficient to ensure that one of the data items is uniquely identified. Look, for example, at the fifth line of Figure 20.9. To refer to this particular e, the name e is clearly not enough, since two other data items are also called e. Reference to e **in** c would not be enough, for there is another e **in** c in record g; nor would e **in** a, since there is another e **in** a subordinate to f. The only possible way of referring to this e is therefore e **in** c **in** a. Study Figure 20.9 and you should be able to deduce the rules for qualification. Figure 20.9 assumes that the names concerned are not used for any other things in the program.

When a qualified name is subscripted, the subscripts follow the complete qualified name. If, for example, a group item x includes an array of items called y, the first of these items may be referenced as y **in** $x(1)$.

It is unlikely that any programmer would assign names quite as strangely as in Figure 20.9. But data-names may sometimes usefully be duplicated when two files contain identical record types, or when a program can take advantage of the **corresponding** option.

20.9 CORRESPONDING DATA ITEMS

Consider the three record definitions in Figure 20.10. As we have seen, every program reference to *credits, debits,* or *adjustments* needs to be qualified. But an advantage of duplicating these data-names is that statements like

---

```
Definitions              Acceptable references

01  a.                   a
     02  b  ...           b;  b  in  a
     02  c.               c  in  a
          03  d  ...      d  in  c  in  a;  d  in  a
          03  e  ...      e  in  c  in  a
     02  f.               f;  f  in  a
          03  e  ...      e  in  f  in  a;  e  in  f

01   g.                   g
     02  c.               c  in  g
          03  e  ...      e  in  c  in  g;  e  in  g
          03  h  ...      h;  h  in  c  in  g;  h  in  g
     02  d  ...           d  in  g

01  ...
```

Figure 20.9:   Qualification of duplicated names

```
01   day-totals.
     02 debits          pic 9(5)v99.
     02 credits         pic 9(5)v99.
     02 forms           pic 9(5).

01   month-totals.
     02 adjustments pic 9(7)v99.
     02 credits         pic 9(7)v99.
     02 debits          pic 9(7)v99.

01   year-totals.
     02 credits         pic 9(8)v99.
     02 debits          pic 9(8)v99.
     02 adjustments pic 9(8)v99.
```

Figure 20.10:   Three record descriptions which include items with common names

---

    move corresponding *month-totals* **to** *year-totals*

can be used. This statement is equivalent to the three statements

    move *credits*   **in** *month-totals* **to** *credits*   **in** *year-totals*
    move *debits*   **in** *month-totals* **to** *debits*   **in** *year-totals*
    move *adjustments* **in** *month-totals* **to** *adjustments* **in** *year-totals*

because *credits, debits,* and *adjustments* are all data-names which are subordinate to both *month-totals* and *year-totals*. (Notice that the effect is very different from that of **move** *month-totals* **to** *year-totals*.) Similarly, the statement

    add corresponding *day-totals* **to** *month-totals, year-totals*

is equivalent to the pair of statements

    add corresponding *day-totals* **to** *month-totals*
    add corresponding *day-totals* **to** *year-totals*

which, in turn, are equivalent to

    add *debits*   **in** *day-totals* **to** *debits*   **in** *month-totals*
    add *credits* **in** *day-totals* **to** *credits* **in** *month-totals*
    add *debits*   **in** *day-totals* **to** *debits*   **in** *year-totals*
    add *credits* **in** *day-totals* **to** *credits* **in** *year-totals*

but the data items *forms* and *adjustments* are not involved since their names are not common to *day-totals* and *month-totals* or to *day-totals* and *year-totals*.

    At least one of each pair of items whose names are the same must be elementary. A further rule is illustrated by the example of Figure 20.11. The statement

    move corresponding *rail* **to** *fastest*

is equivalent to

    move *hours*   **in** *out* **in** *rail* **to** *hours*   **in** *out* **in** *fastest*
    move *minutes* **in** *out* **in** *rail* **to** *minutes* **in** *out* **in** *fastest*

```
01  rail.
    02 out.
        03 hours    pic 999.
        03 minutes  pic 99.
        03 route    pic x.
    02 ret.
        03 hours    pic 999.
        03 minutes  pic 99.
        03 route    pic x.
    02 delay.
        03 hours    pic 99.
        03 minutes  pic 99.

01  fastest.
    02 out.
        03 hours    pic 99.
        03          pic x,  value space.
        03 minutes  pic 99.
        03          pic xx, value spaces.
    02 ret.
        03 hours    pic 99.
        03          pic x,  value space.
        03 minutes  pic 99.
        03          pic xx, value spaces.
    02 route        pic x.
```

Figure 20.11: Two record descriptions to illustrate name correspondences

---

move *hours* **in** *ret* **in** *rail* **to** *hours* **in** *ret* **in** *fastest*
move *minutes* **in** *ret* **in** *rail* **to** *minutes* **in** *ret* **in** *fastest*

because each pair of elementary data items involved has an identical 'chain of qualification' (e.g. *hours* **in** *out* **in** . . .) to the items named in the **move corresponding** statement. The three occurrences of *route* give rise to no correspondences because their chains of qualification are all different.

The **corresponding** option is available only in **add, subtract**, and **move** statements, and, when it is used in **add** and **subtract** statements, numeric data items alone are regarded as corresponding. The option can be particularly useful in reformatting the records of a file. If two record areas (*a* and *b*) are described using identical subordinate names but different formats, then the statement

> **move corresponding** *a* **to** *b*

is often sufficient to effect the complete reformatting of a record. But it is not always sufficient, for data items whose descriptions contain, or are subordinate to, a **redefines, occurs,** or **usage index** clause are never regarded as corresponding.

The advantage of using the **corresponding** option is probably outweighed by the problems it can cause during program maintenance. Even quite experienced Cobol programmers often slip up when they use it.

20.10 GROUPING OF PARAGRAPHS IN THE PROCEDURE DIVISION

Up to now we have equated procedures with paragraphs. A procedure may also consist of several paragraphs. The need for this facility arises from the existence of a **go to** statement and from the curious fact that a paragraph-name may be used both as a procedure-name and as the destination of a **go to** statement (i.e. as a label); if a **go to** is used within a procedure, it will probably be necessary for the procedure to consist of more than one paragraph.

There are two ways in which such a grouping can be achieved. One is for a **perform** statement to name the entry and exit paragraphs of the procedure which is to be executed. The statement

   perform *p1* **thru** *p2*

causes a transfer of control to the beginning of the paragraph named *p1*; thereafter, control returns to the **perform** statement when the end of paragraph *p2* (instead of the end of *p1*) is reached. (If the last statement executed in a paragraph is not **go to, stop run,** or **exit program**, and if the end of a **perform**ed procedure has not been reached, then execution continues at the first statement of the next paragraph in textual sequence. This is consistent with the use of paragraph-names as labels.) Paragraph *p2* need not follow *p1* textually; all that is necessary is that during execution the end of *p2* is reachable from *p1*. The **thru** option may be used in any variant of the out-of-line **perform** statement.

The other method of grouping paragraphs together is by writing the procedure division as a sequence of sections. A **section** consists of zero or more consecutive paragraphs, as illustrated in Figure 20.12, where the procedure division consists of three sections which the programmer has named *main, input-handling,* and *report-handling*. These sections consist respectively of two, three, and two paragraphs. The statement

```
procedure division.
main section.
m1. -
     -
     -
m2. -
     -
     -
     -
input-handling section.
i1. -
     -
i2. -
     -
     -
     -
i3. -
     -
report-handling section.
r1. -
     -
     -
     -
r2. -
     -
     -
```

Figure 20.12: A procedure division organized as three sections

  perform *input-handling*

is equivalent to

  perform *i1* **thru** *i3*

and the statement

  perform *input-handling* **thru** *report-handling*

is equivalent to

  perform *i1* **thru** *r2*

Section-names, rather than paragraph-names, may be used in any variant of the out-of-line **perform** statement.

 Sections add nothing to the functional capabilities of the language, but many people find that their use makes programs more readable.

21. Sorting, and other file-handling facilities

21.1 SORTING RECORDS

Sorting of records has long been an important part of data processing. It was especially important in computing 20 to 30 years ago, when the use of very large indexed or relative files was not economically feasible. Large files were at that time stored on magnetic tape in key order, and batches of transactions to be applied to such a file were sorted into key order, then processed during a single pass through the file. As large-capacity direct-access storage devices became cheaper, the importance of sorting declined.

Nevertheless, sorting of large numbers of records is still a common operation. For instance, users often require their output presented in a particular order. Also, where there is no requirement for on-line working, even processing transactions on an indexed file may be significantly more efficient when done sequentially, especially when there is a high hit rate; where this is done, the transactions must first be sorted into key order.

Many programming languages provide no facilities for sorting; sorting has therefore to be achieved by operating system commands—peculiar, of course, to the particular operating system being used, and perhaps not accessible from a program. Cobol, however, has a **sort** statement which offers considerable flexibility.

A **sort** statement sorts a collection of records according to the values of specified embedded data items known as *sort keys*. In order to use a **sort** statement it is necessary to define a 'sort file'. A sort file is described in the file section of the data division in the same way as any other file but, instead of starting with the reserved word **fd** (file description), the description starts with the reserved word **sd** (sort-file description). In the environment division, the **select** sentence for a sort file has only an **assign** clause—no organization or access method is specified. The basic action of a **sort** statement is that the records to be sorted are first placed in the sort file, then the records in the sort file are sorted, and then these records are made available in sorted order.

The simplest, and probably the commonest, way of using a **sort** statement is illustrated in Figure 21.1, where a file of product data is sorted on descending profitability of the products and, within any one profitability value, on ascending product number. The sort file is named *9products*; the file which supplies the records to be sorted (**using**) is *1products*; and the file to contain the records as

```
fd 1products ...                          fd 2products ...
01 1product-record.                       01 2product-record.
   02 1description    pic x(20).              02 2description    pic x(20).
   02 1product-no     pic x(5).               02 2product-no     pic x(5).
   02 1unit-price     pic 999v99.             02 2unit-price     pic 999v99.
   02 1reorder-level  pic 9(5).               02 2reorder-level  pic 9(5).
   02 1profitability  pic s99v9.              02 2profitability  pic s99v9.
   02 1supplier       pic x(10).              02 2supplier       pic x(10).

sd 9products.
01 9product-record.
   02                 pic x(20).
   02 9product-no     pic x(5).
   02                 pic x(10).
   02 9profitability  pic s99v9.
   02                 pic x(10).

   -
   -


   sort 9products on descending 9profitability,
               ascending 9product-no,
       using 1products,  giving 2products

   -
   -
```

Figure 21.1:   *Simple use of a **sort** statement*

---

sequenced by the sorting process (**giving**) is *2products*. On the assumption that other statements in the program refer to the data items in *1product-record* and *2product-record*, these records are described in full. The only items which need to be named in the sort file are the sort keys *9product-no* and *9profitability*. The **sort** statement in the example produces, in the file *2products*, the records from *1products* sorted in the required sequence.

More than one 'input' file may be specified after the word **using**, in which case the records from all the named files are sorted to form a single sequence. More than one 'output' file may be specified after the word **giving**, in which case the named files will each consist of all the records in sorted order. Input and output files may have sequential, relative, or indexed organization. If an output file has relative organization, the first record in the sorted sequence is assigned relative key value 1, the next record relative key value 2, and so on. If an output file has indexed organization, then sorting must, reasonably enough, be on **ascending** values of the item specified as the **record key** for that file. The files named in **using** and **giving** phrases must not be open when the **sort** statement is executed; **sort** opens and closes these files automatically.

Sometimes we want to sort only certain selected records from the input file or files. For instance, in the previous example, we may want to sort only records for products with *positive* profitability. To achieve this, we can replace the **using** phrase in the **sort** statement by specification of an **input procedure**, as in Figure 21.2. Each execution of the **release** statement in *select-records* sends one record to the sorting process; in other words, a **release** statement behaves like a **write** to a sort file. An input procedure thus acts as a means of creating a set of records to be sorted.

```
main section.
      -
      -

      sort 9products on descending 9profitability,
                     ascending 9product-no,
             input procedure select-records,    giving 2products
      -
      -
  select-records section.
  s-r1.
      open input 1products
      perform with test after until eof = "t"
          read 1products next
          at end        move "t" to eof
          not at end move "f" to eof
              if 1profitability > 0
              then move 1product-record to 9product-record
                   release 9product-record
              end-if
          end-read
      end-perform
      close 1products.
```

*Figure 21.2: Use of a **sort** statement with an input procedure. (Assume
that* eof *is a working-storage data item.)*

The records sorted by a **sort** statement need not all have the same length or
the same format; an **sd** sentence may therefore be followed by several record
descriptions (01 entries). But each sort key must occupy the same character
positions in all the record formats, in the same way as record keys in indexed
files must occupy the same character positions in all record formats. Where this
is not the case, an input procedure may be used to reformat records so that the
sort key positions in all records correspond, and an output procedure may be
used to restore the set of sorted records to their original formats.

An input procedure creates a set of records to be sorted; an output procedure
obtains the records one by one after sorting and performs any required processing
on them. For instance, the output of the sorting process may require formatting
for printing and the omission of some data items, as in the example of Figure
21.3. (Note the use of **move corresponding** for reformatting, and the resulting
qualification of data-names in the **sort** statement.) The **return** statement, in the
output procedure *format-records*, obtains the next record in sorted order from
the sort file. When all records have been obtained, the **at end** condition exists.
A **return** statement thus behaves like a sequential **read** statement applied to a
sort file.

Execution of a **sort** statement, then, may be considered as consisting of these
three phases:

(1) A sort file is formed *either* by copying all records from one or more named
files (**using**) *or* by execution of a procedure written for the purpose (**input
procedure**).

(2) The records in the sort file are sequenced according to the values of the key
or keys specified by the **sort** statement.

```
data division.
file section.
fd   products.
01   product-record   pic x(48).

sd   sorted-products.
01   sorted-record.
     02 description      pic x(20).
     02 product-no       pic x(5).
     02 unit-price       pic 999v99.
     02 reorder-level    pic 9(5).
     02 profitability    pic s99v9.
     02 supplier         pic x(10).

fd   output-products.
01   output-record.
     02 profitability    pic ++9.9bb.
     02 product-no       pic x(7).
     02 description      pic x(22).
     02 supplier         pic x(10).

     -
     -

procedure division.
     -
     -
     -

     sort sorted-products on
         descending profitability in sorted-record
         ascending  product-no    in sorted-record
         using products
         output procedure format-records
     -
     -
     -

format-records section.
f-r1.
     open output output-products
     perform with test after until eof = "t"
        return sorted-products
        at end      move "t" to eof
        not at end  move "f" to eof
                    move corresponding sorted-record to output-record
                    write output-record
        end-return
     end-perform
     close output-products.
```

*Figure 21.3:   Use of a **sort** statement with an output procedure*

---

(3) The sorted records are *either* copied in sequence to one or more named files (**giving**) *or* disposed of in sequence by a procedure written for the purpose (**output procedure**).

21.2 MERGING ORDERED FILES

If two or more files are each ordered on values of the same key data items, a **merge** statement may be used to merge these files into a single sequence of records ordered on the same keys. For instance, an organization may produce each day a summary file in which records represent orders placed by customers. Suppose that three of these files, named *day-1, day-2,* and *day-3,* are each sorted on ascending value of customer number. These files may be merged by a statement like

> **merge** *merge-file* **on ascending** *customer-number*
>   **using** *day-1 day-2 day-3*
>   **giving** *days-123*

to form a single file, in ascending *customer-number* sequence, named *days-123*. The file *merge-file* is akin to a sort file in a **sort** statement and, like such a file, is defined by an **sd** entry in the file section of the data division; *customer-number* is the name of a data item in a record description associated with *merge-file*.

Like **sort**, a **merge** statement may operate on files of any organization, containing records of diverse lengths and formats; the key used for merging must occupy the same character positions in all record formats. Like **sort,** a **merge** statement may specify more than one output file after the word **giving**; or the **giving** phrase may be replaced by specification of an **output procedure** which uses **return** statements to obtain the merged records one by one. Unlike **sort**, the **merge** statement has no provision for specifying an **input procedure**.

21.3 FILE STATUS

In earlier chapters it was assumed that execution of any file-accessing statement would either be successfully completed or give rise to the **invalid key** or the **at end** condition. But, of course, other situations may arise when a file is accessed. We may run out of allocated space when we are writing to a file; or the length of a record in a file may not match any of those in the program's record descriptions; or a hardware fault may make a record or a complete file inaccessible.

Information about success or failure in the execution of a file-accessing statement may be communicated to the Cobol program through a **file status** data item. A program may optionally specify a file status item for any file it uses. Then, every time an **open, close, read, write, rewrite, delete,** or **start** statement for that file is executed, the file status item is set to an appropriate value. A file status item consists of two character positions and is usually described in the working-storage section. The first character indicates whether execution was successful and, if not, the broad category of failure; the second character may give further information.

For example, the working-storage section of a program may contain

> 01   *status-key-x*.
>   02   *skx1*   **pic** x.
>   02   *skx2*   **pic** x.

The **select** sentence for a file may include a **file status** clause:

> **select** *x*, **assign to** . . .
>   **organization** . . .
>   —
>   —
>   **file status**   *status-key-x*.

Then each execution of a statement which accesses file *x* will result in a value being automatically assigned to *status-key-x*. The first character of the assigned value (i.e. the value assigned to *skx1*) will be one of the following:

"0": successful execution.
"1": unsuccessful execution—**at end** condition.
"2": unsuccessful execution—**invalid key** condition.
"3": unsuccessful execution—"permanent error" (e.g. **open i–o** attempted on a file not stored on a mass storage medium).
"4": unsuccessful execution—"logic error" (e.g. **write** attempted on a file which is not open or is open for **input**).
"9": unsuccessful execution—implementor-defined error.

As illustrations of the detailed information given by the second character (*skx2* in our example), the following are the status code values for the **invalid key** condition. (This list is included here merely to indicate the kind of information supplied by status codes. Exhaustive lists can be found in the Standard or in your implementor's manual.)

"21": A sequence error exists for a sequentially accessed indexed file. The prime record key value has been changed by the program between the successful execution of a **read** statement and the execution of the next **rewrite** statement for that file, or the ascending sequence requirements for successive record key values are violated by a **write** statement.
"22": An attempt is made to **write** or **rewrite** a record that would create a duplicate key value in the file, and the key is not an alternate record key for which duplicates are allowed.
"23": An attempt is made to access randomly a record which does not exist in the file.
"24": An attempt is made to write outside the space allocated to the file.

Similar detailed information is given in the other cases of unsuccessful execution, and even in the case of successful execution.

A Cobol program can therefore determine the result of attempted execution of any statement which accesses file *x* and, in the event of unsuccessful execution, can avoid being aborted by the operating system. This facility is of the utmost practical importance.

As a simple example of handling invalid key situations, suppose that file *x* is an indexed file accessed sequentially, and that the associated record area is named *xr*. A **write** statement may take the form shown in Figure 21.4. Alternatively, condition-names might be used for the status codes, as shown in Figure 21.5.

21.4 DECLARATIVE PROCEDURES

Unsuccessful execution of a file-accessing statement is due to what is sometimes called an *exception condition*. From the programmer's point of view there are two types of exception:

```
write xr; invalid key
    evaluate skx2
        when "2"   perform process-key-clash
        when "4"   perform get-more-space
    end-evaluate
end-write
```

Figure 21.4:   Examining status codes on an invalid key condition

---

```
01   skx pic xx.
     88 x-duplicate-key value "22".
     88 x-overflow      value "24".
     -
     -
     -

     write xr; invalid key
         evaluate true
             when x-duplicate-key  perform process-key-clash
             when x-overflow       perform get-more-space
         end-evaluate
     end-write
```

Figure 21.5:   Using condition-names for status codes

(a) those which can be expected to occur even if the file and the program contain no errors and whose detection is part of the application logic (normally the **at end** and **invalid key** conditions);

(b) those which arise from situations unconnected with the application logic and which indicate hardware or software faults (e.g. permanent errors, logic errors).

Usually a programmer will want to include tests for exceptions of type (a) in the application program. But, though the programmer may also want to catch any exceptions of type (b), tests for these exceptions would destroy the program structure—the application program would be cluttered with tests for conditions which would be unlikely to arise during normal execution of the program. It is therefore useful for the coding associated with type (b) exceptions to be isolated from the main application logic, and for that coding to be invoked *automatically* when an exception condition arises. (Readers with a PL/1 background will recognize here the principle of ON-units.)

Suppose that we want to specify program code to handle exception conditions which may arise in the processing of file x. We do this by writing a **declarative procedure** such as the section *x-error* in Figure 21.6. The program need never explicitly perform *x-error*. Instead, *x error* is automatically executed when an exception condition arises during execution of a statement (**open, read**, etc.) which accesses file x. For example, if during execution of the statement

read x

a parity error is detected, the system will first take any appropriate standard action (such as attempting to reread the block) and will then pass control to the section *x-error*; this is the meaning of **after standard exception procedure** in the

```
      environment division.
         -
         -
      select x,   assign ...
          file status status-key-x.
         -
         -
  data division.
  file section.
    fd   x ...
      -
      -
  working-storage section.
      -
      -
  01   status-key-x.
       02 skx1   pic x.
       02 skx2   pic x.
      -
      -
      -

  procedure division.

  declaratives.
  x-error section.
      use after standard exception procedure on x.
  xe1.  evaluate skx1
          when "3"   perform x-perm-error
          when "4"   perform x-logic-error
        end-evaluate
        go to xe-exit.
  x-perm-error.
      evaluate skx2
          when ...
       -
       -
  x-logic-error.
      evaluate skx2
          when ...
       -
       -
  xe-exit.
  end declaratives.

  p1 section.
      -
      -
      -
```

Figure 21.6: Outline of a declarative procedure to handle permanent error and logic error exception conditions for file x

---

use statement of Figure 21.6. On completion of execution of *x-error* (i.e. when control reaches the end of the last paragraph of the section—in this case, an empty paragraph), control will be returned to the program statement logically following the **read** which gave rise to the exception condition, unless, of course, an **exit program** or **stop run** statement is executed in *x-error*.

More than one file may be named in the **use** statement of a declarative procedure, as in

use after standard exception procedure on *x, y, z.*

In this case the procedure will be automatically invoked if an exception condition arises during access to any of the named files *x, y,* or *z.* It is also possible to specify a declarative procedure which will be invoked on the occurrence of an exception condition during access to *any* file which is open, or being opened, as an **input** file:

use after standard exception procedure on input.

Declarative procedures may similarly be specified for:

(a) all **output** files;
(b) all **i–o** files;
(c) all **extend** files;

and these procedures will be automatically invoked on the occurrence of an exception on any file open, or being opened, in the stated mode.

A declarative procedure whose **use** statement names a file takes precedence over one whose **use** statement names an open mode. For example, suppose that file *x* is used as an input file and that there is one declarative procedure for exceptions on file *x* and another for exceptions on **input** files. Then, if an exception condition arises during access to *x*, only the first of these is executed.

When a program contains declarative procedures, the **procedure division** header is followed by the header

declaratives.

This is followed by the declarative procedures themselves, each written in the form of a **section** and each beginning with an appropriate **use** statement. The last declarative procedure is followed by

end declaratives.

This in turn is followed by the first section of the procedure division proper. (When declaratives are present the procedure division must be in the form of sections; the paragraphs following the declaratives may of course constitute a single section.) When the program is called, entry is at the start of the first non-declarative section.

Within a declarative procedure there must be no reference to non-declarative procedures, but a declarative procedure may be explicitly **perform**ed from within another procedure, either declarative or non-declarative.

Two classes of exception condition *must* be provided for. These are the **at end** and **invalid key** conditions. A sequential **read** statement may include an **at end** phrase; if it does, occurrence of the **at end** condition causes the code specified in the **at end** phrase to be executed, and no declarative procedure is executed. If a sequential **read** statement does *not* include an **at end** phrase, then there must be a declarative procedure whose **use** statement names either the file or the appropriate open mode; that procedure is invoked during execution of the **read** statement if the **at end** condition arises. In the same way, an **invalid key** phrase takes precedence over declarative procedures; and the program must include a suitable declarative procedure if the **invalid key** phrase is omitted in any of the following statements:

(a) a **start** or a random **read** statement;
(b) a **write** statement for an indexed or a relative file;
(c) a **delete** or **rewrite** statement for an indexed or relative file in random or dynamic access mode.

Detection of **at end** and **invalid key** conditions is often part of the logic of an application. Where it is, it is normal to include **at end** and **invalid key** phrases in the program. But, as we have seen in earlier chapters, cases often exist in which the **invalid key** condition can only indicate a software or hardware error. In these cases the **invalid key** phrase is best omitted and a declarative procedure used. Handling of other exception conditions could be left to the whim of your operating system, but you will very often want the Cobol program to retain control at least long enough to display suitable terminal messages and to do some tidying up. For this purpose, declarative procedures are invaluable.

22. Provisions for portability

22.1 INTRODUCTION

Programs and data files are important corporate resources. Ideally their use should not be restricted to particular hardware or a particular operating system. We would like to be able to transfer files and programs unchanged from one machine to another. This ideal of *portability* of programs and data between different environments is rarely fully achieved in practice, but Cobol approaches the ideal more closely than other traditional programming languages—and, indeed, more closely than many more modern programming languages.

Nearly 30 years ago the far-seeing designers of the first version of Cobol showed their concern for portability in a rigid separation between data definition and data manipulation (data and procedure divisions) and in their attempt to isolate in the environment division those aspects of a program which were dependent on the characteristics of a specific computer. They also required that every numeric data item be defined in terms of the precise range of values it could assume (the range limits being integral powers of ten); together with their careful specification of arithmetic operations, this ensured that a calculation which executed successfully in one environment would also execute successfully, and give the same results, in another. For reasons which need not be gone into here, the designers were not entirely successful in realizing their objectives; their achievement was nevertheless remarkable, and their successors on Cobol committees have perpetuated the emphasis on portability.

Few of the features outlined in this chapter are available in other programming languages. To achieve equivalent effects, programmers who use these languages usually have to attain some degree of mastery of operating system utilities and commands and of their interfaces with the programming language; when a program is run under a different operating system, this process of learning has to be repeated. Cobol programs are more portable partly because the range of facilities offered by the language itself is wider.

22.2 PORTABILITY OF PROGRAMS

The **environment division** of a Cobol program consists of a **configuration section** followed by an **input–output section**. Both these sections, and the individual paragraphs within them, are optional; so is the environment division itself. But most Cobol programs use files, so an **input–output section** is usually required except in some nested programs and small sub-programs.

The **configuration section** consists of three paragraphs. One of these describes the **source computer**—the machine on which the program is intended to be compiled. Another describes the **object computer**—the machine on which the compiled code is to be run. The language originally provided a means of specifying such information as memory size and program segmentation strategy; but nowadays these two paragraphs are rarely used except for specification of the program collating sequence, the use of which is described later in this chapter.

The third paragraph of the configuration section is called **special-names**. It may be used to equate names used in the program with those used by an implementor to identify hardware features of the system. The paragraph may also contain definitions of **symbolic characters** and **currency sign** and the **decimal point is comma** clause, all of which were explained in Chapter 20, **class** definitions as mentioned in Chapter 10, and **alphabet** definitions, which will be described later in this chapter.

The **input–output section** consists of two paragraphs. A **file-control** paragraph contains a **select** sentence for each file defined in the data division. A **select** sentence links a file-name used in the program with a name known to the operating system. It also specifies the organization and the access method, as well as possibly the buffering strategy, the file status data item, and other file-related information which will be discussed later in this chapter. The other paragraph of the input–output section, called **i–o-control**, specifies any sharing of main store areas between files (described in Chapter 23) as well as the allocation of multiple files to a single reel of magnetic tape.

Thoughtful comparison of the above features with those provided in the data division shows that the functional boundary between the environment and data divisions is not as satisfactory as it should be. A more logical allocation of features to these two divisions was proposed in drafts of the 1985 Standard but later abandoned.

Provision of an environment division is only one aspect of Cobol's facilities for portability. As we have seen, sorting and merging of files can be achieved simply, entirely within Cobol, and in a manner which is independent of machine and operating system. Another example is the provision of **source text manipulation** facilities.

Cobol source text is often wearisome to type or write; a programmer may like to use a personal shorthand (e.g. 'ik' for 'invalid key' and 'nik' for 'not invalid key') and to have it converted later to proper Cobol. Or perhaps the names of certain data items are to be changed. Cases of systematic text replacement such as these can be effected at compile time by use of **replace** statements in a program.

Another aspect of source text manipulation is the language's provision for the existence of 'Cobol libraries'—collections of named texts which are available to the compiler. A **copy** statement in a Cobol source program enables any text from any of these libraries to be incorporated into the source program at the point where the **copy** statement occurs. By use of a **replacing** option in the **copy** statement, systematic text replacement of the kind mentioned in the preceding paragraph may be included in the copying process.

Usually a data file is used by a number of different Cobol programs. It is therefore convenient to store Cobol descriptions of files, and perhaps common procedures for handling particular files, in a Cobol library. The descriptions and procedures can then be included in a program at compile time by use of **copy** statements.

Cobol applications often make use of the current date or time. In machines where this information is available, it can be obtained through the medium of Cobol without any need to use operating system commands. There are four reserved words which denote the following 'conceptual data items':

date: treated as though described by picture 9(6). The value of **date** is the current date in the form *yymmdd*, where *yy* is year within century, *mm* is month within year, and *dd* is day within month. For example, the value 880121 represents 21 January 1988.

day: treated as though described by picture 9(5). The value of **day** is the current date in the form *yyddd*, where *yy* is year within century and *ddd* is day within year. For example, the value 88034 represents 3 February 1988.

time: treated as though described by picture 9(8). The value of **time** is in the form *hhmmssdd*, where *hh* is the hour, *mm* the minute, *ss* the second, and *dd* the hundredth of a second. For example, the value 13052900 represents 1.05.29 p.m.

day-of-week: treated as though described by picture 9. The value of **day-of-week** is an integer representing the day of the week. The value 1 represents Monday, 2 represents Tuesday, and so on. The value 7 represents Sunday.

These items may be referenced only by an **accept** statement. In this context, **accept** behaves like a **move** statement, in accordance with the rules given earlier for **move** statements. For example, given the data item descriptions

x **pic** 9(6).
y **pic** 9(7).
z **pic** 99,99,99,99.

Then, at precisely 2.15 p.m. on 5 November 1987, execution of the statements

    accept *x* **from date**
    accept *y* **from date**
    accept *z* **from time**

would assign the strings

    871105
    0871105
    14,15,00,00

to *x*, *y*, and *z* respectively.

A major problem of program portability was mentioned in Chapter 2. Given a pair of character-strings to compare, a program in one machine may give a different result from the same program in another machine. As we saw, this is due to the fact that different machines may have different character collating sequences. Quite apart from the portability problem, a program may occasionally need to compare or sort alphanumeric data according to some sequence other than that implied by the machine's native collating sequence.

Cobol caters for these situations by allowing **alphabets** to be named and defined in the **special-names** paragraph of the environment division. In the clauses

> **alphabet** *ascii77* **is standard-1**
> **alphabet** *iso* **is standard-2**

the reserved words **standard-1** and **standard-2** represent respectively the ASCII and the (seven-bit) ISO Standard codes. (The implementor is allowed to introduce further reserved words indicating particular alphabets.) The effect of the above clauses is that the names *ascii77* and *iso* may be used in the program to refer to these encodings and to the collating sequence implied by them. The programmer may also define any other alphabet in the manner indicated by the following examples:

> **alphabet** *al* **is** "AaBbCc . . .
> defines a collating sequence *al* in which "A" is the first character, "a" is the second, and so on.

> **alphabet** *a2* **is** 1 **thru** 9, 31, 10 **thru** 30, 32 **thru** 256
> indicates that *a2* is the machine's native collating sequence, but with the thirty-first character in that sequence moved to the tenth position.

> **alphabet** *a3* **is** "#", 200
> indicates that *a3* is the machine's native collating sequence, but with "#" moved to the first position in the sequence and the two-hundredth character moved to the second position. All characters of the native collating sequence other than "#" and the two-hundredth character are assigned the remaining positions in the alphabet being defined and retain their original ordering. Thus, for example, the predecessor and the successor of "#" in the native collating sequence are adjacent in alphabet *a3*.

It is also possible to define an alphabet in which two or more characters have the same position in the collating sequence.

By themselves, alphabet definitions have no effect on a program. But the environment division may also contain a **program collating sequence** clause which names one of the alphabets, as in

> **program collating sequence is** *al*

the effect of which is that the collating sequence defined by alphabet *al* is used throughout the program (and any contained programs) in place of the native collating sequence. The graphic representation of **low-value** will be "A", and the following will be evaluated in terms of *al*:

(a) comparisons of alphanumeric data items (for instance, "A" is now less than "a", "B" is greater than "a", etc.);
(b) by default, key comparisons during execution of **sort** and **merge** statements;
(c) the ranges implied by the word **thru** in **evaluate** statements and in the **value** clauses of condition-name descriptions (level 88).

The collating sequence which is currently in force may be overridden by a **collating sequence** phrase in a **sort** statement or a **merge** statement. For example, to sort a file according to the ASCII collating sequence, the **sort** statement might include the phrase

> **collating sequence is** *ascii77*

where *ascii77* had been defined as shown earlier in this chapter.

22.3 PORTABILITY OF DATA

In the Cobol context, data portability is the ability to transfer a file from one machine to another, using the same file description in both machines. This can often be achieved with a sequentially organized file; but, because at a lower level Cobol implementations and operating systems have their own methods of file organization which underlie those of Cobol, it is perhaps unreasonable to expect to take an indexed file or a relative file unchanged to a new environment. To transfer such a file, we usually have to read the records sequentially, writing them to a sequential file; this file is then read in the new environment and the records are written sequentially to create an indexed file or a relative file there.

Sequential files on magnetic tape are often completely portable. Portability is made possible by the fact that Cobol records and their constituent data items are described as character strings. If a file is to be portable, data items of other kinds should not be present (e.g. **sync, comp**—see Chapter 23; signed items without a **sign is separate** clause—see Chapter 7). Such items are introduced into Cobol programs purely to improve efficiency—there is rarely any logical need for their presence. (Though the use of **sync** and **comp** compromises data portability between machines, it can be useful on a given machine in achieving data portability between Cobol and other languages.)

The **block contains** clause in a file description aids portability by describing how records are physically blocked in the file (see Chapter 23). Independent of Cobol, an international standard specifies how the lengths of variable-length records are to be indicated in magnetic tape files: in Cobol, this standard method can be referenced by a **record delimiter** clause in a file's **select** sentence. The **select** sentence also provides a **padding** clause specifying the character used to pad out blocks to a fixed length where this is appropriate to the storage medium.

Two machines between which a file is transferred may differ in their internal encodings of characters. Where a Cobol program has to read a file recorded in a character encoding other than the machine's native encoding, the program may arrange for translation to the native encoding to be performed automatically on input. Similarly, output sent to a file can be translated automatically to a non-native encoding. These translations are achieved by including, in the **fd** sentence for the file, a **code-set** clause which names a defined **alphabet**. For instance, if the environment division of a program contained

> **alphabet** *ascii77* **is standard-1**

and the data division contained

>   **fd** *stranger,* **code-set** *ascii77.*
>   01 . . .

then, if *stranger* were opened as an output file, all data written to that file would
be translated to ASCII code. This facility is available only for sequential files
and only for **standard-1**, **standard-2**, and implementor-defined alphabets.

Generally speaking, a Cobol programmer should wherever possible use only
the standard language, rejecting those features which are implementor-dependent.
It will then be relatively easy to transfer programs and files to a new environment.

23. Provisions for efficiency

23.1 INTRODUCTION

Many programs for commercial data processing handle vast quantities of data and are run for long periods daily over a number of years. It has therefore been important in the past to 'tune' programs, or critical parts of programs, to achieve reductions both in the space required for data storage and in execution time. Data storage costs are not yet so low that they can be disregarded, and acceptable response times for on-line work can sometimes be achieved by reducing the execution time of small parts of a program.

In programming generally, performance improvements are often achieved in a machine-dependent way by writing critical parts of programs in assembly language or by using operating system statements to control such things as blocking factors in files. By contrast, the Cobol philosophy has always been that tuning facilities should, as far as possible, be provided by Cobol itself. The existence of such facilities inevitably increases the size and complexity of the language, and their use can make programs less comprehensible; program portability is sometimes lost, for some aspects of tuning which are implementor-defined have a wider impact on the program as a whole.

In order to understand certain features of Cobol, it is necessary to appreciate the context in which Cobol was originally designed. Few machines were provided with any more than a minimum of operating system software. It was therefore essential that a high-level language which emphasized the use of files should contain provisions for a program to include in a file special information in the form of a 'file label' which identified that file. The **open** statement would write the label to an output file or check the label of an input, i–o, or extend file. The label would typically contain such information as the name of the file, the date on which it was written, and its generation number (to distinguish different files having the same name). Though file-labelling facilities are still provided for in Cobol, there are plans to remove the provision in the next version of the Cobol standard, on the ground that the functions provided are available through operating system commands.

Some people, however, argue that it should not be necessary for a programmer to learn operating system commands at all, since any 'operating system' facilities required by an application program should be made available in the language in which the bulk of the application is written. Operating system commands exist, this argument goes, to simplify the work of the language designer and the compiler writer at the expense of the application programmer. Language designers do not like the untidiness introduced by such considerations as multi-volume files, multi-file volumes, file labels, blocking factors, etc.; but such things do concern the application programmer. Newcomers to programming are perhaps right to wonder why they have to learn two languages ('application language' and 'operating system language') and they are justifiably puzzled by the seemingly arbitrary division of functions between the two.

But, however upsetting the incursion of operating system languages into the application area may be, it is a fact of life. For example, many a Cobol compiler will treat the **block contains** clause (discussed below) as 'documentation only' and will take all information about blocking from operating system commands.

23.2 BLOCKING AND BUFFERING

A Cobol programmer always views a record as being the *logical* unit of transfer between the computer's main store and the storage device on which a file resides. A **read, write, rewrite**, or **delete** statement operates on a single record. But behind the scenes, as it were, there may be a very different situation which is hidden from the application programmer. The *physical* unit of transfer between main store and a file storage device is a *block* (sometimes called a *physical record*, as opposed to a logical record). A block may consist of a single logical record or, more commonly, of a (not necessarily integral) number of logical records. From the software point of view, file processing would be simpler if a block always contained precisely one logical record, but there are good reasons why it often does not:

(a) Some storage devices have fixed-length blocks, and the block size may be very different from the size of a logical record in a given application.
(b) On devices on which the block size may be varied, large blocks each containing several records use the available storage space more economically than small blocks; they also give more efficient sequential access.

The designer of an application system must therefore decide, for each stored file, what the block size is to be. These decisions can be embodied in the file descriptions in a Cobol program without in any way affecting anything else in the program; the logical unit of transfer is still one logical record, and the code generated by the Cobol compiler ensures that any blocking or deblocking of records takes place automatically. A change in block size to improve efficiency does not involve any change in the program logic.

The block size for a file is specified by a **block contains** clause in the data division description of that file. Thus, for example, a file description might be

    fd *file-1*
       block contains 6 **records**.

Applied to a sequentially organized file, this specifies that there are six records in each block (except possibly the last block of the file). If *file-1* is opened as an **output** file, then the system will ensure that the **write** statements place the records in a six-record buffer area in main store and, when six **write** statements have been executed (or when the file is closed), the content of the buffer is written as a block to the file storage device. If *file-1* is opened as an **input** file, then the system will ensure that each block in turn is read into a buffer and that the records in that buffer are presented to the program one by one in response to **read** statements, the buffer being refilled when necessary.

Alternatively, the block size may be specified as a number of characters instead of a number of records. Thus

> **block contains** 2000 **characters**

specifies a fixed block length of 2000 characters. If every record in the file were 500 characters in length, then each block would contain four records. Variable-length blocks may be specified by stating the minimum and maximum sizes, as in

> **block contains** 2000 **to** 2200 **characters**

The **block contains** clause may be omitted when there is one logical record per block and/or the hardware device (or the implementor's software interface with the device) has a standard fixed block size.

A number of questions are raised by the ANSI Standard description of the **block contains** clause, and you would do well to consult your implementor's manual to see how the clause is interpreted. You may even find that your implementor treats the clause as 'for documentation only' and requires the block size to be specified by operating system commands.

Now suppose that a sequential file called *file2* has five records per block. The compiler may arrange that, when *file2* is opened as an input file, the first block is read into the buffer. The first

> **read** *file2*

statement executed will result in the first record in the buffer being presented to the program, the second such statement executed will result in the second record being presented, and so on. After the fifth record has been presented, execution of the sixth **read** statement may take a considerable time, since no record can be presented to the program until the buffer has been refilled. The delay arises from the fact that typically the time to obtain a block from the file storage device exceeds the processing time for the last record in the preceding block. In a multi-programming environment, therefore, control will regularly be lost to other programs, and in a dedicated machine run time will be longer than it need be for a program which processes a large file.

In order to increase the efficiency of such a program, *double buffering* may be used. Two buffers, say *a* and *b*, are allocated to a file so that, while records in *a* are being processed, the next block is being read into *b*; and, while the records in *b* are being processed, the next block is being read into *a*. The time to read a block is thus shared with the processing of all records, rather than just the last record, of the preceding block. Irregularities of processing time can sometimes be evened out by allocating more than two buffers to a file. In general, the technique is known as *multiple buffering*. Similar considerations apply to output files.

The number of buffers allocated to a file may be specified by a **reserve** clause in the file's **select** sentence. To achieve double buffering for *file2*, the environment division might include:

> **select** *file2;* **assign to** . . .
>> **organization sequential**
>> **reserve** 2 **areas**.

If no **reserve** clause is specified for à file, the implementor determines the number of buffers allocated.

23.3 SHARING OF STORAGE AREAS

Consider the data and procedure divisions shown in Figure 23.1. The program makes a copy of *a-file*, naming the copy *b-file*. (Both files are, by default, sequentially organized and accessed.) Every record, after reading, has to be moved from storage area *a-rec* to storage area *b-rec*. In order to avoid such copying and (historically) to save space in main store, it is possible to specify that two or more files are to share a common record area. In the example of Figure 23.1, *a-rec* and *b-rec* would then be different names for the same area of main store; *b-rec* would be a redefinition of *a-rec*.

To achieve this effect, a **same record area** entry would be used in an optional paragraph of the environment division known as **i–o-control**. The complete environment division might then be that shown in Figure 23.2; the data and

```
data division.
file section.

fd a-file.
01 a-rec  pic x(200).

fd b-file.
01 b-rec  pic x(200).

working-storage section.
01 a-end  pic x.


procedure division.
main.
    open input a-file, output b-file
    perform, with test after, until a-end = "t"
        read a-file next
          at end
             move "t" to a-end
          not at end
             move "f" to a-end
             move a-rec to b-rec
             write b-rec
        end-read
    end-perform
    stop run.
```

Figure 23.1: A simple file-copying program

```
environment division.
input-output section.
file-control.
    select a-file   assign to ...
        reserve 2 areas.
    select b-file   assign to ...
        reserve 2 areas.
i-o-control.
    same record area for a-file, b-file.
```

Figure 23.2: An environment division for the program of Figure 23.1. The **same record area** *clause enables the procedure division statement* **move** *a-rec* **to** *b-rec to be omitted*

---

procedure divisions would remain as shown in Figure 23.1, except that the statement

> **move** *a-rec* **to** *b-rec*

would be omitted. (Notice, by the way, that the **reserve** clauses specify double buffering.) In general, any number of files may share a single record area.

It is possible for two or more files to share not only a common record area but also common storage for input–output buffers and file control information. Such sharing can be achieved by listing the file-names in a **same area** clause. Thus, if the clause

> **same area for** *x, y*

appears in the **i–o-control** paragraph, then the areas of main store used in connection with accesses to file *x* will also be used in connection with accesses to file *y*; in particular, there will not be separate buffer areas for the two files. Files *x* and *y* must never be open at the same time during program execution; the reason for this rule should be obvious. The **same area** clause, then, enables space in main store to be saved when it is known that only one of the files concerned will be open at any given time. This facility was important in the days when main store was a scarce and expensive resource.

23.4 SYNCHRONIZATION OF DATA ITEMS

The Cobol programmer sees computer storage as a sequence of character positions. At the hardware level, however, the storage in some machines is arranged as a sequence of *words*; a word can typically contain several characters. A 'word' in this context is not a Cobol word, nor is it a word in the normal everyday sense. It is a fixed-length unit of storage by which main store is addressed and accessed at the hardware level. Machine language instructions may operate exclusively on words, or on words and half-words, or on words, half-words, and double-words. Better machine languages provide facilities for addressing either words or characters at the programmer's choice. If a machine provides for addressing and manipulation of character-strings, Cobol can usually be implemented reasonably efficiently.

When the Cobol view of store is mapped on to a word-oriented machine, even a simple **move** statement can generate quite a few machine instructions. Consider the following:

01 *a*.
    02 *b* **pic** xxx.
    02 *c* **pic** xxx.
    02 *d* **pic** xx.

In Cobol terms, nothing could be simpler than the statement

    move *b* **to** *c*

yet consider what has to happen if this statement is compiled on a machine which does not have reasonable character-handling facilities. Suppose the machine is such that four characters can be accommodated in a word. Then *a* will be mapped on to two words, as shown in Figure 23.3(a) (most implementors arrange to map the first character of a record to the first character position of a word).

If you are familiar with machine-level programming, you will appreciate that, with a single-accumulator architecture, the statement

    move *b* **to** *c*

can result in the Cobol compiler generating something like fifteen machine instructions. Contrast the situation if *b* and *c* are instead mapped as shown in Figure 23.3(b). The **move** statement will now generate only one machine instruction if storage-to-storage operations are provided, or two instructions if a register or an accumulator must be used.

The second of these two mappings can be achieved in Cobol by describing the record thus:

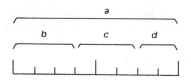

(a) Storage mapping of a record description with unsynchronized data items. The record occupies two four-character words.

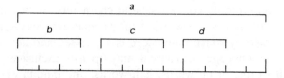

(b) Storage mapping using left-synchronization. The record occupies three four-character words.

Figure 23.3: Effect of synchronization

01 *a*.
    02 *b* **pic** xxx **sync left**.
    02 *c* **pic** xxx **sync left**.
    02 *d* **pic** xx **sync left**.

The word **sync** is an abbreviation of **synchronized**. The storage allocated to a synchronized data item is always an integral number of words; any character positions in the allocated words which are not required for storage of the data item are treated as unnamed data items, so that the length of *a* implied by the above description is 12 characters. Only elementary items may be synchronized.

Synchronization of data items, properly used, can have a significant effect on execution time, but it undermines the basis of data structures in Cobol and removes the possibility of transporting a program to a machine with a different storage architecture. Notice, in the example given above, that:

(a) the length of *a* is now greater than the sum of the lengths of *b*, *c*, and *d*; furthermore, this must be borne in mind in any redefinition of *a*;
(b) the record area *a* contains four 'garbage' characters;
(c) if the program were transported to a machine which had six character positions in each word, the length of *a* would be increased by six character positions and there would be *ten* garbage characters in the record area.

For these reasons, use of synchronized data items is best avoided unless it is absolutely necessary for efficiency or for transfer of a file from a program written in a different language.

23.5 REPRESENTATIONS OF NUMERIC DATA

So far, we have considered any numeric value stored in the computer's main store or in a file as being represented as a string of characters, each character in the string being a decimal digit, and the scaling being indicated by a picture. This representation is, of course, eminently suited to data presented to a program from the outside world, or presented to the outside world by a program. It also enables programmers to think of numbers in an entirely natural way and to predict easily the accuracy of arithmetic operations. There is not usually any need for a Cobol programmer to consider any other representation of numbers.

At the hardware level, regrettably, many computers cannot perform arithmetic directly on numbers which are represented as character strings. In many machines, the operands in arithmetic operations must be represented in binary form. Typically, a machine may offer a choice between fixed-point binary and floating-point binary representation and may additionally, for either or both of these, offer a choice of operand size (half-word for integers, full-word or double-word for integers and reals). Some machines also provide for arithmetic to be performed on operands in *packed decimal* representation. (The number of bits required to represent any of the decimal digits 0 to 9 is four; if a character position in store is eight bits in length, then it can accommodate two digits, rather than one. In packed decimal representation, a number is stored in decimal form in consecutive character positions with two digits per character position and one of the 'half-character' positions used for sign representation.) These various forms will be referred to as **computational** representations.

If a machine cannot perform arithmetic on operands which are represented as character-strings, then a Cobol compiler for that machine must convert the operands to an appropriate form. For example, execution of the Cobol statement

    add *a* **to** *b*

includes the following steps:

(a) convert operand *a* from character-string representation to a computational representation in some temporary storage location;
(b) convert operand *b* similarly;
(c) add the two values and store the result in some temporary storage location;
(d) convert the result to character-string representation and store it as the new value of operand *b*.

While machines differ in the degree of efficiency with which they can perform these conversions, the conversions typically take several times as long to execute as the addition operation itself. For this reason, Cobol provides a facility for defining numeric data items in such a way that their values are stored not as character-strings but in some suitable computational form.

This form of data item is defined by data division entries such as

    01 *x* **pic** s9(7)v9 **comp**.
    01 *y* **pic** s999 **binary**.
    01 *z* **pic** s9(5) **packed decimal**.

(The word **comp** is a standard abbreviation for **usage computational** or **usage comp**, **binary** for **usage binary**, **packed decimal** for **usage packed decimal**. Programmers rarely use the longer forms.) Some implementors employ also non-standard usages like **comp-1**, **comp-2**, etc. Implementors decide (on the basis of machine architecture and of the range of values indicated by an item's picture) precisely what representations of the numbers will be used, and may or may not choose to apply automatic synchronization to such items. Your implementor's manual will tell you what form of representation is used for each combination of usage and picture.

In arithmetic and conditional expressions, data items having any of these computational representations may be freely mixed with each other and with data items in character-string form, and most Cobol statements can have operands with different representations. Any necessary conversions are done during program execution.

In some cases a computational representation may use less storage than a character-string representation; this can be important with large files on disk storage. The other major advantage of using computational representations is the execution time saved by avoiding conversions which would otherwise be needed for arithmetic operations. The saving can be considerable when a lot of calculation is done by a program.

These advantages are bought at the cost of increased complexity and decreased portability of data and programs. As with synchronized items, you cannot know the size of a group item which contains computational items unless you know which Cobol compiler is to be used; you cannot sensibly use **inspect** or **unstring** statements on such group items; you cannot transport data files containing computational items from one Cobol implementation to a different one; and a program which uses computational items may give rise to subtle execution-time errors if taken unchanged to a different compiler. Where possible it is best to use character-string representation for all data. Other representations should be introduced only when there is a clear need for the improvements they offer.

23.6 EFFICIENT ARRAY ACCESSING

When a procedure division statement refers to an item of an array, 'behind-the-scenes' arithmetic usually takes place to convert a subscript to a storage address. Data items used in subscripts are therefore prime candidates for computational usage. But Cobol also provides a special **index** usage exclusively for accessing array items.

Opinions differ on the value of this facility and of other language features associated with it. The small attention given to it here reflects the author's view that the quite minimal functional enhancement to Cobol which indexing offers does not merit the complexities for which it is responsible in the language specification. The main contribution of indexing is in the area of run-time efficiency. With the passing years this becomes less important while the advantage of using an internally consistent programming language becomes more widely recognized.

An index may be associated with any dimension of an array. The specification

    02 *x* **pic** 9(5), **occurs** 50, **indexed by** *i*.

defines *i* as an index for *x*. No further definition of *i* is needed (or, indeed, permitted). The **index-name**, *i*, must be unique in the program. Similarly

    02 *y* **occurs** 50, **indexed by** *j*.

defines *j* as an index for *y*. It is also possible to define index data items which are not associated with particular arrays (for use, perhaps, for temporary storage of array index values), as in

    01 *k* **index**.

(**Index** is a standard abbreviation for **usage index**; there must be no picture clause with this usage.) But indexes and index data items are subject to very circumscribed operations. For instance, they cannot appear as operands in **move** statements; instead, the **set** statement must be used, as in

    set *j* **to** *i*

which assigns the value of *i* to *j*.

The operands of this form of **set** statement must be indexes or index data items, except that the operand following **to** may instead be an integer or a data item whose picture indicates that it is an integer, as in

    set *k* **to** 1

or

>   **set** *i* **to** *n*

where *n* has a picture like 99.

The normal arithmetic statements cannot be used with index or index data item operands. Instead, to add 3 to *j*, we must say

>   **set** *j* **up by** 3

and, to subtract 3 from *j*, we must say

>   **set** *j* **down by** 3

We cannot use arithmetic expressions, and only very restricted use may be made of comparisons. Subject to certain restrictions, an index-name may be used in a **perform varying** statement.

To set against all its restrictions and peculiarities, indexing offers two advantages—a gain in efficiency of subscripting and the use of the **search** statement. Since each implementor may represent an index in the manner most suitable to the array and to the hardware concerned, subscripts in the form of index-names should give faster access to array items than those in the form of data-names. A subscript involving the use of an index may be *either* the index-name associated with the array or that index-name with addition or subtraction of an integer literal. Thus one of the items *x*, as defined above, could be accessed by references such as *x* (*i*) or *x* (*i* + 4) or *x* (*i* − 5). References like *x* (*k*) and *x* (*i* + *j*) are not permitted.

The **search** statement can search an array for an item which satisfies any specified condition or any one of a number of specified conditions. It allows the embedded specification of statements which are to be executed in the event of such an item being found, and of those to be executed if such an item is not found. The search is performed serially through the array, but need not start at the first item.

A variant form (**search all**) can be used to effect a binary search (or, as the Standard puts it, 'a non-serial type of search') on the items of an array for an item satisfying a specified condition. Such a search, of course, presupposes that the items are ordered on the values of 'key' subordinate items and that the condition specified involves these subordinate items. The ordering must be specified in the description of the array. For example, Figure 23.4 shows a description of an array containing details of a timetable arranged in ascending order of destination and, within each destination, in ascending order of departure

```
01   trains.
     02 train occurs 200
            ascending key dest
            ascending key dep-time
            indexed by t-ind.
        03 dep-time  pic 9(4).
        03 dest      pic x(15).
        03 t-details pic x(51).
```

Figure 23.4:   Description of an ordered array

```
search all train
    at end
        display "No train"
    when dest (t-ind) = "Dundee" and dep-time (t-ind) = 0800
        display dep-time (t-ind), " to ", dest (t-ind)
        display t-details (t-ind)
end-search
```

*Figure 23.5:   A **search all** statement for the array of Figure 23.4*

---

time. To display details of the 8 a.m. service to Dundee, a program might use the **search** statement shown in Figure 23.5.

These **search** statements are undoubtedly useful, but a competent programmer can easily achieve equivalent effects without using them. The main advantage they offer is that a compiler writer can arrange for efficient object code to be generated.

24 The 1974 Cobol Standard

24.1 INTRODUCTION

You may find that you have to use an old Cobol compiler or that you have to modify old Cobol programs written by someone else. If so, it is important that you be aware of the major differences between the 1974 Standard and the 1985 Standard.

This is mainly a matter of knowing which features of 1985 Cobol were not present in 1974 Cobol, since the differences are mainly additions made to the language in 1985. Most programs written for 1974 compilers will run successfully after compilation by an 1985 compiler; but a few ambiguities in the 1974 Standard were resolved in 1985 in a manner which may be inconsistent with the interpretation applied by some 1974 compilers. A complete list of the differences between the standards can be found in the 1985 Standard. Many of these are at a level of detail not reached by this book. The object of this chapter is to list the more important limitations of 1974 Cobol.

You will notice that only upper-case letters are used in the 1974 Cobol examples in this chapter. Whatever individual compilers may have done, the 1974 Standard did not allow the use of lower-case letters except in non-numeric literals. Also, in order to compare the two versions of Cobol realistically, no changes of typeface are used in the examples.

24.2 CONTROL STRUCTURES

It was in its control structures that the 1974 Standard was most seriously deficient. The following features of 1985 Cobol were not available:

(1) explicit scope terminators (**end-if**, **end-perform**, etc.);
(2) alternatives to exception conditions (**not at end**, **not size error**, etc.);
(3) in-line **perform**;
(4) **perform with test after**;
(5) **evaluate**.

24.2.1 EXPLICIT SCOPE TERMINATORS

Throughout this book, two conventions of programming style have been adopted:

(a) any Cobol statement which contained other statements has been terminated by an explicit scope terminator. For example, **if** statements have been

terminated by **end-if**, and **compute** statements with **size error** phrases have
been terminated by **end-compute**;

(b) full stops (i.e. periods) have never been used between statements within a
paragraph.

When we use 1974 Cobol we have to abandon these conventions, for 1974 Cobol
has no explicit scope terminators. Statements which contain other statements can
be terminated only by a full stop or by the ELSE of an enclosing IF statement.

Let us start with the IF statement. (Notice, by the way, that the word **then**,
which is optional in 1985 Cobol, is not allowed at all in 1974 Cobol; some 1974
compilers, however, do accept it.) Figure 24.1 shows a program fragment written
in 1985 Cobol and 1974 Cobol. You will see that in 1974 Cobol the IF statements
are terminated by full stops instead of **end-if**.

Because Cobol was originally designed to be a specialized form of 'English',
an important syntactic unit was the 'sentence'. A sentence, of course, is terminated
by a single full stop, not by two or more. Thus the full stop shown in the 1974
version in Figure 24.2 terminates both the IF C1 and IF C3 statements. In general,
a full stop in 1974 Cobol terminates all statements which have not so far been
terminated. (This is still true in 1985 Cobol and it is the reason why this book
shows full stops in the procedure division at the ends of paragraphs only. Use of
full stops *within* paragraphs is extremely dangerous and should be avoided.)

As a compiler scans a 1974 Cobol program, it matches each ELSE with the
most recent (unterminated) IF for which no ELSE has yet been encountered. In
Figure 24.2, therefore, the IFs and ELSEs are matched in the manner implied
by the indentation. Notice that the ELSE corresponding to IF C1 acts as a
terminator for the statement which begins IF C2. The three IF statements in
Figure 24.2 are therefore terminated as follows:

(1) IF C1: by the full stop;
(2) IF C2: by the ELSE of IF C1;
(3) IF C3: by the full stop.

These rules can give rise to very 'unnatural' programming. Consider the 1985
Cobol program fragment shown in Figure 24.3. If we are to write an equivalent
piece of program in 1974 Cobol (i.e. without **end-if**), how are we to terminate
the statement beginning IF C2? (Clearly we have to indicate somehow that ADD
B TO C is not part of that statement.) It does not come immediately before the

```
if    c1                                    IF    C1
then add 1 to a                                   ADD 1 TO A
     add 1 to b                                   ADD 1 TO B.
end-if                                      IF    C2
if    c2                                           ADD B TO A
then add b to a                             ELSE ADD A TO B.
else add a to b                             MOVE 0 TO B
end-if
move 0 to b


      (1985 Cobol)                                 (1974 Cobol)
```

Figure 24.1

```
if    c1                           IF    C1
then move 1 to a                         MOVE 1 TO A
     if    c2                            IF    C2
     then move 1 to b                          MOVE 1 TO B
     else move 2 to b                    ELSE MOVE 2 TO B
          move 2 to c                         MOVE 2 TO C
     end-if                        ELSE MOVE 2 TO A
else move 2 to a                         IF    C3
     if    c3                                  MOVE 0 TO B
     then move 0 to b                    ELSE MOVE 1 TO B.
     else move 1 to b              MOVE 0 TO D
     end-if
end-if
move 0 to d


         (1985 Cobol)                        (1974 Cobol)
```

Figure 24.2

```
if    c1                           IF    C1
then move 1 to a                         MOVE 1 TO A
     if    c2                            PERFORM TEST-C2
     then move 1 to b                    ADD B TO C
     else move 2 to b              ELSE MOVE 2 TO A
          move 2 to c                    IF    C3
     end-if                                    MOVE 0 TO B
     add b to c                               PERFORM TEST-C4
else move 2 to a                              MOVE B TO C.
     if    c3
     then move 0 to b             -
          if    c4                -
          then add 1 to b    TEST-C2.
          end-if                  IF    C2
          move b to c                   MOVE 1 TO B
     end-if                       ELSE MOVE 2 TO B
end-if                                   MOVE 2 TO C.
                             TEST-C4.
                                   IF    C4
                                       ADD 1 TO B.


         (1985 Cobol)                        (1974 Cobol)
```

Figure 24.3

ELSE of IF C1, so that ELSE cannot terminate it; and, if we insert a full stop
before ADD B TO C, the full stop will terminate not only the IF C2 statement
but also the IF C1 statement. In short, there is no way of textually nesting the
IF C2 within the IF C1. One way to solve the problem is shown in the 1974
Cobol version in Figure 24.3—remove the inner IF to a procedure and replace
it by a PERFORM. This has the undesirable effect that the final modular structure
of a program is partly the result of a deficiency in the language syntax. The
program usually becomes unduly fragmented. Alternative solutions based on GO
TO exist, but most people today seem to prefer the use of PERFORM.

    A further consequence of the 1974 syntax is exemplified in Figure 24.4. The
rule for matching IF with ELSE implies that every nested IF has a corresponding

```
if   c1                                IF    C1
then if   c2                                 IF    C2
         then add 1 to a                           ADD 1 TO A
         end-if                                ELSE NEXT SENTENCE
else move 0 to a                       ELSE MOVE 0 TO A.
end-if                                 DISPLAY A
display a


        (1985 Cobol)                          (1974 Cobol)
```

Figure 24.4

ELSE. Where this is not the case, as in this example, the words ELSE NEXT SENTENCE must be inserted in order to ensure correct matching.

Conditional statements other than IF may also be nested within an IF statement. The scopes of these other statements too are terminated by a full stop or by the ELSE of an enclosing IF. Thus, in the 1974 version of Figure 24.5, the ADD statement is terminated by ELSE and the READ statement by the full stop which also terminates the IF. When such a statement is to be nested but would not immediately precede ELSE or a full stop, it can be removed to a PERFORMed procedure, as shown in Figure 24.6.

Except for an IF statement, no conditional statement in 1974 Cobol may contain another conditional statement (i.e. another statement which itself contains further statements). Thus a READ statement cannot, for example, contain (within its AT END or INVALID KEY phrase) an IF, a further READ with either of these phrases, or a COMPUTE with a SIZE ERROR phrase. Once again we are driven to PERFORM a procedure, as in Figure 24.7.

24.2.2 ALTERNATIVES TO EXCEPTION CONDITIONS

Most of Cobol's so-called 'conditional statements' are concerned with the detection of 'exception conditions', such as **at end, invalid key, size error**, and **overflow**. Cobol standards before 1985 made no provision for the inclusion of statements to be executed in the event of the exception condition *not* arising. Thus in 1974 Cobol there is no provision for such phrases as **not at end, not invalid key, not**

```
if   c1                                IF    C1
then add 1 to a                            ADD 1 TO A
         size error move 1 to s                SIZE ERROR MOVE 1 TO S
         end-add                         ELSE MOVE 1 TO B
else move 1 to b                           READ X
         read x                                INVALID KEY MOVE 1 TO K.
         invalid key move 1 to k
         end-read
end-if


        (1985 Cobol)                          (1974 Cobol)
```

Figure 24.5

```
if   c1                              IF    C1
then add 1 to a                            PERFORM INC-A
       size error move 1 to s             MOVE 0 TO P
     end-add                       ELSE MOVE 1 TO B
     move 0 to p                         PERFORM INP-X
else move 1 to b                          MOVE 0 TO Q.
     read x                             -
       invalid key move 1 to k          -
     end-read                           -
     move 0 to q                 INC-A. ADD 1 TO A
end-if                                   SIZE ERROR MOVE 1 TO S.
                                 INP-X. READ X
                                         INVALID KEY MOVE 1 TO K.



       (1985 Cobol)                        (1974 Cobol)
```
Figure 24.6

```
    read x; invalid key                   READ X; INVALID KEY
        if   c2                               PERFORM TEST-C2.
        then display a                       -
        end-if                               -
    end-read                                -
                                 TEST-C2. IF   C2
                                             DISPLAY A.



         (1985 Cobol)                        (1974 Cobol)
```
Figure 24.7

---

size error, and **not overflow**—statements like READ, COMPUTE, and STRING may therefore resemble an IF statement without an ELSE.

This limitation can be overcome by appending to the statement an IF statement which provides the 'two-way branch' required. Figure 24.8 shows how this can be done, using a 'flag' variable called I-K. The flag here is introduced purely to overcome a syntactic limitation of the language; it creates no confusion, and its textual scope is four lines of code. A single variable can safely be used for all such situations in the program. Notice that the READ and IF statements of Figure 24.8 are terminated by full stops. So, if this solution were adopted in a

---

```
    read x; invalid key                   MOVE "F" TO I-K
        add a to y                        READ X; INVALID KEY
        display d                             MOVE "T" TO I-K.
      not invalid key                     IF I-K = "T"
        add b to y                            ADD A TO Y
        display c                             DISPLAY D
    end-read                              ELSE ADD B TO Y
    add 1 to y                                DISPLAY C.
                                          ADD 1 TO Y



         (1985 Cobol)                        (1974 Cobol)
```
Figure 24.8

nested situation, the MOVE, READ, and IF statements would be displaced into a PERFORMed procedure.

24.2.3 IN-LINE PERFORM

In 1974 Cobol, all PERFORM statements call procedures. There is no in-line PERFORM. This is particularly irksome in the case of a PERFORM VARYING statement, when the initialization and incrementation of the control variable have to be textually separated from its use. See Figure 24.9.

24.2.4 TESTING TERMINATING CONDITIONS

In 1974 Cobol, there is no **with test after** phrase in a PERFORM statement. Figure 24.10 shows how an equivalent effect can be achieved.

24.2.5 MULTI-BRANCH MULTI-JOIN STRUCTURES

Such a structure is provided in 1985 Cobol by the **evaluate** statement. There is no **evaluate** in 1974 Cobol but, as we have seen in Chapter 19, an equivalent effect can be achieved by use of nested IF statements.

24.3 CONDITIONAL EXPRESSIONS

We saw in Section 13.5 how 1985 Cobol evaluates a conditional expression. The 1974 Standard did not specify an order of evaluation for a single level of precedence. It would be dangerous, therefore, to present the expression

$$B = 0 \quad OR \quad A / B > 3.5$$

```
perform varying i from 1 by 1          PERFORM T-CLEAR VARYING I
    until i > 10                           FROM 1 BY 1 UNTIL I > 10
      add a (i) to t                        -
      move 0 to a (i)                       -
end-perform                                 -
                                       T-CLEAR.  ADD A (I) TO T
                                                 MOVE 0 TO A (I).


       (1985 Cobol)                         (1974 Cobol)
```

Figure 24.9

```
perform proc-x with test after         PERFORM PROC-X
    until c2                           PERFORM PROC-X UNTIL C2


       (1985 Cobol)                         (1974 Cobol)
```

Figure 24.10

to a 1974 compiler. The only means of ensuring safe evaluation is to use nested IFs. These cannot, of course, be used in the UNTIL phrase of a PERFORM; Figure 24.11 demonstrates the complexity which has to be introduced to get round the problem. If the required loop had not been of the **with test after** variety, it would have been necessary to repeat the pair of IFs before the PERFORM statement; 1974 Cobol shares this awkwardness with other languages, including Pascal.

In 1974 Cobol, there is no provision for a **class** condition to be defined in a program (see Section 10.4). The classes **alphabetic-upper** and **alphabetic-lower** are also missing.

1974 Cobol does not provide the operators $<=$ and $>=$. Equivalent effects are of course obtained by using NOT $>$ and NOT $<$ respectively.

24.4 PROCEDURE DIVISION STATEMENTS

The **evaluate**, **initialize**, and **continue** statements are not available in 1974 Cobol. The effect of a **continue** (i.e. do nothing) can be obtained by PERFORMing an empty paragraph, as illustrated in Figure 24.12, where the empty paragraph is P-2. (Notice again in this example the fragmenting effect of having no in-line PERFORM.)

```
perform with test after until            PERFORM P-X
   b = 0    or   a / b > 3.5             PERFORM P-X UNTIL X1 = "T"
      compute a = a + 1                   -
      compute b = b - 1                   -
end-perform                               -
                                 P-X. COMPUTE A = A + 1
                                      COMPUTE B = B - 1
                                      IF    B = 0
                                           MOVE "T" TO X1
                                      ELSE IF    A / B > 3.5
                                                MOVE "T" TO X1
                                           ELSE MOVE "F" TO X1.


      (1985 Cobol)                        (1974 Cobol)
```

Figure 24.11

```
accept d                                 ACCEPT D
perform until d = "end"                  PERFORM P-1 UNTIL D = "end"
   perform varying n from 1 by 1          -
      until dc (n) = space                -
         continue               ,         -
   end-perform                    P-2.
   display n                      P-1. PERFORM P-2 VARYING N FROM 1
   accept d                               BY 1 UNTIL DC (N) = SPACE
end-perform                             DISPLAY N
                                        ACCEPT D.


      (1985 Cobol)                        (1974 Cobol)
```

Figure 24.12

Several other statements, though available, are less powerful in 1974 Cobol:

(a) a SORT or MERGE statement can have only one destination file and that file must have sequential organization; input and output procedures must be SECTIONs; and the SORT statement has no **duplicates** phrase;

(b) 'de-editing' MOVE statements (i.e. MOVE from an edited numeric item to an ordinary numeric item) are not permitted;

(c) an EXIT PROGRAM statement must be the only statement in a paragraph;

(d) it is not possible to SET a condition-name (i.e. a level 88 name) to TRUE (see Section 20.6);

(e) there is no statement ACCEPT DAY-OF-WEEK.

This list is by no means exhaustive, but it covers the cases most likely to be of practical interest.

24.5 STRING HANDLING

In 1974 Cobol, there is no provision for reference modification (see Section 16.3). To achieve equivalent effects, the data item concerned should be redefined as an array of characters; subscripting can then be used in place of reference modification but the programming is likely to be more complex.

There is no **converting** option in the 1974 version of the INSPECT statement. The same effect can be achieved using INSPECT REPLACING, as shown in Figure 24.13.

24.6 INTER-PROGRAM RELATIONSHIPS

Programs cannot be nested in 1974 Cobol and therefore data items and files cannot be **global**. There is also no provision for **external** data items and files.

There are no **initial** programs in 1974 Cobol. The effect of an **initial** program can be obtained by preceding each CALL by a CANCEL statement.

All parameters are passed by reference in 1974 Cobol, so the phrases **by reference** and **by content** cannot be included in a CALL statement. In 1974 Cobol it is required that all parameters passed in a CALL statement are level 01 (or level 77—see below) data items and that they are not subscripted.

Because 1974 Cobol has no nested programs, it is not unreasonable that it requires the presence of all four divisions (identification, environment, data, and procedure) in every program. Less reasonably perhaps, it also requires the

```
      inspect m converting              INSPECT M REPLACING
          "abc" to "def"                    ALL "a" BY "d"
                                            ALL "b" BY "e"
                                            ALL "c" BY "f"


          (1985 Cobol)                      (1974 Cobol)
```

Figure 24.13

environment division to include a configuration section; the configuration section, in turn, must include SOURCE-COMPUTER and OBJECT-COMPUTER paragraphs. Many compilers, however, simply ignore these paragraphs; the implementor's manual should be consulted.

24.7 DATA ITEM DESCRIPTIONS

When you look at a 1974 Cobol program written by someone else, you may be surprised to see data items with level number 77. This is a redundant feature of Cobol, since a level 77 item is the same as an *elementary* level 01 item. However, 77 cannot be substituted for 01 in the file section of the data division.

Unnamed data items are not permitted in 1974 Cobol; the reserved word FILLER must be used in place of a name. Instead of writing

        02   pic x(5)

we write

        02 FILLER PIC X(5)

but the word FILLER cannot be used elsewhere to refer to this (or any other) data item. Also, when a data item A redefines another item B, both must be the same length. This involves using a FILLER to extend the shorter item to the length of the longer one, as in Figure 24.14.

In 1974 Cobol, data items cannot be described as **binary** or **packed-decimal**. This does not mean that such representations are excluded; usually the implementor provides a variation of COMP (like COMP-1 or COMP-2) for each representation of numeric data which the compiler can handle.

24.8 ARRAYS

In 1985 Cobol an array is allowed to have up to seven dimensions, but in 1974 Cobol the limit is three dimensions. Thus the maximum depth of nesting of OCCURS clauses is three, as is the maximum number of subscripts following a data-name.

In 1974 Cobol, the description

        02 A OCCURS 0 TO 5 DEPENDING ON B

```
02  a   pic x(5).                02  A   PIC X(5).
02  b   redefines a, pic 9(4).   02  B-1 REDEFINES A.
                                 03  B   PIC 9(4).
                                 03  FILLER  PIC X.


        (1985 Cobol)                     (1974 Cobol)
```

Figure 24.14

is not permitted, but

    02 A OCCURS 1 TO 5 DEPENDING ON B

is, because the integer following the word OCCURS must be non-zero and positive. This limitation proved to be so restrictive that some 1974 compilers accept the first of these forms.

In 1985 Cobol, the description

    01 y.
        02 z occurs 3 pic x value "*".

causes each of the items z(1), z(2), and z(3) to have the initial value "*". But in 1974 Cobol a VALUE clause cannot appear in the same description as an OCCURS clause, nor in the description of any data item subordinate to an item with an OCCURS clause. Initial values of array elements have to be specified at a higher level, as in

    01 Y   VALUE   ALL "*".
        02   Z   OCCURS   3   PIC   X.

Finally, where a data item is used as a subscript, 1974 Cobol does not allow addition or subtraction of an integer. For example, the operation expressed in 1985 Cobol as

    move space to a (n + 1)

would, in 1974 Cobol, have to be written in another way, such as

    COMPUTE P = N + 1
    MOVE SPACE TO A (P)

24.9 FILES

In relation to files, the major differences you will find when you use the 1974 Standard are these:

(1) In the file section of the data division, the description (FD) of every file must include a clause which says either

    LABEL RECORDS STANDARD

or

    LABEL RECORDS OMITTED

Usually the former is specified when the file is stored internally (e.g. on disk or magnetic tape) and the latter when the file is assigned to an external device (e.g. a printer or a terminal).

(2) There is no provision for the use of a data item to indicate the size of a record which is to be written or which has been read. The clause

    record varying . . . depending on . . .

cannot therefore be used in a file description.

(3) Relative files and indexed files cannot be opened in EXTEND mode.

(4) A REWRITE statement must send to the file a record of the same length as the record being replaced. (In 1985 Cobol, this restriction applies only to sequential files; in 1974 Cobol, it applies to *all* files.)

(5) The values assigned to a FILE STATUS data item at the time of a file operation are different from those in 1985 Cobol.

24.10 SUMMARY

This chapter has not listed all the differences between the two standards. It includes only those which you are likely to meet in practice during your early grapplings with 1974 Cobol. There are other differences at a lower level of detail, and some of them are quite subtle. If you are doing serious programming in 1974 Cobol, you should consult an appropriate manual or textbook.

25. The structure of the 1985 Standard

As 1985 Cobol is a large language, it would be unrealistic to expect every implementor to provide everything in it. Accordingly, the Standard specifies three subsets of the language—minimum, intermediate, and high.

The facilities of the language are divided into functional 'modules':

(a) Nucleus (i.e. the 'core' of the language);
(b) Sequential I–O;
(c) Relative I–O;
(d) Indexed I–O;
(e) Inter-program Communication (**call**, **cancel**, nested programs, etc.);
(f) Sort-merge;
(g) Source Text Manipulation (**copy**, **replace**, etc.).

The Sort-merge module must be implemented in full or not at all, but each of the other required modules may be implemented at level 1 or at level 2. Level 2 offers full facilities of the module and level 1 a subset of the facilities. For instance, level 1 of the Relative I–O and Indexed I–O modules have no dynamic access and no **start** statement. The level 1 limitations of each module are detailed in the 1985 Standard.

The **minimum subset** consists of the Nucleus, Sequential I–O, and Inter-program Communication, all at level 1. The **intermediate subset** consists of the Sort-merge module together with the other six modules all at level 1. The **high subset** consists of the Sort-merge module together with the other six modules all at level 2.

This book has described the major facilities offered by the modules listed above, which the Standard calls the 'required modules'. The Standard also specifies four 'optional modules', any or all of which may be included in an implementation, regardless of which of the three subsets is implemented. The four optional modules are:

(a) Report Writer;
(b) Communication;
(c) Debug;
(d) Segmentation.

The Report Writer must be implemented in full or not at all, but each of the other three modules may be implemented at level 1 or level 2.

The Report Writer provides a facility for producing reports by specifying the physical appearance of a report and the sources of its data, rather than the

243

detailed procedure necessary to produce that report. It takes care of such features as headings and footings, control breaks, subtotals, and totals. The basic difference between a program which uses the Report Writer and one which does not is that in the former the data division is larger and the procedure division smaller, since most of the program requirement is stated in a declarative, rather than an algorithmic, way. Additional procedure division statements **initiate**, **generate**, and **terminate** make reference to the report description written in the data division.

You will find the Report Writer described in a separate section of the Standard or your implementor's manual. Its use can be mastered quickly if you already know the basics of Cobol. Learning to use it can be a worthwhile investment if you often have to prepare report-writing programs in Cobol—it greatly simplifies such tasks as page layout, control of page changes, and totalling. But, if you are not using it regularly, you are likely to forget its details and to use those language features that are of more general application.

The Communication module provides the ability to access, process, and create messages or parts of messages, interfacing through a message control system with communication devices. It thus acts as an interface between a Cobol program and a network of communication devices, taking care of such tasks as dial-up, polling, and synchronization. The Communication module of 1974 Cobol was not widely implemented.

The Debug and Segmentation modules are obsolete parts of Cobol. The ANSI Standard Committee has declared that they will not be included in the next Cobol standard.

It is important therefore, if you are buying a Cobol implementation, to be aware of what your supplier is offering. Is it the minimum, the intermediate, or the high subset? Which optional modules, if any, are provided, and at what level? What extensions are provided for areas not covered by standard Cobol—is there, for instance, an extension for database access?

Whatever implementation of 1985 Cobol you choose, you will have a language which is a considerable advance on a comparable implementation of 1974 Cobol.

Appendix 1: A simplified guide to the details of Cobol syntax

INTRODUCTION

This appendix does not describe the full syntax of the language. The general form of a program should be apparent from the main chapters; each of the higher-level syntactic units, such as a file description or an individual procedure division statement, has its own syntax, details of which can be found in Appendix 3. What usually troubles beginners is the *detailed* syntax. 'Do I need a space here?' 'How do I continue this to the next line?' 'At what position in the line can I start this statement?' These are questions to which a beginner, even armed with a manual, often cannot quickly find answers.

Even the aspects decribed here are not exhaustively treated, and the definitions given are, for the sake of brevity, less rigorous than those in the ANSI Standard. This guide should, however, be all that is needed in most programming situations.

DETAILS

(1) The major symbols of the language are:

Words: A Cobol **word** consists of up to 30 characters, all of which are significant. Permissible characters are the hyphen (-), the upper-case letters A to Z, the lower-case letters a to z, and the digits 0 to 9. Lower-case letters are equivalent to the corresponding upper-case letters. A word must contain at least one letter (except when used as a procedure-name) and must not begin or end with a hyphen. A word is either a **reserved word** (i.e. a word which has a special meaning in the language, such as pic, add, read, end) or a **user-defined word** (e.g. a word used as a file-name, a data-name, or a procedure-name). A user-defined word can be any character string which conforms to the above definition of a word but is not a reserved word. Reserved words are not distinguished typographically from user-defined words. Appendix 2 lists the reserved words in standard Cobol; your implementor may have added a few more.

In the ANSI Standard, the operators $=$, $+$, $-$, $*$, $/$, $**$, $<$, $>$, $<=$ and $>=$ are regarded as reserved words of a special kind called 'special character words'.

Non-numeric literals: A non-numeric literal is a string of characters starting and ending with a quotation mark (the single character "). In a non-numeric literal, upper-case and lower-case letters are distinct characters. There are special rules for the continuation of a non-numeric literal from one line to another—see

(4) below. An embedded quotation mark is represented by two contiguous quotation marks.

Numeric literals: A numeric literal is a number written in conventional notation, i.e. consisting of numeric digits optionally preceded by a sign (+ or −) and optionally containing one decimal point (period). A decimal point must not be the last character of a numeric literal.

Picture character strings: A picture character string (referred to in this book as a 'picture') is used in the description of an elementary data item. A picture follows the word 'pic' and is separated from it by one or more spaces. A picture is followed by one or more spaces or by one of the separators—period, semicolon, and comma—followed by one or more spaces (see (2) below). Within a picture, normal syntax rules do not apply. Thus, in the context of a picture, 999 is not regarded as a numeric literal, nor is a comma or a period regarded as a separator—spaces cannot occur within a picture.

(2) A program can be regarded as a sequence of the above 'symbols' (and a few more), with **separators** between one and the next. Usually the separator used consists of one space or, equivalently, two or more consecutive spaces. Any arithmetic or relational operator must be immediately preceded by at least one space and immediately followed by at least one space. Notice that

$$-1$$

is a numeric literal and

$$-\ a$$

consists of a unary operator followed by a data-name; the intervening space separator is therefore necessary in the latter case.

A comma (,) or a semi-colon (;), when either of them is immediately followed by at least one space, is equivalent to a space separator. These characters may be inserted for readability; they have no semantic effect and they need never be used.

A period (.), immediately followed by at least one space, is a separator which has semantic significance. It is used as the terminator of some higher-level syntactic units. In the procedure division of a program, the period separator must appear after each paragraph-name (at the head of a paragraph) and at the end of each paragraph. Due to the history of the language, it is dangerous to use a period anywhere else in the procedure division, except after the division heading and section headings. Throughout this book, all periods shown in program examples are obligatory.

Left and right parentheses are also defined as separators in the ANSI Standard. They have semantic significance—properly paired, they enclose sub-expressions, subscripts, etc. A left or a right parenthesis, or a sequence of either left or right parentheses, may optionally be immediately preceded by one or more spaces and/ or immediately followed by one or more spaces. A right parenthesis, or a sequence of right parentheses, may be followed by any other separator described here.

(3)   A Cobol program is presented to a compiler as a sequence of lines, every line consisting of character positions numbered serially from 1. The implementor decides how many character positions there are in a line. (Sometimes this number

is smaller than the number of character positions in a *physical* line on an input medium. But usually a line is what a programmer at a terminal would expect it to be.) The format of a line is:

(a) positions 1 to 6: 'sequence number' area;
(b) position 7: indicator area;
(c) positions 8 to 11: area A;
(d) positions 12 to end: area B.

The sequence number area is present for historical reasons associated with punched cards, and its content does not form part of the Cobol program. Most programmers today do not use the sequence number area; some compilers, indeed, allow us to dispense with this area altogether and to regard position 1 as the indicator area.

The indicator area is used for indicating continuation (-), comments (*, /), and 'debugging lines' (D).

Program code is normally written in area B only, but the following language elements must start in area A (i.e. at position 8, 9, 10, or 11):

(a) division and section headings (e.g. **data division**, **file section**);
(b) paragraph-names at heads of paragraphs (e.g. **program-id**, **file-control**, and the paragraph-names in the procedure division);
(c) **fd**, **sd**, **rd**, **cd**;
(d) level number 01.

Level numbers other than 01 may start in area A or area B. (For readability, indentation by level number is nearly always used in practice, but it is not required.)

Statements need not be written one per line, and a statement may continue from one line to the next. Since each procedure division statement starts with a reserved word, there are no general statement separators or terminators in the procedure division.

(4) Normally one additional space character is assumed to be present at the end of each line of a program. Thus the program fragment (a) shown in Figure A1.1 is syntactically correct—the **stop run** statement is followed by a separator consisting of a period and a space.

Examples (b) and (c) show two syntactically correct fragments (though not a recommended method of program layout!), which are logically equivalent.

Example (d), again syntactically correct, shows the effects of placing a hyphen in the indicator area:

(i) the normal additional space character is *not* provided at the end of the preceding line;
(ii) the last character of the preceding line is regarded as immediately preceding *the first non-space character* in area B of the line in which the hyphen appears, thus enabling indentation to be maintained.

The above facilities are in general little used, for they hamper readability. But continuation of a **non-numeric literal** from one line to the next is often unavoidable. (A literal which is to function as a heading for printed output, for example, may

```
    I A    B
(a)                                          write mr        stop run.
      proc1.
            move a to b

(b)         move "report" to print-line    write print-line after
            page

(c)  .      move "report"
                  to print-line
            write print-line after page

(d)           move "report" to print-line    write print-line af
     -        ter page
```

Figure A1.1: Formatting of Cobol procedure division statements

be longer than area B of a program line.) To enable indentation to be maintained, a further quotation mark is required immediately before the first character of the literal's continuation. See Figure A1.2. (For clarity, Figures A1.1 and A1.2 show fixed-length lines; lines input from a terminal will normally be of variable length.)

```
    I A    B

            if    details-reqd
            then move "The number of retail outlets in England a
     -                "nd Wales is " to print-line
```

Figure A1.2: Continuation of a non-numeric literal

An asterisk (∗) in the indicator area denotes that the line is a comment. Any characters may appear in a comment line, which has no effect on program compilation or execution.

An oblique (/) in the indicator area has the same effect as an asterisk, but additionally causes a page throw to take place before the line is printed on a program listing. The programmer can thus have complete control over the pagination of listings.

Blank lines may be inserted in a program to improve the layout of the listing. A blank line is treated as a sequence of spaces and cannot be inserted immediately before a line which has a hyphen in the indicator area.

Appendix 2: Cobol reserved words

ACCEPT
ACCESS
ADD
ADVANCING
AFTER
ALL
ALPHABET
ALPHABETIC
ALPHABETIC-LOWER
ALPHABETIC-UPPER
ALPHANUMERIC
ALPHANUMERIC-EDITED
ALSO
ALTER
ALTERNATE
AND
ANY
ARE
AREA
AREAS
ASCENDING
ASSIGN
AT
AUTHOR

BEFORE
BINARY
BLANK
BLOCK
BOTTOM
BY

CALL
CANCEL
CD
CF
CH
CHARACTER
CHARACTERS
CLASS
CLOCK-UNITS
CLOSE
COBOL
CODE
CODE-SET
COLLATING
COLUMN
COMMA
COMMON
COMMUNICATION
COMP
COMPUTATIONAL
COMPUTE

CONFIGURATION
CONTAINS
CONTENT
CONTINUE
CONTROL
CONTROLS
CONVERTING
COPY
CORR
CORRESPONDING
COUNT
CURRENCY

DATA
DATE
DATE-COMPILED
DATE-WRITTEN
DAY
DAY-OF-WEEK
DE
DEBUG-CONTENTS
DEBUG-ITEM
DEBUG-LINE
DEBUG-NAME
DEBUG-SUB-1
DEBUG-SUB-2
DEBUG-SUB-3
DEBUGGING
DECIMAL-POINT
DECLARATIVES
DELETE
DELIMITED
DELIMITER
DEPENDING
DESCENDING
DESTINATION
DETAIL
DISABLE
DISPLAY
DIVIDE
DIVISION
DOWN
DUPLICATES
DYNAMIC

EGI
ELSE
EMI
ENABLE
END
END-ADD
END-CALL
END-COMPUTE

END-DELETE
END-DIVIDE
END-EVALUATE
END-IF
END-MULTIPLY
END-OF-PAGE
END-PERFORM
END-READ
END-RECEIVE
END-RETURN
END-REWRITE
END-SEARCH
END-START
END-STRING
END-SUBTRACT
END-UNSTRING
END-WRITE
ENTER
ENVIRONMENT
EOP
EQUAL
ERROR
ESI
EVALUATE
EVERY
EXCEPTION
EXIT
EXTEND
EXTERNAL

FALSE
FD
FILE
FILE-CONTROL
FILLER
FINAL
FIRST
FOOTING
FOR
FROM

GENERATE
GIVING
GLOBAL
GO
GREATER
GROUP

HEADING
HIGH-VALUE
HIGH-VALUES

I-O

I-O-CONTROL
IDENTIFICATION
IF
IN
INDEX
INDEXED
INDICATE
INITIAL
INITIALIZE
INITIATE
INPUT
INPUT-OUTPUT
INSPECT
INSTALLATION
INTO
INVALID
IS

JUST
JUSTIFIED

KEY

LABEL
LAST
LEADING
LEFT
LENGTH
LESS
LIMIT
LIMITS
LINAGE
LINAGE-COUNTER
LINE
LINE-COUNTER
LINES
LINKAGE
LOCK
LOW-VALUE
LOW-VALUES

MEMORY
MERGE
MESSAGE
MODE
MODULES
MOVE
MULTIPLE
MULTIPLY

NATIVE
NEGATIVE
NEXT

NO	QUOTE	SELECT	THRU
NOT	QUOTES	SEND	TIME
NUMBER		SENTENCE	TIMES
NUMERIC	RANDOM	SEPARATE	TO
NUMERIC-EDITED	RD	SEQUENCE	TOP
	READ	SEQUENTIAL	TRAILING
OBJECT-COMPUTER	RECEIVE	SET	TRUE
OCCURS	RECORD	SIGN	TYPE
OF	RECORDS	SIZE	
OFF	REDEFINES	SORT	UNIT
OMITTED	REEL	SORT-MERGE	UNSTRING
ON	REFERENCE	SOURCE	UNTIL
OPEN	REFERENCES	SOURCE-COMPUTER	UP
OPTIONAL	RELATIVE	SPACE	UPON
OR	RELEASE	SPACES	USAGE
ORDER	REMAINDER	SPECIAL-NAMES	USE
ORGANIZATION	REMOVAL	STANDARD	USING
OTHER	RENAMES	STANDARD-1	
OUTPUT	REPLACE	STANDARD-2	VALUE
OVERFLOW	REPLACING	START	VALUES
	REPORT	STATUS	VARYING
PACKED-DECIMAL	REPORTING	STOP	
PADDING	REPORTS	STRING	WHEN
PAGE	RERUN	SUB-QUEUE-1	WITH
PAGE-COUNTER	RESERVE	SUB-QUEUE-2	WORDS
PERFORM	RESET	SUB-QUEUE-3	WORKING-STORAGE
PF	RETURN	SUBTRACT	WRITE
PH	REVERSED	SUM	
PIC	REWIND	SUPPRESS	ZERO
PICTURE	REWRITE	SYMBOLIC	ZEROES
PLUS	RF	SYNC	ZEROS
POINTER	RH	SYNCHRONIZED	
POSITION	RIGHT		+
POSITIVE	ROUNDED	TABLE	−
PRINTING	RUN	TALLYING	*
PROCEDURE		TAPE	/
PROCEDURES	SAME	TERMINAL	**
PROCEED	SD	TERMINATE	>
PROGRAM	SEARCH	TEST	<
PROGRAM-ID	SECTION	TEXT	=
PURGE	SECURITY	THAN	>=
	SEGMENT	THEN	<=
QUEUE	SEGMENT-LIMIT	THROUGH	

Appendix 3: Cobol language formats

GENERAL FORMAT FOR IDENTIFICATION DIVISION

IDENTIFICATION DIVISION.

PROGRAM-ID. program-name $\left[\text{IS} \left\{ \left| \begin{matrix} \underline{\text{COMMON}} \\ \underline{\text{INITIAL}} \end{matrix} \right| \right\} \text{PROGRAM} \right]$.

[AUTHOR. [comment-entry] ...]

[INSTALLATION. [comment-entry] ...]

[DATE-WRITTEN. [comment-entry] ...]

[DATE-COMPILED. [comment-entry] ...]

[SECURITY. [comment-entry] ...]

GENERAL FORMAT FOR ENVIRONMENT DIVISION

[ENVIRONMENT DIVISION.

[CONFIGURATION SECTION.

[SOURCE-COMPUTER. [computer-name [WITH DEBUGGING MODE].]]

[OBJECT-COMPUTER. [computer-name

$$\left[\text{MEMORY SIZE integer-1} \left\{ \begin{array}{l} \text{WORDS} \\ \text{CHARACTERS} \\ \text{MODULES} \end{array} \right\} \right]$$

[PROGRAM COLLATING SEQUENCE IS alphabet-name-1]

[SEGMENT-LIMIT IS segment-number].]]

[SPECIAL-NAMES. [[implementor-name-1

$$\left\{ \begin{array}{l} \text{IS mnemonic-name-1 [ON STATUS IS condition-name-1 [OFF STATUS IS condition-name-2]]} \\ \text{IS mnemonic-name-2 [OFF STATUS IS condition-name-2 [ON STATUS IS condition-name-1]]} \\ \underline{\text{ON}} \text{ STATUS IS condition-name-1 [OFF STATUS IS condition-name-2]} \\ \underline{\text{OFF}} \text{ STATUS IS condition-name-2 [ON STATUS IS condition-name-1]} \end{array} \right\} \dots$$

[ALPHABET alphabet-name-1 IS

$$\left\{ \begin{array}{l} \underline{\text{STANDARD-1}} \\ \underline{\text{STANDARD-2}} \\ \underline{\text{NATIVE}} \\ \text{implementor-name-2} \\ \left\{ \text{literal-1} \left[\left\{ \begin{array}{l} \underline{\text{THROUGH}} \\ \underline{\text{THRU}} \end{array} \right\} \text{literal-2} \\ \{\underline{\text{ALSO}} \text{ literal-3}\} \dots \right] \right\} \dots \end{array} \right\} \dots \right]$$

$$\left[\underline{\text{SYMBOLIC}} \text{ CHARACTERS} \left\{ \left\{ \{\text{symbolic-character-1}\} \dots \left\{ \begin{array}{l} \text{IS} \\ \text{ARE} \end{array} \right\} \{\text{integer-1}\} \dots \right\} \dots \right. \right.$$

$$\left. \left. [\underline{\text{IN}} \text{ alphabet-name-2}] \right\} \right] \dots$$

$$\left[\underline{\text{CLASS}} \text{ class-name-1 IS} \left\{ \text{literal-4} \left[\left\{ \begin{array}{l} \underline{\text{THROUGH}} \\ \underline{\text{THRU}} \end{array} \right\} \text{literal-5} \right] \right\} \dots \right] \dots$$

[CURRENCY SIGN IS literal-6]

[DECIMAL-POINT IS COMMA].]]]

GENERAL FORMAT FOR ENVIRONMENT DIVISION

[INPUT-OUTPUT SECTION.

FILE-CONTROL.

    {file-control-entry} ...

[I-O-CONTROL.

$$\left[\left[\text{RERUN }\left[\underline{\text{ON}}\ \left\{\begin{array}{l}\text{file-name-1}\\\text{implementor-name-1}\end{array}\right\}\right]\ \text{EVERY}\ \left\{\begin{array}{l}\left\{[\underline{\text{END}}\ \text{OF}]\left\{\begin{array}{l}\underline{\text{REEL}}\\\underline{\text{UNIT}}\end{array}\right\}\right\}\text{OF file-name-2}\\\text{integer-1 }\underline{\text{RECORDS}}\\\text{integer-2 }\underline{\text{CLOCK-UNITS}}\\\text{condition-name-1}\end{array}\right\}\right]\ \dots\right.$$

$$\left[\underline{\text{SAME}}\ \left[\begin{array}{l}\text{RECORD}\\\text{SORT}\\\text{SORT-MERGE}\end{array}\right]\ \text{AREA FOR file-name-3 }\{\text{file-name-4}\}\ \dots\ \right]\ \dots$$

    [MULTIPLE FILE TAPE CONTAINS {file-name-5 [POSITION integer-3]} ...] ... .]]]]

GENERAL FORMAT FOR FILE CONTROL ENTRY

SEQUENTIAL FILE:

SELECT [OPTIONAL] file-name-1

   ASSIGN TO $\left\{ \begin{matrix} \text{implementor-name-1} \\ \text{literal-1} \end{matrix} \right\}$ ...

   $\left[\underline{\text{RESERVE}} \text{ integer-1} \left[\begin{matrix} \text{AREA} \\ \text{AREAS} \end{matrix} \right] \right]$

   [[ORGANIZATION IS] SEQUENTIAL]

   $\left[\underline{\text{PADDING}} \text{ CHARACTER IS } \left\{ \begin{matrix} \text{data-name-1} \\ \text{literal-2} \end{matrix} \right\} \right]$

   $\left[\underline{\text{RECORD}} \underline{\text{ DELIMITER}} \text{ IS } \left\{ \begin{matrix} \underline{\text{STANDARD-1}} \\ \text{implementor-name-2} \end{matrix} \right\} \right]$

   [ACCESS MODE IS SEQUENTIAL]

   [FILE STATUS IS data-name-2].

RELATIVE FILE:

SELECT [OPTIONAL] file-name-1

   ASSIGN TO $\left\{ \begin{matrix} \text{implementor-name-1} \\ \text{literal-1} \end{matrix} \right\}$ ...

   $\left[\underline{\text{RESERVE}} \text{ integer-1} \left[\begin{matrix} \text{AREA} \\ \text{AREAS} \end{matrix} \right] \right]$

   [ORGANIZATION IS] RELATIVE

   $\left[\underline{\text{ACCESS}} \text{ MODE IS } \left\{ \begin{matrix} \underline{\text{SEQUENTIAL}} \text{ [\underline{RELATIVE} KEY IS data-name-1]} \\ \left\{ \begin{matrix} \underline{\text{RANDOM}} \\ \underline{\text{DYNAMIC}} \end{matrix} \right\} \underline{\text{RELATIVE}} \text{ KEY IS data-name-1} \end{matrix} \right\} \right]$

   [FILE STATUS IS data-name-2].

GENERAL FORMAT FOR FILE CONTROL ENTRY

INDEXED FILE:

SELECT [OPTIONAL] file-name-1

   ASSIGN TO $\begin{Bmatrix} \text{implementor-name-1} \\ \text{literal-1} \end{Bmatrix}$ ...

   $\left[\text{RESERVE integer-1} \begin{bmatrix} \text{AREA} \\ \text{AREAS} \end{bmatrix} \right]$

   [ORGANIZATION IS] INDEXED

   $\left[\text{ACCESS MODE IS} \begin{Bmatrix} \text{SEQUENTIAL} \\ \text{RANDOM} \\ \text{DYNAMIC} \end{Bmatrix} \right]$

   RECORD KEY IS data-name-1

   [ALTERNATE RECORD KEY IS data-name-2 [WITH DUPLICATES]] ...

   [FILE STATUS IS data-name-3].

SORT OR MERGE FILE:

SELECT file-name-1 ASSIGN TO $\begin{Bmatrix} \text{implementor-name-1} \\ \text{literal-1} \end{Bmatrix}$ ... .

GENERAL FORMAT FOR FILE CONTROL ENTRY

REPORT FILE:

SELECT [OPTIONAL] file-name-1

   ASSIGN TO $\begin{Bmatrix} \text{implementor-name-1} \\ \text{literal-1} \end{Bmatrix}$ ...

   $\left[\text{RESERVE integer-1} \begin{bmatrix} \text{AREA} \\ \text{AREAS} \end{bmatrix} \right]$

   [[ORGANIZATION IS] SEQUENTIAL]]

   $\left[\text{PADDING CHARACTER IS} \begin{Bmatrix} \text{data-name-1} \\ \text{literal-2} \end{Bmatrix} \right]$

   $\left[\text{RECORD DELIMITER IS} \begin{Bmatrix} \text{STANDARD-1} \\ \text{implementor-name-2} \end{Bmatrix} \right]$

   [ACCESS MODE IS SEQUENTIAL]

   [FILE STATUS IS data-name-2].

<u>GENERAL FORMAT FOR DATA DIVISION</u>

[<u>DATA</u> <u>DIVISION</u>.

[<u>FILE</u> <u>SECTION</u>.

$$\begin{bmatrix} \text{file-description-entry \{record-description-entry\} ...} \\ \text{sort-merge-file-description-entry \{record-description-entry\} ...} \\ \text{report-file-description-entry} \end{bmatrix} ... \Bigg]$$

[<u>WORKING-STORAGE</u> <u>SECTION</u>.

$$\begin{bmatrix} \text{77-level-description-entry} \\ \text{record-description-entry} \end{bmatrix} ...$$

[<u>LINKAGE</u> <u>SECTION</u>.

$$\begin{bmatrix} \text{77-level-description-entry} \\ \text{record-description-entry} \end{bmatrix} ...$$

[<u>COMMUNICATION</u> <u>SECTION</u>.

[communication-description-entry [record-description-entry] ...] ...]

[<u>REPORT</u> <u>SECTION</u>.

[report-description-entry {report-group-description-entry} ...] ...]]

GENERAL FORMAT FOR FILE DESCRIPTION ENTRY

SEQUENTIAL FILE:

FD   file-name-1

   [IS EXTERNAL]

   [IS GLOBAL]

$$\left[\text{BLOCK CONTAINS [integer-1 } \underline{\text{TO}} \text{] integer-2 } \left\{ \begin{array}{l} \underline{\text{RECORDS}} \\ \text{CHARACTERS} \end{array} \right\} \right]$$

$$\left[\underline{\text{RECORD}} \left\{ \begin{array}{l} \text{CONTAINS integer-3 CHARACTERS} \\ \text{IS } \underline{\text{VARYING}} \text{ IN SIZE [[FROM integer-4] [}\underline{\text{TO}} \text{ integer-5] CHARACTERS]} \\ \qquad \text{[}\underline{\text{DEPENDING}} \text{ ON data-name-1]} \\ \text{CONTAINS integer-6 } \underline{\text{TO}} \text{ integer-7 CHARACTERS} \end{array} \right\} \right]$$

$$\left[\underline{\text{LABEL}} \left\{ \begin{array}{l} \underline{\text{RECORD}} \text{ IS} \\ \underline{\text{RECORDS}} \text{ ARE} \end{array} \right\} \left\{ \begin{array}{l} \underline{\text{STANDARD}} \\ \underline{\text{OMITTED}} \end{array} \right\} \right]$$

$$\left[\underline{\text{VALUE}} \ \underline{\text{OF}} \ \left\{ \text{implementor-name-1 IS } \left\{ \begin{array}{l} \text{data-name-2} \\ \text{literal-1} \end{array} \right\} \right\} \ \dots \right]$$

$$\left[\underline{\text{DATA}} \left\{ \begin{array}{l} \underline{\text{RECORD}} \text{ IS} \\ \underline{\text{RECORDS}} \text{ ARE} \end{array} \right\} \ \{ \text{data-name-3} \} \ \dots \right]$$

$$\left[\underline{\text{LINAGE}} \text{ IS } \left\{ \begin{array}{l} \text{data-name-4} \\ \text{integer-8} \end{array} \right\} \text{ LINES } \left[\text{WITH } \underline{\text{FOOTING}} \text{ AT } \left\{ \begin{array}{l} \text{data-name-5} \\ \text{integer-9} \end{array} \right\} \right] \right.$$

$$\left. \left[\text{LINES AT } \underline{\text{TOP}} \left\{ \begin{array}{l} \text{data-name-6} \\ \text{integer-10} \end{array} \right\} \right] \left[\text{LINES AT } \underline{\text{BOTTOM}} \left\{ \begin{array}{l} \text{data-name-7} \\ \text{integer-11} \end{array} \right\} \right] \right]$$

   [CODE-SET IS alphabet-name-1].

GENERAL FORMAT FOR FILE DESCRIPTION ENTRY

RELATIVE FILE:

<u>FD</u> file-name-1

   [IS <u>EXTERNAL</u>]

   [IS <u>GLOBAL</u>]

$$
\left[\underline{BLOCK}\ CONTAINS\ [integer\text{-}1\ \underline{TO}]\ \ integer\text{-}2\ \left\{ \begin{array}{l} \underline{RECORDS} \\ CHARACTERS \end{array} \right\} \right]
$$

$$
\left[\underline{RECORD} \left\{ \begin{array}{l} CONTAINS\ integer\text{-}3\ CHARACTERS \\ IS\ \underline{VARYING}\ IN\ SIZE\ [[FROM\ integer\text{-}4]\ [\underline{TO}\ integer\text{-}5]\ CHARACTERS] \\ \qquad [\underline{DEPENDING}\ ON\ data\text{-}name\text{-}1] \\ CONTAINS\ integer\text{-}6\ \underline{TO}\ integer\text{-}7\ CHARACTERS \end{array} \right\} \right]
$$

$$
\left[\underline{LABEL} \left\{ \begin{array}{l} \underline{RECORD}\ IS \\ \underline{RECORDS}\ ARE \end{array} \right\} \left\{ \begin{array}{l} \underline{STANDARD} \\ \underline{OMITTED} \end{array} \right\} \right]
$$

$$
\left[\underline{VALUE}\ \underline{OF} \left\{ implementor\text{-}name\text{-}1\ IS \left\{ \begin{array}{l} data\text{-}name\text{-}2 \\ literal\text{-}1 \end{array} \right\} \right\} \dots \right]
$$

$$
\left[\underline{DATA} \left\{ \begin{array}{l} \underline{RECORD}\ IS \\ \underline{RECORDS}\ ARE \end{array} \right\} \ \{data\text{-}name\text{-}3\} \dots \right].
$$

GENERAL FORMAT FOR FILE DESCRIPTION ENTRY

INDEXED FILE:

<u>FD</u> file-name-1

   [IS <u>EXTERNAL</u>]

   [IS <u>GLOBAL</u>]

$$
\left[\underline{BLOCK}\ CONTAINS\ [integer\text{-}1\ \underline{TO}]\ \ integer\text{-}2\ \left\{ \begin{array}{l} \underline{RECORDS} \\ CHARACTERS \end{array} \right\} \right]
$$

$$
\left[\underline{RECORD} \left\{ \begin{array}{l} CONTAINS\ integer\text{-}3\ CHARACTERS \\ IS\ \underline{VARYING}\ IN\ SIZE\ [[FROM\ integer\text{-}4]\ [\underline{TO}\ integer\text{-}5]\ CHARACTERS] \\ \qquad [\underline{DEPENDING}\ ON\ data\text{-}name\text{-}1] \\ CONTAINS\ integer\text{-}6\ \underline{TO}\ integer\text{-}7\ CHARACTERS \end{array} \right\} \right]
$$

$$
\left[\underline{LABEL} \left\{ \begin{array}{l} \underline{RECORD}\ IS \\ \underline{RECORDS}\ ARE \end{array} \right\} \left\{ \begin{array}{l} \underline{STANDARD} \\ \underline{OMITTED} \end{array} \right\} \right]
$$

$$
\left[\underline{VALUE}\ \underline{OF} \left\{ implementor\text{-}name\text{-}1\ IS \left\{ \begin{array}{l} data\text{-}name\text{-}2 \\ literal\text{-}1 \end{array} \right\} \right\} \dots \right]
$$

$$
\left[\underline{DATA} \left\{ \begin{array}{l} \underline{RECORD}\ IS \\ \underline{RECORDS}\ ARE \end{array} \right\} \ \{data\text{-}name\text{-}3\} \dots \right].
$$

GENERAL FORMAT FOR FILE DESCRIPTION ENTRY

SORT-MERGE FILE:

SD file-name-1

```
┌                                                                              ┐
│           ⎧ CONTAINS integer-1 CHARACTERS                                  ⎫ │
│           ⎪ IS VARYING IN SIZE [[FROM integer-2] [TO integer-3] CHARACTERS]⎪ │
│  RECORD   ⎨      [DEPENDING ON data-name-1]                                 ⎬ │
│           ⎪ CONTAINS integer-4 TO integer-5 CHARACTERS                     ⎪ │
│           ⎩                                                                 ⎭ │
│  ┌                                                     ┐                      │
│  │       ⎧ RECORD IS   ⎫                               │                      │
│  │ DATA  ⎨ RECORDS ARE ⎬  {data-name-2} ...            │  .                   │
│  │       ⎩             ⎭                               │                      │
│  └                                                     ┘                      │
└                                                                              ┘
```

SORT-MERGE FILE:

SD file-name-1

REPORT FILE:

FD file-name-1

   [IS EXTERNAL]

   [IS GLOBAL]

```
┌                                                       ⎧ RECORDS    ⎫ ┐
│ BLOCK CONTAINS  [integer-1 TO]   integer-2 ⎨ CHARACTERS ⎬ │
└                                                       ⎩            ⎭ ┘
```

```
┌          ⎧ CONTAINS integer-3 CHARACTERS              ⎫ ┐
│ RECORD   ⎨ CONTAINS integer-4 TO integer-5 CHARACTERS ⎬ │
└          ⎩                                            ⎭ ┘
```

```
┌        ⎧ RECORD IS   ⎫ ⎧ STANDARD ⎫ ┐
│ LABEL  ⎨ RECORDS ARE ⎬ ⎨ OMITTED  ⎬ │
└        ⎩             ⎭ ⎩          ⎭ ┘
```

```
┌                                      ⎧ data-name-1 ⎫   ┐
│ VALUE OF  ⎨ implementor-name-1 IS ⎨ literal-1   ⎬ ⎬ ... │
└                                      ⎩             ⎭   ┘
```

   [CODE-SET IS alphabet-name-1]

```
⎧ REPORT IS   ⎫
⎨ REPORTS ARE ⎬  {report-name-1} ...    .
⎩             ⎭
```

GENERAL FORMAT FOR DATA DESCRIPTION ENTRY

FORMAT 1:

```
level-number  ⎡data-name-1⎤
              ⎣FILLER     ⎦

    [REDEFINES data-name-2]

    [IS EXTERNAL]

    [IS GLOBAL]

    ⎡⎧PICTURE⎫  IS character-string⎤
    ⎢⎩PIC    ⎭                     ⎥

    ⎡            ⎛BINARY        ⎞⎤
    ⎢            ⎜COMPUTATIONAL ⎟⎥
    ⎢[USAGE IS]  ⎜COMP          ⎟⎥
    ⎢            ⎜DISPLAY       ⎟⎥
    ⎢            ⎜INDEX         ⎟⎥
    ⎣            ⎝PACKED-DECIMAL⎠⎦

    ⎡[SIGN IS] ⎧LEADING ⎫ [SEPARATE CHARACTER]⎤
    ⎣          ⎩TRAILING⎭                     ⎦

    ⎡OCCURS integer-2 TIMES                                          ⎤
    ⎢                                                                ⎥
    ⎢     ⎡⎧ASCENDING ⎫ KEY IS  {data-name-3} ... ⎤ ...              ⎥
    ⎢     ⎣⎩DESCENDING⎭                           ⎦                  ⎥
    ⎢                                                                ⎥
    ⎢        [INDEXED BY {index-name-1} ... ]                        ⎥
    ⎢                                                                ⎥
    ⎢OCCURS integer-1 TO integer-2 TIMES DEPENDING ON data-name-4    ⎥
    ⎢                                                                ⎥
    ⎢     ⎡⎧ASCENDING ⎫ KEY IS  {data-name-3} ... ⎤ ...              ⎥
    ⎢     ⎣⎩DESCENDING⎭                           ⎦                  ⎥
    ⎢                                                                ⎥
    ⎣        [INDEXED BY {index-name-1} ... ]                        ⎦

    ⎡⎧SYNCHRONIZED⎫ ⎡LEFT ⎤⎤
    ⎣⎩SYNC        ⎭ ⎣RIGHT⎦⎦

    ⎡⎧JUSTIFIED⎫ RIGHT⎤
    ⎣⎩JUST     ⎭      ⎦

    [BLANK WHEN ZERO]

    [VALUE IS literal-1].
```

<u>GENERAL FORMAT FOR DATA DESCRIPTION ENTRY</u>

<u>FORMAT 2</u>:

66 data-name-1 <u>RENAMES</u> data-name-2 $\left[\left\{ \begin{array}{l} \underline{THROUGH} \\ \underline{THRU} \end{array} \right\} \text{ data-name-3} \right]$.

<u>FORMAT 3</u>:

88 condition-name-1 $\left\{ \begin{array}{l} \underline{VALUE} \text{ IS} \\ \underline{VALUES} \text{ ARE} \end{array} \right\}$ $\left\{ \text{literal-1} \left[\left\{ \begin{array}{l} \underline{THROUGH} \\ \underline{THRU} \end{array} \right\} \text{ literal-2} \right] \right\}$ ... .

<u>GENERAL FORMAT FOR COMMUNICATION DESCRIPTION ENTRY</u>

<u>FORMAT 1</u>:

<u>CD</u> cd-name-1

FOR [<u>INITIAL</u>] <u>INPUT</u>

$\left[\begin{array}{l} \text{[[SYMBOLIC } \underline{QUEUE} \text{ IS data-name-1]} \\[4pt] \quad \text{[SYMBOLIC } \underline{SUB\text{-}QUEUE\text{-}1} \text{ IS data-name-2]} \\[4pt] \quad \text{[SYMBOLIC } \underline{SUB\text{-}QUEUE\text{-}2} \text{ IS data-name-3]} \\[4pt] \quad \text{[SYMBOLIC } \underline{SUB\text{-}QUEUE\text{-}3} \text{ IS data-name-4]} \\[4pt] \quad \text{[}\underline{MESSAGE} \text{ } \underline{DATE} \text{ IS data-name-5]} \\[4pt] \quad \text{[}\underline{MESSAGE} \text{ } \underline{TIME} \text{ IS data-name-6]} \\[4pt] \quad \text{[SYMBOLIC } \underline{SOURCE} \text{ IS data-name-7]} \\[4pt] \quad \text{[}\underline{TEXT} \text{ } \underline{LENGTH} \text{ IS data-name-8]} \\[4pt] \quad \text{[}\underline{END} \text{ } \underline{KEY} \text{ IS data-name-9]} \\[4pt] \quad \text{[}\underline{STATUS} \text{ } \underline{KEY} \text{ IS data-name-10]} \\[4pt] \quad \text{[}\underline{MESSAGE} \text{ } \underline{COUNT} \text{ IS data-name-11]]} \\[4pt] \text{[data-name-1, data-name-2, data-name-3,} \\[4pt] \quad \text{data-name-4, data-name-5, data-name-6,} \\[4pt] \quad \text{data-name-7, data-name-8, data-name-9,} \\[4pt] \quad \text{data-name-10, data-name-11]} \end{array} \right]$

GENERAL FORMAT FOR COMMUNICATION DESCRIPTION ENTRY

FORMAT 2:

CD cd-name-1 FOR OUTPUT

    [DESTINATION COUNT IS data-name-1]

    [TEXT LENGTH IS data-name-2]

    [STATUS KEY IS data-name-3]

    [DESTINATION TABLE OCCURS integer-1 TIMES

        [INDEXED BY {index-name-1} ...]]

    [ERROR KEY IS data-name-4]

    [SYMBOLIC DESTINATION IS data-name-5].

FORMAT 3:

CD cd-name-1

```
                       ┌                                          ┐
                       │ [[MESSAGE DATE IS data-name-1]           │
                       │                                          │
                       │    [MESSAGE TIME IS data-name-2]         │
                       │                                          │
                       │    [SYMBOLIC TERMINAL IS data-name-3]    │
                       │                                          │
                       │    [TEXT LENGTH IS data-name-4]          │
       FOR  [INITIAL]  I-O                                        │
                       │    [END KEY IS data-name-5]              │
                       │                                          │
                       │    [STATUS KEY IS data-name-6]]          │
                       │                                          │
                       │ [data-name-1, data-name-2, data-name-3,  │
                       │                                          │
                       │    data-name-4, data-name-5, data-name-6]│
                       └                                          ┘
```

GENERAL FORMAT FOR REPORT DESCRIPTION ENTRY

RD report-name-1

[IS GLOBAL]

[CODE literal-1]

$$\left[\begin{Bmatrix} \underline{CONTROL} \text{ IS} \\ \underline{CONTROLS} \text{ ARE} \end{Bmatrix} \begin{Bmatrix} \{data\text{-}name\text{-}1\} \dots \\ \underline{FINAL} \text{ [data-name-1] } \dots \end{Bmatrix} \right]$$

$$\left[\underline{PAGE} \begin{bmatrix} \underline{LIMIT} \text{ IS} \\ \underline{LIMITS} \text{ ARE} \end{bmatrix} \text{integer-1} \begin{bmatrix} \underline{LINE} \\ \underline{LINES} \end{bmatrix} [\underline{HEADING} \text{ integer-2}] \right.$$

$$[\underline{FIRST} \ \underline{DETAIL} \text{ integer-3}] \quad [\underline{LAST} \ \underline{DETAIL} \text{ integer-4}]$$

$$\left. [\underline{FOOTING} \text{ integer-5}] \right] .$$

GENERAL FORMAT FOR REPORT GROUP DESCRIPTION ENTRY

FORMAT 1:

01 [data-name-1]

$$\left[\underline{LINE} \text{ NUMBER IS} \begin{Bmatrix} \text{integer-1 [ON } \underline{NEXT} \ \underline{PAGE}] \\ \underline{PLUS} \text{ integer-2} \end{Bmatrix} \right]$$

$$\left[\underline{NEXT} \ \underline{GROUP} \text{ IS} \begin{Bmatrix} \text{integer-3} \\ \underline{PLUS} \text{ integer-4} \\ \underline{NEXT} \ \underline{PAGE} \end{Bmatrix} \right]$$

$$\underline{TYPE} \text{ IS} \begin{Bmatrix} \begin{Bmatrix} \underline{REPORT} \ \underline{HEADING} \\ \underline{RH} \end{Bmatrix} \\ \begin{Bmatrix} \underline{PAGE} \ \underline{HEADING} \\ \underline{PH} \end{Bmatrix} \\ \begin{Bmatrix} \underline{CONTROL} \ \underline{HEADING} \\ \underline{CH} \end{Bmatrix} \begin{Bmatrix} \text{data-name-2} \\ \underline{FINAL} \end{Bmatrix} \\ \begin{Bmatrix} \underline{DETAIL} \\ \underline{DE} \end{Bmatrix} \\ \begin{Bmatrix} \underline{CONTROL} \ \underline{FOOTING} \\ \underline{CF} \end{Bmatrix} \begin{Bmatrix} \text{data-name-3} \\ \underline{FINAL} \end{Bmatrix} \\ \begin{Bmatrix} \underline{PAGE} \ \underline{FOOTING} \\ \underline{PF} \end{Bmatrix} \\ \begin{Bmatrix} \underline{REPORT} \ \underline{FOOTING} \\ \underline{RF} \end{Bmatrix} \end{Bmatrix}$$

[[USAGE IS] DISPLAY].

GENERAL FORMAT FOR REPORT GROUP DESCRIPTION ENTRY

FORMAT 2:

level-number [data-name-1]

$$\left[\underline{\text{LINE}} \text{ NUMBER IS } \left\{ \begin{array}{l} \text{integer-1 } [\text{ON } \underline{\text{NEXT}} \underline{\text{PAGE}}] \\ \underline{\text{PLUS}} \text{ Integer-2} \end{array} \right\} \right]$$

[[<u>USAGE</u> IS] <u>DISPLAY</u>].

FORMAT 3:

level-number [data-name-1]

$$\left\{ \begin{array}{l} \underline{\text{PICTURE}} \\ \underline{\text{PIC}} \end{array} \right\} \text{ IS character-string}$$

[[<u>USAGE</u> IS] <u>DISPLAY</u>]

$$\left[[\underline{\text{SIGN}} \text{ IS] } \left\{ \begin{array}{l} \underline{\text{LEADING}} \\ \underline{\text{TRAILING}} \end{array} \right\} \underline{\text{SEPARATE}} \text{ CHARACTER} \right]$$

$$\left[\left\{ \begin{array}{l} \underline{\text{JUSTIFIED}} \\ \underline{\text{JUST}} \end{array} \right\} \text{ RIGHT} \right]$$

[<u>BLANK</u> WHEN <u>ZERO</u>]

$$\left[\underline{\text{LINE}} \text{ NUMBER IS } \left\{ \begin{array}{l} \text{integer-1 } [\text{ON } \underline{\text{NEXT}} \underline{\text{PAGE}}] \\ \underline{\text{PLUS}} \text{ integer-2} \end{array} \right\} \right]$$

[<u>COLUMN</u> NUMBER IS integer-3]

$$\left\{ \begin{array}{l} \underline{\text{SOURCE}} \text{ IS identifier-1} \\ \underline{\text{VALUE}} \text{ IS literal-1} \\ \{\underline{\text{SUM}} \ \{\text{identifier-2}\} \ \dots \ [\underline{\text{UPON}} \ \{\text{data-name-2}\} \ \dots \ ]\} \ \dots \\ \qquad \left[\underline{\text{RESET}} \text{ ON } \left\{ \begin{array}{l} \text{data-name-3} \\ \underline{\text{FINAL}} \end{array} \right\} \right] \end{array} \right\}$$

[<u>GROUP</u> INDICATE].

GENERAL FORMAT FOR PROCEDURE DIVISION

FORMAT 1:

[PROCEDURE DIVISION [USING {data-name-1} ...].

[DECLARATIVES.

{section-name SECTION [segment-number].

    USE statement.

[paragraph-name.

    [sentence] ...] ... } ...

END DECLARATIVES.]

{section-name SECTION [segment-number].

[paragraph-name.

    [sentence] ...] ... } ...]

FORMAT 2:

[PROCEDURE DIVISION [USING {data-name-1} ...].

{paragraph-name.

    [sentence] ... } ...]

GENERAL FORMAT FOR COBOL VERBS

<u>ACCEPT</u> identifier-1 [<u>FROM</u> mnemonic-name-1]

<u>ACCEPT</u> identifier-2 <u>FROM</u> $\begin{Bmatrix} \underline{DATE} \\ \underline{DAY} \\ \underline{DAY-OF-WEEK} \\ \underline{TIME} \end{Bmatrix}$

<u>ACCEPT</u> cd-name-1 MESSAGE <u>COUNT</u>

<u>ADD</u> $\begin{Bmatrix} identifier-1 \\ literal-1 \end{Bmatrix}$ ... <u>TO</u> {identifier-2 [<u>ROUNDED</u>]} ...

   [ON <u>SIZE</u> <u>ERROR</u> imperative-statement-1]

   [<u>NOT</u> ON <u>SIZE</u> <u>ERROR</u> imperative-statement-2]

   [<u>END-ADD</u>]

<u>ADD</u> $\begin{Bmatrix} identifier-1 \\ literal-1 \end{Bmatrix}$ ... TO $\begin{Bmatrix} identifier-2 \\ literal-2 \end{Bmatrix}$

   <u>GIVING</u> {identifier-3 [<u>ROUNDED</u>]} ...

   [ON <u>SIZE</u> <u>ERROR</u> imperative-statement-1]

   [<u>NOT</u> ON <u>SIZE</u> <u>ERROR</u> imperative-statement-2]

   [<u>END-ADD</u>]

<u>ADD</u> $\begin{Bmatrix} \underline{CORRESPONDING} \\ \underline{CORR} \end{Bmatrix}$ identifier-1 <u>TO</u> identifier-2 [<u>ROUNDED</u>]

   [ON <u>SIZE</u> <u>ERROR</u> imperative-statement-1]

   [<u>NOT</u> ON <u>SIZE</u> <u>ERROR</u> imperative-statement-2]

   [<u>END-ADD</u>]

<u>ALTER</u> {procedure-name-1 <u>TO</u> [<u>PROCEED</u> <u>TO</u>] procedure-name-2} ...

<u>CALL</u> $\begin{Bmatrix} identifier-1 \\ literal-1 \end{Bmatrix}$ $\left[\underline{USING} \begin{Bmatrix} [BY \underline{REFERENCE}] \ \{identifier-2\} \ ... \\ BY \underline{CONTENT} \ \{identifier-2\} \ ... \end{Bmatrix} ... \right]$

   [ON <u>OVERFLOW</u> imperative-statement-1]

   [<u>END-CALL</u>]

GENERAL FORMAT FOR COBOL VERBS

CALL $\begin{Bmatrix} \text{identifier-1} \\ \text{literal-1} \end{Bmatrix}$ $\left[\underline{USING} \begin{Bmatrix} [\text{BY } \underline{REFERENCE}] \quad \{\text{identifier-2}\} \dots \\ \text{BY } \underline{CONTENT} \quad \{\text{identifier-2}\} \dots \end{Bmatrix} \dots \right]$

    [ON EXCEPTION imperative-statement-1]

    [NOT ON EXCEPTION imperative-statement-2]

    [END-CALL]

CANCEL $\begin{Bmatrix} \text{identifier-1} \\ \text{literal-1} \end{Bmatrix}$ ...

SW CLOSE $\left\{ \text{file-name-1} \left[\begin{Bmatrix} \underline{REEL} \\ \underline{UNIT} \end{Bmatrix} [\text{FOR } \underline{REMOVAL}] \\ \text{WITH} \begin{Bmatrix} \underline{NO} \ \underline{REWIND} \\ \underline{LOCK} \end{Bmatrix} \right] \right\}$ ...

RI CLOSE {file-name-1 [WITH LOCK]} ...

COMPUTE {identifier-1 [ROUNDED]} ... = arithmetic-expression-1

    [ON SIZE ERROR imperative-statement-1]

    [NOT ON SIZE ERROR imperative-statement-2]

    [END-COMPUTE]

CONTINUE

DELETE file-name-1 RECORD

    [INVALID KEY imperative-statement-1]

    [NOT INVALID KEY imperative-statement-2]

    [END-DELETE]

DISABLE $\begin{Bmatrix} \text{INPUT } [\underline{TERMINAL}] \\ \underline{I-O} \ \underline{TERMINAL} \\ \underline{OUTPUT} \end{Bmatrix}$ cd-name-1 $\left[\text{WITH } \underline{KEY} \begin{Bmatrix} \text{identifier-1} \\ \text{literal-1} \end{Bmatrix} \right]$

GENERAL FORMAT FOR COBOL VERBS

DISPLAY $\begin{Bmatrix} \text{identifier-1} \\ \text{literal-1} \end{Bmatrix}$ ... [UPON mnemonic-name-1] [WITH NO ADVANCING]

DIVIDE $\begin{Bmatrix} \text{identifier-1} \\ \text{literal-1} \end{Bmatrix}$ INTO {identifier-2 [ROUNDED]} ...

   [ON SIZE ERROR imperative-statement-1]

   [NOT ON SIZE ERROR imperative-statement-2]

   [END-DIVIDE]

DIVIDE $\begin{Bmatrix} \text{identifier-1} \\ \text{literal-1} \end{Bmatrix}$ INTO $\begin{Bmatrix} \text{identifier-2} \\ \text{literal-2} \end{Bmatrix}$

   GIVING {identifier-3 [ROUNDED]} ...

   [ON SIZE ERROR imperative-statement-1]

   [NOT ON SIZE ERROR imperative-statement-2]

   [END-DIVIDE]

DIVIDE $\begin{Bmatrix} \text{identifier-1} \\ \text{literal-1} \end{Bmatrix}$ BY $\begin{Bmatrix} \text{identifier-2} \\ \text{literal-2} \end{Bmatrix}$

   GIVING {identifier-3 [ROUNDED]} ...

   [ON SIZE ERROR imperative-statement-1]

   [NOT ON SIZE ERROR imperative-statement-2]

   [END-DIVIDE]

DIVIDE $\begin{Bmatrix} \text{identifier-1} \\ \text{literal-1} \end{Bmatrix}$ INTO $\begin{Bmatrix} \text{identifier-2} \\ \text{literal-2} \end{Bmatrix}$ GIVING identifier-3 [ROUNDED]

   REMAINDER identifier-4

   [ON SIZE ERROR imperative-statement-1]

   [NOT ON SIZE ERROR imperative-statement-2]

   [END-DIVIDE]

GENERAL FORMAT FOR COBOL VERBS

DIVIDE $\left\{ \begin{array}{l} \text{identifier-1} \\ \text{literal-1} \end{array} \right\}$ BY $\left\{ \begin{array}{l} \text{identifier-2} \\ \text{literal-2} \end{array} \right\}$ GIVING identifier-3 [ROUNDED]

    REMAINDER identifier-4

    [ON SIZE ERROR imperative-statement-1]

    [NOT ON SIZE ERROR imperative-statement-2]

    [END-DIVIDE]

ENABLE $\left\{ \begin{array}{l} \text{INPUT [TERMINAL]} \\ \text{I-O TERMINAL} \\ \text{OUTPUT} \end{array} \right\}$ cd-name-1 $\left[\text{WITH KEY} \left\{ \begin{array}{l} \text{identifier-1} \\ \text{literal-1} \end{array} \right\} \right]$

ENTER language-name-1 [routine-name-1].

EVALUATE $\left\{ \begin{array}{l} \text{identifier-1} \\ \text{literal-1} \\ \text{expression-1} \\ \text{TRUE} \\ \text{FALSE} \end{array} \right\}$ $\left[\text{ALSO} \left\{ \begin{array}{l} \text{identifier-2} \\ \text{literal-2} \\ \text{expression-2} \\ \text{TRUE} \\ \text{FALSE} \end{array} \right\} \right]$ ...

  {{WHEN

$\left\{ \begin{array}{l} \text{ANY} \\ \text{condition-1} \\ \text{TRUE} \\ \text{FALSE} \\ \text{[NOT]} \left\{ \begin{array}{l} \text{identifier-3} \\ \text{literal-3} \\ \text{arithmetic-expression-1} \end{array} \right\} \left[\left\{ \begin{array}{l} \text{THROUGH} \\ \text{THRU} \end{array} \right\} \left\{ \begin{array}{l} \text{identifier-4} \\ \text{literal-4} \\ \text{arithmetic-expression-2} \end{array} \right\} \right] \end{array} \right\}$

  [ALSO

$\left[\left\{ \begin{array}{l} \text{ANY} \\ \text{condition-2} \\ \text{TRUE} \\ \text{FALSE} \\ \text{[NOT]} \left\{ \begin{array}{l} \text{identifier-5} \\ \text{literal-5} \\ \text{arithmetic-expression-3} \end{array} \right\} \left[\left\{ \begin{array}{l} \text{THROUGH} \\ \text{THRU} \end{array} \right\} \left\{ \begin{array}{l} \text{identifier-6} \\ \text{literal-6} \\ \text{arithmetic-expression-4} \end{array} \right\} \right] \end{array} \right\} \right]$ ... } ...

  imperative-statement-1} ...

  [WHEN OTHER imperative-statement-2]

  [END-EVALUATE]

GENERAL FORMAT FOR COBOL VERBS

EXIT

EXIT PROGRAM

GENERATE $\begin{Bmatrix} \text{data-name-1} \\ \text{report-name-1} \end{Bmatrix}$

GO TO [procedure-name-1]

GO TO {procedure-name-1} ...   DEPENDING ON identifier-1

IF condition-1 THEN $\begin{Bmatrix} \{\text{statement-1}\} \ ... \\ \underline{\text{NEXT}} \ \underline{\text{SENTENCE}} \end{Bmatrix}$ $\begin{Bmatrix} \underline{\text{ELSE}} \ \{\text{statement-2}\} \ ... \ [\underline{\text{END-IF}}] \\ \underline{\text{ELSE}} \ \underline{\text{NEXT}} \ \underline{\text{SENTENCE}} \\ \underline{\text{END-IF}} \end{Bmatrix}$

INITIALIZE {identifier-1} ...

$$\left[\underline{\text{REPLACING}} \ \begin{Bmatrix} \begin{pmatrix} \underline{\text{ALPHABETIC}} \\ \underline{\text{ALPHANUMERIC}} \\ \underline{\text{NUMERIC}} \\ \underline{\text{ALPHANUMERIC-EDITED}} \\ \underline{\text{NUMERIC-EDITED}} \end{pmatrix} \end{Bmatrix} \text{DATA} \ \underline{\text{BY}} \ \begin{Bmatrix} \text{identifier-2} \\ \text{literal-1} \end{Bmatrix} \ ... \right]$$

INITIATE {report-name-1} ...

INSPECT identifier-1 TALLYING

$$\left\{ \text{identifier-2} \ \underline{\text{FOR}} \ \left\{ \begin{matrix} \underline{\text{CHARACTERS}} \ \left[\begin{Bmatrix} \underline{\text{BEFORE}} \\ \underline{\text{AFTER}} \end{Bmatrix} \text{INITIAL} \begin{Bmatrix} \text{identifier-4} \\ \text{literal-2} \end{Bmatrix} \right] \ ... \\ \begin{Bmatrix} \underline{\text{ALL}} \\ \underline{\text{LEADING}} \end{Bmatrix} \begin{Bmatrix} \text{identifier-3} \\ \text{literal-1} \end{Bmatrix} \left[\begin{Bmatrix} \underline{\text{BEFORE}} \\ \underline{\text{AFTER}} \end{Bmatrix} \text{INITIAL} \begin{Bmatrix} \text{identifier-4} \\ \text{literal-2} \end{Bmatrix} \right] \ ... \end{matrix} \right\} \ ... \right\} \ ...$$

INSPECT identifier-1 REPLACING

$$\left\{ \begin{matrix} \underline{\text{CHARACTERS}} \ \underline{\text{BY}} \begin{Bmatrix} \text{identifier-5} \\ \text{literal-3} \end{Bmatrix} \left[\begin{Bmatrix} \underline{\text{BEFORE}} \\ \underline{\text{AFTER}} \end{Bmatrix} \text{INITIAL} \begin{Bmatrix} \text{identifier-4} \\ \text{literal-2} \end{Bmatrix} \right] \ ... \\ \begin{Bmatrix} \underline{\text{ALL}} \\ \underline{\text{LEADING}} \\ \underline{\text{FIRST}} \end{Bmatrix} \begin{Bmatrix} \text{identifier-3} \\ \text{literal-1} \end{Bmatrix} \ \underline{\text{BY}} \begin{Bmatrix} \text{identifier-5} \\ \text{literal-3} \end{Bmatrix} \left[\begin{Bmatrix} \underline{\text{BEFORE}} \\ \underline{\text{AFTER}} \end{Bmatrix} \text{INITIAL} \begin{Bmatrix} \text{identifier-4} \\ \text{literal-2} \end{Bmatrix} \right] \ ... \end{matrix} \right\} \ ...$$

GENERAL FORMAT FOR COBOL VERBS

```
INSPECT identifier-1 TALLYING
    ⎧                ⎧           ⎡⎧BEFORE⎫         ⎧identifier-4⎫⎤    ⎫
    ⎪identifier-2 FOR ⎨CHARACTERS ⎢⎨AFTER ⎬ INITIAL ⎨literal-2   ⎬⎥ ...⎪
    ⎨                ⎪           ⎣⎩     ⎭         ⎩            ⎭⎦    ⎬ ... ⎫ ...
    ⎪                ⎪⎧ALL    ⎫ ⎧identifier-3⎫ ⎡⎧BEFORE⎫         ⎧identifier-4⎫⎤    ⎪      ⎬
    ⎩                ⎩⎨LEADING⎬ ⎨literal-1   ⎬ ⎢⎨AFTER ⎬ INITIAL ⎨literal-2   ⎬⎥ ...⎪ ...⎭      ⎭
```

REPLACING

```
⎧                ⎧identifier-5⎫ ⎡⎧BEFORE⎫         ⎧identifier-4⎫⎤    ⎫
⎪CHARACTERS BY ⎨literal-3   ⎬ ⎢⎨AFTER ⎬ INITIAL ⎨literal-2   ⎬⎥ ...⎪
⎨               ⎩            ⎭ ⎣⎩     ⎭         ⎩            ⎭⎦    ⎬ ...
⎪⎧ALL    ⎫ ⎧identifier-3⎫    ⎧identifier-5⎫ ⎡⎧BEFORE⎫         ⎧identifier-4⎫⎤    ⎪
⎪⎨LEADING⎬ ⎨literal-1   ⎬ BY ⎨literal-3   ⎬ ⎢⎨AFTER ⎬ INITIAL ⎨literal-2   ⎬⎥ ...⎪
⎩⎩FIRST  ⎭ ⎩            ⎭    ⎩            ⎭ ⎣⎩     ⎭         ⎩            ⎭⎦    ⎭
```

```
INSPECT identifier-1 CONVERTING  ⎧identifier-6⎫ TO ⎧identifier-7⎫
                                 ⎨literal-4   ⎬    ⎨literal-5   ⎬
                                 ⎩            ⎭    ⎩            ⎭

    ⎡⎧BEFORE⎫         ⎧identifier-4⎫⎤
    ⎢⎨AFTER ⎬ INITIAL ⎨literal-2   ⎬⎥ ...
    ⎣⎩     ⎭         ⎩            ⎭⎦
```

```
MERGE file-name-1  ⎧ON ⎧ASCENDING ⎫ KEY {data-name-1} ... ⎫ ...
                   ⎩   ⎨DESCENDING⎬                       ⎭
                       ⎩          ⎭

    [COLLATING SEQUENCE IS alphabet-name-1]

    USING file-name-2  {file-name-3} ...

    ⎧OUTPUT PROCEDURE IS procedure-name-1  ⎡⎧THROUGH⎫ procedure-name-2⎤⎫
    ⎨                                      ⎢⎨THRU   ⎬                 ⎥⎬
    ⎪GIVING  {file-name-4} ...             ⎣⎩       ⎭                 ⎦⎪
    ⎩                                                                 ⎭
```

```
MOVE  ⎧identifier-1⎫ TO  {identifier-2} ...
      ⎨literal-1    ⎬
      ⎩             ⎭
```

```
MOVE  ⎧CORRESPONDING⎫ identifier-1 TO identifier-2
      ⎨CORR         ⎬
      ⎩             ⎭
```

```
MULTIPLY  ⎧identifier-1⎫ BY  {identifier-2 [ROUNDED]} ...
          ⎨literal-1    ⎬
          ⎩             ⎭

    [ON SIZE ERROR imperative-statement-1]

    [NOT ON SIZE ERROR imperative-statement-2]

    [END-MULTIPLY]
```

GENERAL FORMAT FOR COBOL VERBS

$$\underline{\text{MULTIPLY}} \quad \begin{Bmatrix} \text{identifier-1} \\ \text{literal-1} \end{Bmatrix} \quad \underline{\text{BY}} \quad \begin{Bmatrix} \text{identifier-2} \\ \text{literal-2} \end{Bmatrix}$$

$\underline{\text{GIVING}}$ {identifier-3 [$\underline{\text{ROUNDED}}$]} ...

[ON $\underline{\text{SIZE}}$ $\underline{\text{ERROR}}$ imperative-statement-1]

[$\underline{\text{NOT}}$ ON $\underline{\text{SIZE}}$ $\underline{\text{ERROR}}$ imperative-statement-2]

[$\underline{\text{END-MULTIPLY}}$]

S $\underline{\text{OPEN}}$ $\begin{Bmatrix} \underline{\text{INPUT}} \quad \begin{Bmatrix} \text{file-name-1} \begin{bmatrix} \underline{\text{REVERSED}} \\ \text{WITH } \underline{\text{NO}} \ \underline{\text{REWIND}} \end{bmatrix} \end{Bmatrix} \cdots \\ \underline{\text{OUTPUT}} \ \{ \text{file-name-2} \ [\text{WITH } \underline{\text{NO}} \ \underline{\text{REWIND}}] \} \ \cdots \\ \underline{\text{I-O}} \ \{ \text{file-name-3} \} \ \cdots \\ \underline{\text{EXTEND}} \ \{ \text{file-name-4} \} \ \cdots \end{Bmatrix}$ ...

RI $\underline{\text{OPEN}}$ $\begin{Bmatrix} \underline{\text{INPUT}} \ \{ \text{file-name-1} \} \ \cdots \\ \underline{\text{OUTPUT}} \ \{ \text{file-name-2} \} \ \cdots \\ \underline{\text{I-O}} \ \{ \text{file-name-3} \} \ \cdots \\ \underline{\text{EXTEND}} \ \{ \text{file-name-4} \} \ \cdots \end{Bmatrix}$ ...

W $\underline{\text{OPEN}}$ $\begin{Bmatrix} \underline{\text{OUTPUT}} \ \{ \text{file-name-1} \ [\text{WITH } \underline{\text{NO}} \ \underline{\text{REWIND}}] \} \ \cdots \\ \underline{\text{EXTEND}} \ \{ \text{file-name-2} \} \ \cdots \end{Bmatrix}$ ...

$\underline{\text{PERFORM}}$ $\left[\text{procedure-name-1} \left[\begin{Bmatrix} \underline{\text{THROUGH}} \\ \underline{\text{THRU}} \end{Bmatrix} \text{procedure-name-2} \right] \right]$

[imperative-statement-1 $\underline{\text{END-PERFORM}}$]

$\underline{\text{PERFORM}}$ $\left[\text{procedure-name-1} \left[\begin{Bmatrix} \underline{\text{THROUGH}} \\ \underline{\text{THRU}} \end{Bmatrix} \text{procedure-name-2} \right] \right]$

$\begin{Bmatrix} \text{identifier-1} \\ \text{integer-1} \end{Bmatrix}$ $\underline{\text{TIMES}}$ [imperative-statement-1 $\underline{\text{END-PERFORM}}$]

$\underline{\text{PERFORM}}$ $\left[\text{procedure-name-1} \left[\begin{Bmatrix} \underline{\text{THROUGH}} \\ \underline{\text{THRU}} \end{Bmatrix} \text{procedure-name-2} \right] \right]$

$\left[\text{WITH } \underline{\text{TEST}} \begin{Bmatrix} \underline{\text{BEFORE}} \\ \underline{\text{AFTER}} \end{Bmatrix} \right]$ $\underline{\text{UNTIL}}$ condition-1

[imperative-statement-1 $\underline{\text{END-PERFORM}}$]

GENERAL FORMAT FOR COBOL VERBS

PERFORM $\left[\text{procedure-name-1} \left[\begin{Bmatrix} \underline{\text{THROUGH}} \\ \underline{\text{THRU}} \end{Bmatrix} \text{procedure-name-2}\right]\right]$

$\left[\text{WITH } \underline{\text{TEST}} \begin{Bmatrix} \underline{\text{BEFORE}} \\ \underline{\text{AFTER}} \end{Bmatrix}\right]$

$\underline{\text{VARYING}} \begin{Bmatrix} \text{identifier-2} \\ \text{index-name-1} \end{Bmatrix} \underline{\text{FROM}} \begin{Bmatrix} \text{identifier-3} \\ \text{index-name-2} \\ \text{literal-1} \end{Bmatrix}$

$\underline{\text{BY}} \begin{Bmatrix} \text{identifier-4} \\ \text{literal-2} \end{Bmatrix} \underline{\text{UNTIL}} \text{ condition-1}$

$\left[\underline{\text{AFTER}} \begin{Bmatrix} \text{identifier-5} \\ \text{literal-3} \end{Bmatrix} \underline{\text{FROM}} \begin{Bmatrix} \text{identifier-6} \\ \text{index-name-4} \\ \text{literal-3} \end{Bmatrix}\right.$

$\left.\underline{\text{BY}} \begin{Bmatrix} \text{identifier-7} \\ \text{literal-4} \end{Bmatrix} \underline{\text{UNTIL}} \text{ condition-2}\right] \ldots$

[imperative-statement-1 END-PERFORM]

PURGE cd-name-1

RI READ file-name-1 [NEXT] RECORD [INTO identifier-1]

    [AT END imperative-statement-1]

    [NOT AT END imperative-statement-2]

    [END-READ]

R READ file-name-1 RECORD [INTO identifier-1]

    [INVALID KEY imperative-statement-3]

    [NOT INVALID KEY imperative-statement-4]

    [END-READ]

<u>GENERAL FORMAT FOR COBOL VERBS</u>

I <u>READ</u> file-name-1 RECORD [<u>INTO</u> identifier-1]

    [<u>KEY</u> IS data-name-1]

    [<u>INVALID</u> KEY imperative-statement-3]

    [<u>NOT</u> <u>INVALID</u> KEY imperative-statement-4]

    [<u>END-READ</u>]

    <u>RECEIVE</u> cd-name-1 $\left\{ \begin{array}{l} \underline{\text{MESSAGE}} \\ \underline{\text{SEGMENT}} \end{array} \right\}$ <u>INTO</u> identifier-1

    [<u>NO</u> <u>DATA</u> imperative-statement-1]

    [WITH <u>DATA</u> imperative-statement-2]

    [<u>END-RECEIVE</u>]

    <u>RELEASE</u> record-name-1 [<u>FROM</u> identifier-1]

    <u>RETURN</u> file-name-1 RECORD [<u>INTO</u> identifier-1]

    AT <u>END</u> imperative-statement-1

    [<u>NOT</u> AT <u>END</u> imperative-statement-2]

    [<u>END-RETURN</u>]

S <u>REWRITE</u> record-name-1 [<u>FROM</u> identifier-1]

RI <u>REWRITE</u> record-name-1 [<u>FROM</u> identifier-1]

    [<u>INVALID</u> KEY imperative-statement-1]

    [<u>NOT</u> <u>INVALID</u> KEY imperative-statement-2]

    [<u>END-REWRITE</u>]

GENERAL FORMAT FOR COBOL VERBS

SEARCH identifier-1 $\left[\underline{\text{VARYING}} \; \left\{ \begin{array}{l} \text{identifier-2} \\ \text{index-name-1} \end{array} \right\} \right]$

  [AT <u>END</u> imperative-statement-1]

$\left\{ \underline{\text{WHEN}} \; \text{condition-1} \; \left\{ \begin{array}{l} \text{imperative-statement-2} \\ \underline{\text{NEXT}} \; \underline{\text{SENTENCE}} \end{array} \right\} \right\} \dots$

  [<u>END-SEARCH</u>]

<u>SEARCH</u> <u>ALL</u> identifier-1   [AT <u>END</u> imperative-statement-1]

$\underline{\text{WHEN}} \; \left\{ \begin{array}{l} \text{data-name-1} \; \left\{ \begin{array}{l} \text{IS} \; \underline{\text{EQUAL}} \; \text{TO} \\ \text{IS} \; = \end{array} \right\} \; \left\{ \begin{array}{l} \text{identifier-3} \\ \text{literal-1} \\ \text{arithmetic-expression-1} \end{array} \right\} \\ \text{condition-name-1} \end{array} \right\}$

$\left[\underline{\text{AND}} \; \left\{ \begin{array}{l} \text{data-name-2} \; \left\{ \begin{array}{l} \text{IS} \; \underline{\text{EQUAL}} \; \text{TO} \\ \text{IS} \; = \end{array} \right\} \; \left\{ \begin{array}{l} \text{identifier-4} \\ \text{literal-2} \\ \text{arithmetic-expression-2} \end{array} \right\} \\ \text{condition-name-2} \end{array} \right\} \right] \dots$

$\left\{ \begin{array}{l} \text{imperative-statement-2} \\ \underline{\text{NEXT}} \; \underline{\text{SENTENCE}} \end{array} \right\}$

  [<u>END-SEARCH</u>]

<u>SEND</u> cd-name-1 <u>FROM</u> identifier-1

<u>SEND</u> cd-name-1   [<u>FROM</u> identifier-1] $\left\{ \begin{array}{l} \text{WITH identifier-2} \\ \text{WITH} \; \underline{\text{ESI}} \\ \text{WITH} \; \underline{\text{EMI}} \\ \text{WITH} \; \underline{\text{EGI}} \end{array} \right\}$

$\left[\left\{ \begin{array}{l} \underline{\text{BEFORE}} \\ \underline{\text{AFTER}} \end{array} \right\} \; \text{ADVANCING} \; \left\{ \begin{array}{l} \left\{ \begin{array}{l} \text{identifier-3} \\ \text{integer-1} \end{array} \right\} \; \left[\begin{array}{l} \text{LINE} \\ \text{LINES} \end{array} \right] \\ \left\{ \begin{array}{l} \text{mnemonic-name-1} \\ \underline{\text{PAGE}} \end{array} \right\} \end{array} \right\} \right]$

  [<u>REPLACING</u> LINE]

<u>SET</u> $\left\{ \begin{array}{l} \text{index-name-1} \\ \text{identifier-1} \end{array} \right\} \dots \; \underline{\text{TO}} \; \left\{ \begin{array}{l} \text{index-name-2} \\ \text{identifier-2} \\ \text{integer-1} \end{array} \right\}$

GENERAL FORMAT FOR COBOL VERBS

```
SET   {index-name-3} ...   {UP BY  }   {identifier-3}
                           {DOWN BY}   {integer-2   }

SET   {{mnemonic-name-1} ...   TO   {ON }} ...
                                    {OFF}

SET   {condition-name-1} ...   TO TRUE


SORT file-name-1  {ON {ASCENDING }  KEY  {data-name-1} ... } ...
                  {     {DESCENDING}                        }

   [WITH DUPLICATES IN ORDER]

   [COLLATING SEQUENCE IS alphabet-name-1]

   { INPUT PROCEDURE IS procedure-name-1  [{THROUGH}  procedure-name-2] }
   { USING  {file-name-2} ...              {THRU   }                    }

   { OUTPUT PROCEDURE IS procedure-name-3  [{THROUGH}  procedure-name-4] }
   { GIVING  {file-name-3} ...              {THRU   }                    }


                              {IS EQUAL TO                  }
                              {IS =                         }
                              {IS GREATER THAN              }
START file-name-1  [ KEY     {IS >                          }  data-name-1 ]
                              {IS NOT LESS THAN             }
                              {IS NOT <                      }
                              {IS GREATER THAN OR EQUAL TO  }
                              {IS >=                         }

   [INVALID KEY imperative-statement-1]

   [NOT INVALID KEY imperative-statement-2]

   [END-START]


STOP  {RUN      }
      {literal-1}
```

GENERAL FORMAT FOR COBOL VERBS

$$
\underline{STRING} \begin{Bmatrix} \text{identifier-1} \\ \text{literal-1} \end{Bmatrix} \ \dots \ \underline{DELIMITED} \ BY \begin{Bmatrix} \text{identifier-2} \\ \text{literal-2} \\ \underline{SIZE} \end{Bmatrix} \dots
$$

    INTO identifier-3

    [WITH POINTER identifier-4]

    [ON OVERFLOW imperative-statement-1]

    [NOT ON OVERFLOW imperative-statement-2]

    [END-STRING]

$$
\underline{SUBTRACT} \begin{Bmatrix} \text{identifier-1} \\ \text{literal-1} \end{Bmatrix} \ \dots \ \underline{FROM} \ \{\text{identifier-3} \ [\underline{ROUNDED}]\} \ \dots
$$

    [ON SIZE ERROR imperative-statement-1]

    [NOT ON SIZE ERROR imperative-statement-2]

    [END-SUBTRACT]

$$
\underline{SUBTRACT} \begin{Bmatrix} \text{identifier-1} \\ \text{literal-1} \end{Bmatrix} \ \dots \ \underline{FROM} \begin{Bmatrix} \text{identifier-2} \\ \text{literal-2} \end{Bmatrix}
$$

    GIVING {identifier-3 [ROUNDED]} ...

    [ON SIZE ERROR imperative-statement-1]

    [NOT ON SIZE ERROR imperative-statement-2]

    [END-SUBTRACT]

$$
\underline{SUBTRACT} \begin{Bmatrix} \underline{CORRESPONDING} \\ \underline{CORR} \end{Bmatrix} \text{identifier-1} \ \underline{FROM} \ \text{identifier-2} \ [\underline{ROUNDED}]
$$

    [ON SIZE ERROR imperative-statement-1]

    [NOT ON SIZE ERROR imperative-statement-2]

    [END-SUBTRACT]

SUPPRESS PRINTING

TERMINATE {report-name-1} ...

GENERAL FORMAT FOR COBOL VERBS

UNSTRING identifier-1

$$\left[\underline{\text{DELIMITED}} \text{ BY } [\underline{\text{ALL}}] \begin{Bmatrix} \text{identifier-2} \\ \text{literal-1} \end{Bmatrix} \left[\underline{\text{OR}} \; [\underline{\text{ALL}}] \begin{Bmatrix} \text{identifier-3} \\ \text{literal-2} \end{Bmatrix}\right] \dots \right]$$

INTO {identifier-4 [DELIMITER IN identifier-5] [COUNT IN identifier-6]} ...

[WITH POINTER identifier-7]

[TALLYING IN identifier-8]

[ON OVERFLOW imperative-statement-1]

[NOT ON OVERFLOW imperative-statement-2]

[END-UNSTRING]

$$\textit{SRI } \underline{\text{USE}} \; [\underline{\text{GLOBAL}}] \text{ AFTER STANDARD } \begin{Bmatrix} \underline{\text{EXCEPTION}} \\ \underline{\text{ERROR}} \end{Bmatrix} \underline{\text{PROCEDURE}} \text{ ON } \begin{Bmatrix} \{\text{file-name-1}\} \dots \\ \underline{\text{INPUT}} \\ \underline{\text{OUTPUT}} \\ \underline{\text{I-O}} \\ \underline{\text{EXTEND}} \end{Bmatrix}$$

$$\textit{W } \underline{\text{USE}} \; \underline{\text{AFTER}} \text{ STANDARD } \begin{Bmatrix} \underline{\text{EXCEPTION}} \\ \underline{\text{ERROR}} \end{Bmatrix} \underline{\text{PROCEDURE}} \text{ ON } \begin{Bmatrix} \{\text{file-name-1}\} \dots \\ \underline{\text{OUTPUT}} \\ \underline{\text{EXTEND}} \end{Bmatrix}$$

USE [GLOBAL] BEFORE REPORTING identifier-1

$$\underline{\text{USE}} \text{ FOR } \underline{\text{DEBUGGING}} \text{ ON } \begin{Bmatrix} \text{cd-name-1} \\ [\underline{\text{ALL}} \text{ REFERENCES OF}] \text{ identifier-1} \\ \text{file-name-1} \\ \text{procedure-name-1} \\ \underline{\text{ALL}} \; \underline{\text{PROCEDURES}} \end{Bmatrix} \dots$$

GENERAL FORMAT FOR COBOL VERBS

S <u>WRITE</u> record-name-1 [<u>FROM</u> identifier-1]

$$
\left[\left\{ \begin{matrix} \underline{BEFORE} \\ \underline{AFTER} \end{matrix} \right\} \text{ ADVANCING} \left\{ \begin{matrix} \left\{ \begin{matrix} \text{identifier-2} \\ \text{integer-1} \end{matrix} \right\} \left[\begin{matrix} \text{LINE} \\ \text{LINES} \end{matrix} \right] \\ \left\{ \begin{matrix} \text{mnemonic-name-1} \\ \underline{PAGE} \end{matrix} \right\} \end{matrix} \right\} \right]
$$

$$
\left[\text{AT} \left\{ \begin{matrix} \underline{END\text{-}OF\text{-}PAGE} \\ \underline{EOP} \end{matrix} \right\} \text{ imperative-statement-1} \right]
$$

$$
\left[\underline{NOT} \text{ AT} \left\{ \begin{matrix} \underline{END\text{-}OF\text{-}PAGE} \\ \underline{EOP} \end{matrix} \right\} \text{ imperative-statement-2} \right]
$$

[<u>END-WRITE</u>]

RI <u>WRITE</u> record-name-1 [<u>FROM</u> identifier-1]

[<u>INVALID</u> KEY imperative-statement-1]

[<u>NOT</u> <u>INVALID</u> KEY imperative-statement-2]

[<u>END-WRITE</u>]

GENERAL FORMAT FOR COPY AND REPLACE STATEMENTS

<u>COPY</u> text-name-1 $\left[\left\{ \begin{matrix} \underline{OF} \\ \underline{IN} \end{matrix} \right\} \text{ library-name-1} \right]$

$$
\left[\underline{REPLACING} \left\{ \left\{ \begin{matrix} \text{==pseudo-text-1==} \\ \text{identifier-1} \\ \text{literal-1} \\ \text{word-1} \end{matrix} \right\} \underline{BY} \left\{ \begin{matrix} \text{==pseudo-text-2==} \\ \text{identifier-2} \\ \text{literal-2} \\ \text{word-2} \end{matrix} \right\} \right\} \dots \right]
$$

<u>REPLACE</u> {==pseudo-text-1== <u>BY</u> ==pseudo-text-2==} ...

<u>REPLACE</u> <u>OFF</u>

GENERAL FORMAT FOR CONDITIONS

RELATION CONDITION:

$$
\left\{
\begin{array}{l}
\text{identifier-1} \\
\text{literal-1} \\
\text{arithmetic-expression-1} \\
\text{index-name-1}
\end{array}
\right\}
\left\{
\begin{array}{l}
\text{IS [NOT] GREATER THAN} \\
\text{IS [NOT] >} \\
\text{IS [NOT] LESS THAN} \\
\text{IS [NOT] <} \\
\text{IS [NOT] EQUAL TO} \\
\text{IS [NOT] =} \\
\text{IS GREATER THAN OR EQUAL TO} \\
\text{IS >=} \\
\text{IS LESS THAN OR EQUAL TO} \\
\text{IS <=}
\end{array}
\right\}
\left\{
\begin{array}{l}
\text{identifier-2} \\
\text{literal-2} \\
\text{arithmetic-expression-2} \\
\text{index-name-2}
\end{array}
\right\}
$$

CLASS CONDITION:

$$
\text{identifier-1 IS [NOT]}
\left\{
\begin{array}{l}
\text{NUMERIC} \\
\text{ALPHABETIC} \\
\text{ALPHABETIC-LOWER} \\
\text{ALPHABETIC-UPPER} \\
\text{class-name-1}
\end{array}
\right\}
$$

CONDITION-NAME CONDITION:

condition-name-1

SWITCH-STATUS CONDITION:

condition-name-1

SIGN CONDITION:

$$
\text{arithmetic-expression-1 IS [NOT]}
\left\{
\begin{array}{l}
\text{POSITIVE} \\
\text{NEGATIVE} \\
\text{ZERO}
\end{array}
\right\}
$$

NEGATED CONDITION:

NOT condition-1

$$\underline{\text{GENERAL FORMAT FOR CONDITIONS}}$$

<u>COMBINED CONDITION</u>:

$$\text{condition-1} \left\{ \left\{ \begin{array}{c} \underline{\text{AND}} \\ \underline{\text{OR}} \end{array} \right\} \text{condition-2} \right\} \dots$$

<u>ABBREVIATED COMBINED RELATION CONDITION</u>:

$$\text{relation-condition} \left\{ \left\{ \begin{array}{c} \underline{\text{AND}} \\ \underline{\text{OR}} \end{array} \right\} [\underline{\text{NOT}}] \ [\text{relational-operator}] \ \text{object} \right\} \dots$$

$$\underline{\text{GENERAL FORMAT FOR QUALIFICATION}}$$

<u>FORMAT 1</u>:

$$\left\{ \begin{array}{c} \text{data-name-1} \\ \text{condition-name-1} \end{array} \right\} \left\{ \begin{array}{l} \left\{ \left\{ \begin{array}{c} \underline{\text{IN}} \\ \underline{\text{OF}} \end{array} \right\} \text{data-name-2} \right\} \dots \left[\left\{ \begin{array}{c} \underline{\text{IN}} \\ \underline{\text{OF}} \end{array} \right\} \left\{ \begin{array}{l} \text{file-name-1} \\ \text{cd-name-1} \end{array} \right\} \right] \\ \left\{ \begin{array}{c} \underline{\text{IN}} \\ \underline{\text{OF}} \end{array} \right\} \left\{ \begin{array}{l} \text{file-name-1} \\ \text{cd-name-1} \end{array} \right\} \end{array} \right\}$$

<u>FORMAT 2</u>:

$$\text{paragraph-name-1} \left\{ \begin{array}{c} \underline{\text{IN}} \\ \underline{\text{OF}} \end{array} \right\} \text{section-name-1}$$

<u>FORMAT 3</u>:

$$\text{text-name-1} \left\{ \begin{array}{c} \underline{\text{IN}} \\ \underline{\text{OF}} \end{array} \right\} \text{library-name-1}$$

<u>FORMAT 4</u>:

$$\underline{\text{LINAGE-COUNTER}} \left\{ \begin{array}{c} \underline{\text{IN}} \\ \underline{\text{OF}} \end{array} \right\} \text{file-name-2}$$

<u>FORMAT 5</u>:

$$\left\{ \begin{array}{c} \underline{\text{PAGE-COUNTER}} \\ \underline{\text{LINE-COUNTER}} \end{array} \right\} \left\{ \begin{array}{c} \underline{\text{IN}} \\ \underline{\text{OF}} \end{array} \right\} \text{report-name-1}$$

<u>FORMAT 6</u>:

$$\text{data-name-3} \left\{ \begin{array}{l} \left\{ \begin{array}{c} \underline{\text{IN}} \\ \underline{\text{OF}} \end{array} \right\} \text{data-name-4} \left[\left\{ \begin{array}{c} \underline{\text{IN}} \\ \underline{\text{OF}} \end{array} \right\} \text{report-name-2} \right] \\ \left\{ \begin{array}{c} \underline{\text{IN}} \\ \underline{\text{OF}} \end{array} \right\} \text{report-name-2} \end{array} \right\}$$

MISCELLANEOUS FORMATS

SUBSCRIPTING:

$$\begin{Bmatrix} \text{condition-name-1} \\ \text{data-name-1} \end{Bmatrix} \quad (\quad \begin{Bmatrix} \text{integer-1} \\ \text{data-name-2 } [\{\pm\} \text{ integer-2}] \\ \text{index-name-1 } [\{\pm\} \text{ integer-3}] \end{Bmatrix} \quad \dots \quad)$$

REFERENCE MODIFICATION:

data-name-1 (leftmost-character-position: [length])

IDENTIFIER:

$$\text{data-name-1} \quad \left[\begin{Bmatrix} \underline{IN} \\ \underline{OF} \end{Bmatrix} \text{ data-name-2} \right] \quad \dots \quad \left[\begin{Bmatrix} \underline{IN} \\ \underline{OF} \end{Bmatrix} \begin{Bmatrix} \text{cd-name-1} \\ \text{file-name-1} \\ \text{report-name-1} \end{Bmatrix} \right]$$

[({subscript} ...)]   [(leftmost-character-position: [length])]

GENERAL FORMAT FOR NESTED SOURCE PROGRAMS

IDENTIFICATION DIVISION.

PROGRAM-ID. program-name-1 [IS INITIAL PROGRAM].

[ENVIRONMENT DIVISION. environment-division-content]

[DATA DIVISION. data-division-content]

[PROCEDURE DIVISION. procedure-division-content]

[[nested-source-program] ...

END PROGRAM program-name-1.]

GENERAL FORMAT FOR NESTED-SOURCE-PROGRAM

IDENTIFICATION DIVISION.

PROGRAM-ID. program-name-2 $\left[\text{IS} \begin{Bmatrix} \underline{COMMON} \\ \underline{INITIAL} \end{Bmatrix} \text{PROGRAM} \right]$.

[ENVIRONMENT DIVISION. environment-division-content]

[DATA DIVISION. data-division-content]

[PROCEDURE DIVISION. procedure-division-content]

[nested-source-program] ...

END PROGRAM program-name-2.

GENERAL FORMAT FOR A SEQUENCE OF SOURCE PROGRAMS

{ IDENTIFICATION DIVISION.

 PROGRAM-ID. program-name-3 [IS INITIAL PROGRAM].

[ENVIRONMENT DIVISION. environment-division-content]

[DATA DIVISION. data-division-content]

[PROCEDURE DIVISION. procedure-division-content]

[nested-source-program] ...

 END PROGRAM program-name-3.} ...

 IDENTIFICATION DIVISION.

 PROGRAM-ID. program-name-4 [IS INITIAL PROGRAM].

[ENVIRONMENT DIVISION. environment-division-content]

[DATA DIVISION. data-division-content]

[PROCEDURE DIVISION. procedure-division-content]

[[nested-source-program] ...

 END PROGRAM program-name-4.]

Index

285